The Innovation Pyramid

The Innovation Pyramid is a learnable, repeatable, nonlinear, knowledge-based innovation methodology. While traditional books on innovation focus on either assembling an innovation team with the right combination of innate abilities or developing a creativity skillset, the Innovation Pyramid instead trains readers to produce serial innovations successfully. The original method segments innovation into four distinct yet interrelated stages: (1) identification of the root problem, (2) formulation of a solution, (3) development of an execution plan, and (4) implementation. At all stages, it considers the perspectives of both the innovator and the adopter, in order to increase the likelihood that innovations will achieve a significant impact. Part I of the book describes the overarching method of innovating. Part II details the creativity-based process for implementing the Innovation Pyramid methodology. Finally, the book's appendices include advanced techniques to enhance the utility of the Innovation Pyramid method.

TIMOTHY L. FALEY is the Distinguished Professor of Entrepreneurship and Special Assistant to the University President, at the University of the Virgin Islands. His other books include The Entrepreneurial Arch (Cambridge University Press, 2015).

The Innovation Pyramid

A Strategic Methodology for Impactful Problem Solving

TIMOTHY L. FALEY
University of the Virgin Islands

CAMBRIDGE
UNIVERSITY PRESS

CAMBRIDGE
UNIVERSITY PRESS

University Printing House, Cambridge CB2 8BS, United Kingdom

One Liberty Plaza, 20th Floor, New York, NY 10006, USA

477 Williamstown Road, Port Melbourne, VIC 3207, Australia

314–321, 3rd Floor, Plot 3, Splendor Forum, Jasola District Centre, New Delhi – 110025, India

79 Anson Road, #06-04/06, Singapore 079906

Cambridge University Press is part of the University of Cambridge.

It furthers the University's mission by disseminating knowledge in the pursuit of education, learning, and research at the highest international levels of excellence.

www.cambridge.org
Information on this title: www.cambridge.org/9781108843430
DOI: 10.1017/9781108918664

First published 2021

A catalogue record for this publication is available from the British Library.

Library of Congress Cataloging-in-Publication Data

NAMES: Faley, Timothy L., 1956- author.
TITLE: The innovation pyramid : a strategic methodology for impactful problem solving / Timothy L. Faley, University of the Virgin Islands.
DESCRIPTION: Cambridge, United Kingdom ; New York, NY : Cambridge University Press, 2021. | Includes bibliographical references and index.
IDENTIFIERS: LCCN 2020026136 (print) | LCCN 2020026137 (ebook) | ISBN 9781108843430 (hardback) | ISBN 9781108825108 (paperback) | ISBN 9781108918664 (ebook)
SUBJECTS: LCSH: Problem solving. | Creative thinking. | Organizational change. | Diffusion of innovations.
CLASSIFICATION: LCC HD30.29 .F35 2021 (print) | LCC HD30.29 (ebook) | DDC 658.4/063--dc23
LC record available at https://lccn.loc.gov/2020026136
LC ebook record available at https://lccn.loc.gov/2020026137

ISBN 978-1-108-84343-0 Hardback
ISBN 978-1-108-82510-8 Paperback

This book is dedicated to my wife, Kelley, for her love, support, and understanding.

Contents

PART II   THE DIVERGE–ORGANIZE–CONVERGE
PROCESS

Figures

I Introduction

WHAT IS INNOVATION?

Impactful problem-solving. Individually, corporately, and society-wide we face increasingly critical and complex problems. We long for new solutions that will generate meaningful and lasting positive change – not just solutions that are new or creative, but those that are impactful. While there are many definitions of "innovation" (Schaver, 2014) – the word is unfortunately on the brink of becoming a meaningless buzzword – the definition used throughout this book is impactful problem-solving that leverages a product or service or approach that is new, or at least perceived as new by the adopter (Anthony, 2012).

An innovation must solve a problem for someone. People, individually or organizationally, have problems. There is no problem without someone who is suffering from it. It is similar to a tree falling in the woods. If a tree falls in the empty woods, will it be heard? No. The falling tree will certainly produce sound waves, but there needs to be someone or something there for the sound to be "heard." Problems are analogous. Without people (individuals, groups, or organizations) who are directly or indirectly affected by a problem, then there really is no issue that needs to be resolved. For a solution to be impactful, it must both address a real problem and be adopted by the person, individually or corporately, who has the problem. That adoption could be widespread, as in the global adoption of smart phones, or that adoption could be narrow, as when our friend adopts our innovative solution to their relationship issue. No adoption, no impact. No impact, no innovation.

Innovation is therefore, by its very nature, outward facing. It encompasses two separate points of view (POVs). One POV is that of the adopter. An innovation must align with the needs of an adopting individual, group, or organization. The second POV is that of the creator of the innovation. That creator could be an individual, group, or organization. The two POVs could be one and the same if the innovation creator is creating a new solution to a problem of their own, but the two POVs are typically different.

By solving a problem for someone, an innovation creates impact. But impact can be measured in a number of different ways. For corporations, it may be measured in financial terms (reduced cost or increased profits) or in market terms (increased sales or market share). In government, the impact may be raising constituents above the poverty line or increasing their satisfaction index. In our personal lives, impact may be having a stronger relationship with our loved ones or a more satisfying career. It is not important *how* the impact is measured; what is important is that there *is* an impact.

An innovation must be new. However, an innovation does not necessarily need to be "a-brand-new-concept-to-the-universe" new, but rather it must be perceived as new by the adopter (Rogers, 1995). Indeed many innovations take something that is known in one field and apply it to another. Henry Ford's (2013) automobile manufacturing assembly line had its roots in the slaughter houses of Chicago. But the application of the automated "disassembly" processes ("Assembly," n.d.) was new to the manufacturing of goods like automobiles. While the concept of an assembly line was not a "brand new" concept, its application to the problem of automobile manufacturing certainly was new and impactful, and therefore an innovation.

Innovation is not an invention or a discovery. An invention is typically something that is novel, useful, and nonobvious. Flash memory was an invention. An invention can become an innovation, but only when it is adopted. Flash memory's use in digital cameras, for example, is an innovation. Similarly, discovery is also not an innovation, although it could certainly lead to one. A discovery is typically insight into how things work. Electrons flow freely down a copper wire. OK, so what? But that insight can be leveraged into something that is adopted to solve a problem – electric lights.

Innovation is not entrepreneurship. An innovation creates value for the adopter by solving a specific problem for them. That's half the entrepreneurship equation of creating and capturing value (Faley, 2015a). Thought of in this way, innovation is part of the continuum of entrepreneurship. Put another way, as Peter Drucker (1985) stated it, innovation is a tool of entrepreneurship. The two are part of one value-creation/value-capture continuum, although entrepreneurship is often taught solely from a value-capture perspective. There can also be entrepreneurship without innovation and innovation without entrepreneurship. We can create and capture value for a customer without creating something new. A franchise business does that. That's entrepreneurship without innovation. Alternatively, we can innovatively solve a personal problem for a friend. The friend's adoption of our new alternative and the impact it has on our friend makes it an innovation. But there is no "value-capture" portion, so no "entrepreneurship." Figure 1.1 shows the overlap of the entrepreneurship and innovation. There is certainly overlap between the two, but not complete overlap.

Innovation is also not creativity. Similar to innovation being the tool of the entrepreneur, creativity is the tool of the innovator. Creative thinking is the catalyst of innovation (Foursight, n.d.). We can do something "creative" that solves no problem and has no impact. As a result, we can be creative and not innovative as innovation is focused on problem-solving. Even a creative new product or service idea is not an innovation because the idea alone does not solve a problem. That idea could certainly lead to an innovation, but it is not a complete innovation. That idea must target

Entrepreneurship   Innovation   Creativity

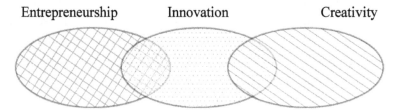

FIGURE 1.1 Creativity, innovation, and entrepreneurship continuum.

a specific problem. No problem, no adoption. No adoption, no impact. No impact, no innovation. The identification of the real, underlying problem that needs resolving is part of the innovation process, but not necessarily part of being creative. Then there is the execution side of innovation which is not part of creativity. For a solution to be adopted, it must exist and be available to the adopter. In other words, that innovation concept must be created and delivered to the adopter. Those actions are part of innovation, but not part of creativity. While there is significant overlap between the two, as Figure 1.1 illustrates, innovation and creativity do not completely overlap.

In short, innovation is impactful problem-solving that leverages something "new." Innovation overlaps with both creativity and entrepreneurship, but is not wholly either. The development of an innovation is a process of discovery; it is nonlinear, iterative, and knowledge-based. The Innovation Pyramid is a visual representation of a design thinking-based repeatable, learnable, nonlinear, iterative methodology that leverages the tools of creativity for its execution.

WHY IS INNOVATION IMPORTANT?

We need critical thinkers who can uncover the underlying root causes of our present situations amidst the vast noise of information that inundates us. We need these thinkers to analyze the facts in an objective manner so that a rational judgment can be reached (Schuster, 2018). And finally, we need them in all aspects of our life: in business, in government, in education, and in our personal lives. In short, we need impactful problem-solvers. We need innovators.

Impactful problem-solving – innovation – is necessary when stasis is no longer dominating or when incremental improvements on today's solutions will not get us where we want to be. We need new, impactful solutions that directly address today's problems, not simply polish yesterday's legacies. There are reasons the old solutions are not working today. The challenge is often not that the "solution" is outdated, but that the underlying cause of the problem has shifted. If the new underlying cause is not addressed, the desired impact will simply not be obtained.

For communities and individuals, innovation represents real change: not just window-dressing on old situations but something new that generates real, significant impact. The world is changing rapidly. We face, or will soon face – individually and corporately – new problems that will need data-supported solutions. We need a systematic way of approaching those problems, gathering the appropriate information, and creating those impactful solutions we long for.

While the need for innovations is in every aspect of our lives, the need is most easily measured in business. While we could certainly use innovations to address our personal issues, and on a larger scale, our societal issues, the corporate world needs them to survive. Innovation is consistently a top-five concern among CEOs according to TEC's Annual Global CEO Survey (TEC, 2018). Why?

> Effect of competition-driven markets is, over time, to commoditize any differentiation a company has and thereby diminish its ability to win customers and win capital and to win sales at attractive margins; to create attractive returns. The only way to respond to that is to continually to come up with new differentiation and to do that you have to innovate.
>
> Geoffrey Moore (2005), author of *Crossing the Chasm*

Peter Drucker (1985) puts it more succinctly. "Businesses must be able to innovate or else their competitors will render them obsolete."

Innovation determines the firm's ability to create future cash flows through new products, services, and ways of operating (business models). Future cash flows determine a firm's market value. It should be of no surprise then that a corporate CEO, whose variable pay is tied to the value of their firm's stock, is focused on innovation.

Given its importance to business, one would think that they would have the innovation process down to a science, but they are not even close. According to the NSF report, of all manufacturing firms only 23 percent have introduced new or significantly improved products/services between 2012 and 2014. It ranged from a high of 56.3 percent for communications equipment companies to a low of 10 percent for wood product firms (Kindlon, 2017).

The story is even worse for nonmanufacturing industries (i.e. services). Only 8.2 percent of firms have introduced new or significantly improved products or services during that period. Software firms led the way with 61.1 percent of firms introducing a new or significantly improved products or services during the 2012–2014 timeframe. The industry laggers were real estate or leasing firms at 4.7 percent.

While these numbers are dismal, the story is actually worse. There is "no correlation between the amount of money a company spends on research and development (R&D) and its overall financial results" (PWC, 2018). That strongly suggests that the conversion of discoveries and/or inventions to innovations is completely ad hoc at best. There appears to be no system for a firm – whose future is dependent on innovations – to become a serial innovator. Innovations occasionally occur, but randomly.

WHY IS IT SO DIFFICULT TO BE A SERIAL INNOVATOR?

Why is it so hard? Innovation requires three elements: people, place, process (Hasso, n.d.), or more generally, people, environment, and methodology.

People

There are actually two groups of people involved in generating impactful solutions: those creating the proposed innovation (the innovators) and those who have an issue they long to resolve (the adopters). While the innovator and adopter can be the same person, say if we are solving a problem for ourselves, would-be innovators too often project themselves as the "adopter" when they are not the ones suffering from the issue. Empathy is critical. The would-be innovator must have empathy for the adopter. The innovator must understand the would-be adopter's general issue and be able to drive that down to a specific need, want, or desire. That requires the innovator to see the world from the adopter's POV. The features of the innovator's proposed solution must align with the adopter's needs, wants, or desires. That requires that the innovator consider both what they can create and how that creation will align with the adopter's needs. That, in turn, requires multiple POV shifts throughout the innovation's development. This alone would make innovating difficult; as F. Scott Fitzgerald puts it, "The test of a first-rate intelligence is the ability to hold two opposed ideas in mind at the same time and still retain the ability to function."

Unfortunately, while this duality of POVs is critical, the focus of innovation training is too often innovator-centric. While creating innovation teams with diverse thinking sets is absolutely necessary, it is simply not sufficient to become a repeatable innovator. "Putting the right people in a room" is not a replicable process. The method element is missing. If we wanted to build a house for someone and were going to put a group of people together that had never built a house before, it would make sense to get a diverse set of skills on the team: carpenters, plumbers, masons, electricians, etc. If the people are clever, they may eventually figure it out. The process would be neither efficient nor predictable, but they could accomplish the task sometimes. Sounds a bit like the noncorrelation between R&D spending and innovation, doesn't it?

Environment

The second piece of the innovation puzzle is the environment. There are actually two environments that matter: the environment of the innovators (often the environment inside the organization in which they work) and that of the potential adopters. For the innovator, knowing what to do and having the right people but not having a supportive environment will not lead to a positive result. "You cannot grow roses in concrete" (Munro, 2018). Let's say that we desire to drive from New York to California. We have a map and a car. We have people who know how to drive and can work together. What we do not have are the necessary fuel stations along the way, as our automobile operates on hydrogen. It is a nonsupportive environment for our trip. Some environments can be supportive, some neutral, while some are simply counterproductive to repetitive innovating. Does the culture of the organization treat failure as a part of the learning process or as a career-ending event? The former is the bare minimum requirement for a supportive innovation-development environment, while the latter is a toxic environment for would-be innovators.

The would-be adopter's environment is also critical. There must be a pathway for the would-be adopter to obtain the proposed innovation. There is no innovation without adoption. If there are significant barriers that separate the target adopter from the would-be innovation, then there will be no adoption. This is true even if every other part of the innovation development was performed perfectly. The adopter-impacting environment ranges from local laws or customs that prohibit or discourage the adoption of the potential innovation to financial or physical access barriers to the would-be innovation.

Methodology

While the other two legs of the stool (people and environment) are definitely challenging, it is often the lack of a methodology that makes or breaks our ability to repeatedly create and deliver new impactful solutions. Figure 1.2 summarizes the impact of the lack of each of these elements on the desired outcome of creating an authentic innovation. Note that an inconsistent output is predicted by a lack of a repeatable methodology. That inconsistency sounds eerily familiar to the previously mentioned lack of a correlation between an organization's

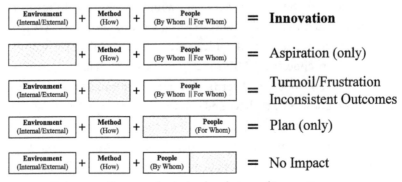

FIGURE 1.2 Impacts of missing key factors of innovation.

R&D spending and its ability to create innovations. Other common organizational outcomes are also identified in Figure 1.2.

A method is not a guarantee for reaching an impactful solution. If we correctly follow a recipe, we will end up with a predictable result. This not the case for a methodology, as will be further explained in Chapter 2. A methodology is a system of procedures and/or techniques that allow the accomplishment of a set of tasks without guarantee of a specific outcome. A repeatable method controls a number of innovation-project variables, but not all of them. Those variables not controlled for will require our judgment. Judgment remains an important element in innovation development. Repeatable use of a consistent method provides a means to improve our judgment and therefore improve on our ability to become serial innovators.

The focus of this book is describing a learnable, repeatable, nonlinear, iterative, knowledge-based methodology for generating innovations. The method's description will seem foreign to some and obvious to others. Naturally gifted serial innovators operate on instinct. They just "know" things should be done a certain way and a certain order. They are very intuitive. That's great. For them. Some do not even realize they are following a methodology, but they are. They may even argue that it cannot be "taught" as they are "born" with this ability. That is simply not true; any method, once identified, can be codified and learned. The methodology described in this book is a codification of methods practiced by successful intuitives. The method presented is certainly not the only viable method, but it is one that works.

The design thinking-based Innovation Pyramid, which is detailed in Part I of this book, describes this needed overarching guide. This part presents the macro-level view of innovation development. Those that prefer to learn from the general-to-specific should begin reading here. The second section of the book (Part II) details the creativity-based Diverge–Organize–Converge (DOC) Process essential to implementing The Pyramid methodology. This is the micro-level view. Those that prefer to learn from specific-to-general could read this part first, and then read Part I. The order of the reading does not matter. The Innovation Pyramid can be thought of as the assembly instructions while the DOC Process provides the toolset necessary to perform the assembly. Together they create a learnable, implementable, repeatable means for developing true innovations. Innovations that will generate real, positive impact.

UNIQUE ASPECTS OF THE INNOVATION PYRAMID METHODOLOGY

The Innovation Pyramid book differentiates itself from other offerings on innovation in several distinct ways. First and foremost, this book is focused on a methodology for innovating. Most other books on innovation target the people side of innovation. They either focus on assembling an innovation team with the right combination of innate abilities or they focus on developing an individual's creativity skillset.

The Innovation Pyramid is a visual representation of a strategic approach for developing impactful solutions to real problems, or in other words, to create innovations. The user-centric, design thinking-based Innovation Pyramid is a physical representation of a repeatable overarching guide, or roadmap for producing innovations. The overarching methodology is articulated in Part I of this book. The methodology leverages the creativity-based DOC Process detailed in Part II of this book. The DOC Process can be used on its own to improve our problem-solving ability, but more importantly, is essential to reducing The Innovation Pyramid to practice. Think of the DOC Process as a set of tools that helps us implement the overarching methodology, similar to a wrench set being the specific tools which allow us to rebuild an engine. The tools alone are not enough. Simply having a set of tools, and having no other knowledge about engine reconstruction, would not allow us to get the job done. On the other hand, if we had a step-by-step guide for rebuilding an engine, but had no tools or understanding of their use, then that guide would be nothing more than a theoretical construct. Together the two parts get us there. The Innovation Pyramid is the overarching pathway for developing an innovation and the DOC Process provides the means to transform that construct into reality. The book can be read in any order. Detail-oriented readers may want to read Part II before moving on to Part I, while those that prefer the big-picture before the details can read it as presented.

The Innovation Pyramid methodology distinguishes itself through its bifurcation of the innovation process. It first separates the innovation's design from its execution. The top two levels of The Pyramid represent the design, while the lower half represents the execution stages. The design and execution levels are each further bifurcated. In the design half, the identification of the problem is separated from the creation of a solution. This requires the recognition and balancing of a number of POVs. In the execution portion of The Pyramid, the planning and resourcing of the innovation project are separated from the plan's implementation. Finally, The Pyramid has built-in assessment at each of the design and execution stages, in addition to providing a structure for reviewing and learning from the entire innovation project.

Design/Execution Separation

One differentiating approach of The Innovation Pyramid methodology is separating design from execution. There are two parts to developing anything. Design it first, then execute it. Or put another way, "All things are created twice. There's a mental, or first creation, and a physical or second creation to all things" (Covey, 2008). The activities of "design" and "execution" are often inadvertently intertwined so as to confuse the two. They, of course, flow back and forth, but design first, then execute. The Innovation Pyramid methodology is segmented into four levels, two design and two execution. Both design and execution transition from a broad purview, to ensure that nothing is overlooked, to a zoomed-in detailed implementable view. Delineating these steps allows for both straightforward innovation development and post-project review.

Problem/Solution Separation

Within the design stages, the method separates the problem from the solution. Other offerings muddle the two or in other ways short-change the identification of the core problem. It is impossible to generate a perfect solution to an ill-defined problem. The reality is that focusing on Problem Identification (i.e. working in the "problem space") for an extended period of time is, however, difficult and unnatural. We human beings think in terms of actions. Those actions are solutions to situations. It likely goes back to our "fight or flight" response. When that saber tooth tiger was charging at our ancient ancestors, they did not pause to consider the root of the problem by asking "why" this tiger may be attacking them. Was the tiger hungry? Did our ancestor inadvertently threaten it? No. They went into action ... they fought it or ran from it to survive. But today's problems are more complex. Just tossing random answers at them no longer works. We need to really understand the problem we are trying to solve before attempting to solve it. That seems obvious, but it is much easier said than done.

Most of us are so solution-oriented that we actually think our proposed solution describes the problem. It does not. The proposed solution is only the mirror image of the problem. When we examine something only by looking at in in a mirror we lose depth. We have to retrain ourselves to "transition" to the other side to get the full immersive experience; to understand the know-how and know-what of the problem before attempting to develop solutions for it. That will be unnatural and feel uncomfortable. We will make excuses to avoid doing it. Excuses like "this is a waste of time; we already know what the problem is." Go slow to go fast. That's the facilitator's axiom and it fully applies here. To avoid a lot of false starts and solutions that do not create the desired impact, we must learn to stay in the problem space as long as we can stand to do so. That will take patience and plenty of empathy for the would-be adopter of the innovation. Without empathy, we will not be able to remain in the problem space long enough to dig down to the root of the real issue. Without empathy we will prematurely jump to "solution space" – start to propose solutions. Without empathy we will not create impact. Diagnose before prescribing. The Innovation Pyramid methodology will keep us in the problem space long enough to fully understand the root-cause issue before moving onto creating solutions.

Plan/Implement Separation

Similar to the design stages, the execution section of The Pyramid is also bifurcated. Execution is separated into Plan and Perform. This separation increases efficiency by focusing us on the activities we need to perform when we need to perform them. It also aids in diagnosis. The implementation team is often vilified when the innovation project fails. Was it really an implementation issue or was it a poor plan? Separating the two makes this diagnosis possible.

Multiple Points-of-View

Yet another differentiator of the approach described in this book is the consideration of multiple POVs. Both the would-be innovator and the would-be adopter POVs, as well as their unique environments, are considered. Generating impact is not just about those creating the innovation, we must also deliver it to the innovator. It must also create value for the adopter. That value-creation is from the adopter's POV, not the innovation creator's. The method of creating an innovation that is laid out in this book requires going back-and-forth between those two POVs at each of the four levels of The Innovation Pyramid, not just during the two design levels. In addition to these two POVs, there may be collaborators inside and outside the innovation-creation organization that will be involved in the project. Their POVs must also be taken into account.

Assessment Throughout

The final differentiator of The Innovation Pyramid methodology is that assessment is performed at each Pyramid level. Each of the two design and each of the two execution stages have evaluative conditions to meet. The assessments start as very qualitative, but increase in rigor as we descend down The Pyramid. This approach allows for quick pivots at the early stages and increasing more rigorous ones as we approach implementation.

Since this is a methodology and not a recipe, even though assessment is performed at each level of the methodology to determine if rational and reasonable choices are being made, the overall outcome may still end up not being what was desired at the start. The final project assessment is a systematic review of each layer of The Pyramid, revealing how choices made at each layer may have resulted in the nondesired outcome. Once the root-issue is uncovered, the innovator iterates back to the appropriate level, alters their original choice, and proceeds again from that point. This is particularly important when utilizing The Pyramid in creating a prototype or pilot program. While it is not uncommon to traverse through The Pyramid multiple times in the development of an innovation, it is guaranteed in the development of a prototype or pilot program. In these cases, all levels of The Innovation Pyramid will be completed during the completion of a prototype or pilot program. After their implementation, a systemic review of the project, utilizing the method of Chapter 7 should be performed. This additional insight gained from the review, plus the knowledge gained from the pilot (or prototype), is then utilized in traversing The Pyramid a second time for the development of the final innovation.

ORGANIZATION OF THE BOOK

This book reflects the nonlinear iterative nature of innovating by not being laid out in a linear fashion. Rather, the book is organized into two integrated, but stand-alone sections. The reader can benefit from reading either section of the book, but combined they constitute a serious step toward becoming a serial innovator. The sections can be read in any order.

The first of the two sections (Part I) lays out the overarching innovation methodology of the design thinking-based Innovation Pyramid. The Innovation Pyramid is the overarching, zoomed-out pathway; it is a project's assembly instructions. The second section (Part II) describes the use of the creativity-based DOC Process. The DOC Process has multiple uses on its own, but more importantly, is essential to reducing The Innovation Pyramid to practice. The DOC Process is a zoomed-in toolset required to complete the assembly described in the first part of the book. Finally, the book's appendixes highlight detailed DOC Process techniques for use in both the problem space and the solution space. The remainder of this chapter highlights the key concepts of the remaining chapters and appendices.

Part I: Innovation Design and Execution

Chapter 2 – Introduction to The Innovation Pyramid

Key Concept: Part I of the book, starts with Chapter 2, an overview of The Innovation Pyramid methodology. The chapter describes the overall approach to using The Innovation Pyramid. The overarching method is visually encompassed as The Innovation Pyramid, an inverted triangular pyramid that is sliced into four layers (see Figure 1.3). The three sides of The Pyramid represent the "What" (desired outcome for that level), the "Who" (those who are leading and/or impacted by the activities at this stage), and the "How" (how the desired outcome of each layer is achieved). Each layer of this section incorporates at least two POVs (the innovation creator and its adopter). The interior of The Pyramid is assessment, which occurs at each level. The top two levels of The Pyramid focus on the innovation's

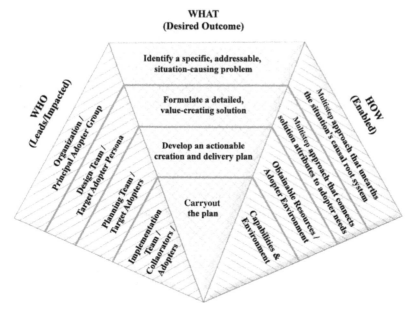

FIGURE 1.3 The Innovation Pyramid laid flat.

design, while the bottom two layers concentrate on the innovation's execution.

This chapter additionally describes the overall layer-by-layer flow necessary to move from the original situation we find ourselves in to implementing a new impactful solution. Given The Pyramid describes a nonlinear process, while there is a general "flow" through The Pyramid, there is no sequential step-by-step checklist to follow. The order is not as important as completing every segment of The Pyramid. Chapters 4–6 detail each layer of The Pyramid. Each of those chapters concludes with a "Common Mistakes" section describing the common errors incurred at that level of the methodology. While each chapter describes specific techniques and examples, one overarching example transcends the design levels of The Pyramid illustrating how the method flows from level to level for a specific project.

Chapter 3 – Level 1: Problem Identification
Key Concept: The Innovation Pyramid segments the innovation's design from its execution. The design stage is further segmented into Problem Identification and Solution Formulation. The first level of The Pyramid, which is the first stage of the innovation's design, describes a procedure for identifying and defining root causes of larger situations. Like The Innovation Pyramid itself, this five-step procedure for Problem Identification is a nonlinear and iterative process of discovery. These steps also incorporate a core tenet of The Pyramid which is: diverge before converge. The methodology consistently prompts us to broaden our purview before narrowing it.

Step 1: Clearly state the starting situation or issue.
Step 2: Zoom out to define the General Problem.
Step 3: Draft a neutral problem statement.
Step 4: Zoom in, layer-by-layer, to a root cause.
Step 5: Identify the Principal Adopter.

Chapter 4 – Level 2: Solution Formulation
Key Concept: The second design stage focuses on creating an impactful solution. The first step is to narrow The Principal Adopter group, the

general group for whom the innovation is being created, identified at the end of Level 1, to a Target Adopter persona with specific needs, wants, and/or desires. The Target Adopter is the specific group for whom the innovation is designed and creates value. The five-step guideline for completing this stage is as follows:

Step 1: Describe a specific Target Adopter persona.
Step 2: Determine a solution approach.
Step 3: Craft a detailed solution.
Step 4: Establish a clear value proposition.
Step 5: Quantify the Target Adopter group size.

The final step in this stage is to quantify the size of this Target Adopter group. This step may be temporarily skipped until that specific information is needed in Level 3. The objective is to keep the design detailed, but qualitative until it is understood that it can be successfully executed.

Chapter 5 – Level 3: Plan
Key Concept: This chapter transitions from the innovation's design to its execution. The purpose of this level is to develop a creation and delivery plan. The plan must include how the innovation will actually be created, of course, but it must additionally articulate how that created innovation will be delivered to the adopter. The complete plan identifies the implementation team as well as the resources required to execute the plan. If those resources are unobtainable, then the plan must be modified. This creation and delivery plan will also be utilized as a "sales" document necessary to pitch this concept to potential supporters or detractors.

Chapter 6 – Level 4: Perform
Key Concept: This chapter is about implementation – getting it done. This level focuses on assessing the performance of the plan; the team and the environment associated with both the innovation's creation and its delivery to the adopter. Too often implementation focuses on the people alone; it must also examine both the innovator's

"internal" environment in addition to externalities that may impact the innovation creators or its adopters.

Chapter 7 – Systematic Pyramid Review

Key Concept: The overall methodology described in this book is both nonlinear and iterative. There are many choices that must be made along the way. While assessment is performed at each level to ensure that rational and reasonable choices are being made, the overall outcome may still end up not being what was desired at the start. The plan's implementation team is typically unfairly vilified when this occurs. This chapter lays out a systematic review of each layer of The Pyramid, revealing how choices made at each layer may have contributed to the nondesired outcome. Once the root-issue is uncovered, the innovator iterates back to the appropriate level, alters their original choice, and proceeds again from that point. This is particularly important when utilizing The Pyramid in creating a prototype or pilot program. In those cases it is known that The Pyramid will be traversed more than once. Once for the development of the prototype and a second time for the development of the final innovation.

Part II: The Diverge–Organize–Converge Process

Chapter 8 – Diverge–Organize–Converge Process Overview

Key Concept: This second part provides details of the creativity-based DOC Process. The DOC Process can be used on its own to improve our problem-solving ability, but more importantly, is essential to reducing The Innovation Pyramid to practice. The DOC Process has three steps: Diverge, Organize, and Converge. This chapter provides an overview of those three steps and how this process can be applied to either the problem space (identifying a root-cause problem) or its more common application to the solution space (generating new solution concepts). Similar to the design chapters, one overarching example transcends all three steps of the DOC Process illustrating how the method flows step to step.

Chapter 9 – Diverge

Key Concept: This chapter describes in detail how to use the first step in the DOC Process – Diverge. As with every step of the DOC Process, Diverge applies to both Problem Identification and Solution Formulation. Most often this technique is used to "brainstorm" new solutions to problems. Rarely is it used to actually identify the problems which these solutions hypothetically fix. Both, however, are necessary. This chapter illuminates the subtle differences between how to apply the technique to the problem space as well as the solution space.

Chapter 10 – Organize

Key Concept. The Organize step, the second step of the DOC Process, is the transition step between the divergent-thinking process of step one and the convergent-thinking process of step three. This important Organize step has characteristics of both the divergent and convergent steps. The Organize step may cause us to return to the Diverge step before proceeding to the Converge step of Chapter 11. This makes the DOC Process a nonlinear process inside the nonlinear methodology that is The Innovation Pyramid. Creative-thinking sessions tend to break down after the divergent-thinking step. This chapter describes how the proper use of the Organize step will resolve this common issue.

Chapter 11 – Converge

Key Concept: This chapter describes the function and use of the third step of the DOC Process, Converge. The ultimate desired outcome for the Converge step of the DOC Process is to make a choice; choose the "best." This is true whether we are working in the problem or solution space. An important element of this step, therefore, is to consciously define the criteria by which we will be selecting the "best" so as to create a "level evaluation field" for all concepts that are being judged. As with the Organize step, the criteria definition may cause us to return to either the Diverge or the Organize step. Despite the number of iterations through the steps, the DOC Process ultimately ends with a single choice.

Chapter 12 – Book Summary
Key Concept: This chapter wraps up the entire book and provides final insights. This book is for innovators, individuals, and corporations who want to become serial innovators. Innovation is a learnable skill that virtually everyone needs today. In various aspects of our lives, we are all confronted with new and challenging problems where the "tried and true" approaches of yesteryear no longer yield the longed-for result. To resolve that dilemma, we must innovate. In both small and large ways, we all need to improve our abilities to innovate. This chapter summarizes the book's methodology for innovating.

Appendices

Appendix A: Interviewing for Insight and Persona Development
Key Concept: Interviewing for Insight (IFI) and Persona Development are unique techniques for applying the DOC Process. Uncovering adopter group's needs/wants/desires is an exercise in tacit knowledge discovery. This appendix provides detailed instructions on how to implement the IFI technique to uncover adopter needs, wants, and/ or desires. Once a plethora of needs/wants/desires are uncovered, the second half of this appendix illustrates how that information is shaped into personas – arch-type adopters that make choices based on a specific and unique combination of needs, wants, and/or desires. Overall, this appendix describes an alternative implementation of the DOC Process. The needs identification via the IFIs is the Diverge step. Persona creation is the Organize step and the selection of one persona to target, the Target Adopter, is the Converge step of that process.

Appendix B: Divergent-thinking prompts
Key Concept: Tools, like a screwdriver, are useful to have and know how to use. In-and-of-themselves, however, tools alone do not fix anything. Once armed with an innovation methodology, however, having a wide assortment of tools can expand our ability to innovate. This appendix reviews a number of tools and techniques aimed at expanding divergent thinking. These tools generally fall into two categories: ones that coax us to shift our POV and others that help us alter our perspective.

PART I Innovation Design and Execution

2 Introduction to The Innovation Pyramid

The Innovation Pyramid is a strategic methodology for developing impactful solutions to real problems, or in other words, to create innovations. The design thinking–based Innovation Pyramid is a physical representation of a repeatable overarching guide or roadmap for producing innovations. The user-centric, design thinking–based methodology provides a pathway that extends from identifying the real underlying problem, and the specific group that is in need of a solution, to executing a plan for its resolution. The methodology leverages the creativity-based Diverge–Organize–Converge (DOC) Process detailed in Part II of this book. The DOC Process gets us "out of the box," by ensuring that we diverge our thinking before converging on a single idea or solution. This process can be used on its own to improve problem-solving ability, but more importantly, is an essential process for reducing The Innovation Pyramid to practice. Think of the DOC Process as a set of tools that aid in the accomplishment of a larger objective, similar to a wrench set being the specific tools that allow us to rebuild an engine. The tools alone are not enough. Simply having a set of tools, and having no other knowledge about engine reconstruction, would not allow us to get the job done. On the other hand, if we had a step-by-step guide for rebuilding an engine, but had no tools or understanding of their use, then that guide would be nothing more than a theoretical construct. Together the two elements get us there. The Innovation Pyramid is the overarching pathway for developing an innovation and the DOC Process is an important tool utilized in transforming that construct into reality.

NONLINEAR, ITERATIVE, LEARNABLE, REPEATABLE METHODOLOGY

The Innovation Pyramid is a visual representation of a repeatable, nonlinear, iterative, learnable methodology. Being nonlinear, there is no "right" place to start. Typically, one would start at the top, Level 1, and work down level-by-level, but that is not always the case, nor does it need to be. What is important is that we traverse through every segment of The Pyramid at least once.

The method is also iterative. We may find ourselves completing one segment of The Pyramid and discover that we need to go back and repeat a previously completed segment, that is the nature of a learning system. The Innovation Pyramid is a pathway to understanding as well as a pathway to developing innovations. Such iterations would not be necessary if we learned everything we needed to know about creating an impactful solution all at once. Learning, however, does not work that way. We will continue to learn as we move through The Pyramid. That increased understanding may impact decisions made at previous junctures in The Pyramid, causing us to go back and repeat a step with this new insight.

The Innovation Pyramid is a learnable methodology. Many of the great innovators are incredibly intuitive. The wondrous innovations they conjure up seem to come out of thin air, but they do not. These innovators follow a methodology, albeit one that is usually unknown even to themselves. The Innovation Pyramid is the codification of a critical pathway leading to an innovation. It organizes and rationally sequences all the activities necessary to create an innovation. It is certainly not the only way to create innovations, but it provides a teachable means to create new innovations, develop new innovators, and enable organizations to become more innovative.

The Innovation Pyramid is a repeatable methodology, but not a recipe. If we correctly follow a recipe, we will end up with a predictable result. This is true when we are making bread or wiring an electrical outlet; however, this is not the case for a methodology. A methodology is a system of procedures and/or techniques that allow the accomplishment of a set of tasks without guarantee of a specific outcome. The reason the outcome is not guaranteed is that while the methodology controls for a number of innovation-development variables, it does not eliminate them all. Judgment remains important. A repeatable method provides a means for our judgment to improve.

Consider the archer: if the archer holds the bow consistently, draws back the arrow consistently, and aims consistently, then the errant shot is a result of the archer's judgment of how the wind, humidity, and other environmental variables might have impacted the shot. All the variability in the outcome cannot be eliminated, but having a consistent method will reduce the parameters impacting the ultimate outcome to those that are dependent on the archer's judgments. A consistent method, combined with a consistent review of the outcome of the shot, allows the archer to improve their judgment. By repeated experience using the same method for firing the arrow in different conditions, the archer's ability to judge the impact of the wind on the flight of their arrow improves. Contrarily, if the archer held the bow differently and aimed differently in every different weather condition, there is no way to discern which change most impacted the final outcome. There is no learning, just random attempt after random attempt. Some attempts will succeed and some will fail miserably, but there will be no way to discern what caused which outcome nor will there be any ability to improve upon the next attempt. The method provides the foundation on which learning can occur, but only if the method is repeatable.

Similar to the archer comparing the result of their shot versus its intended target, a review of the ultimate impact of the innovation versus our initial desired outcome will allow the organization to improve their decision-making judgments that occur throughout the development of an innovation, thus allowing the organization to become better serial innovators. The feedback loop is significantly longer for the innovator than it is for the archer. For the archer, the result of their judgment occurs in seconds. For the innovator, particularly for the innovator designer, the measure of the actual versus anticipated (hoped for) impact could be months or even years.

That is why documenting the judgments we make as we progress through The Innovation Pyramid methodology is very important. The overarching guide to reviewing and making adjustments to the judgments we made as we traversed through The Innovation Pyramid is detailed in Chapter 7.

In addition to the systematic review of the overall impact of the innovation versus our anticipated outcome, The Pyramid incorporates assessment criteria as part of each level. These assessment criteria accomplish two objectives. First, they force us to make rational and reasonable judgments. More importantly, they also force us to make conscious ones and discourage "guessing" or other logical leaps. While making rational and reasonable judgments will not guarantee the overall results we desire, they provide us a place to pivot from should the ultimate innovation impact not turn out as we had hoped. There is no rational pivoting from a logical leap; it only leads to more of the same.

THE INNOVATION PYRAMID STRUCTURE

The Innovation Pyramid is an inverted triangular pyramid, or to get technical, a tetrahedron. The Pyramid is "inverted" with the broadest part (typically thought of as the "base") at the top. Its appearance reflects the fact that we generally start with some broad conditions and narrow to the specific execution of a detailed solution. Ordinarily, it all begins with a "situation" in which we find ourselves. That situation could be personal, organizational, or societal. That situation is generally broad and vague. Our desire is to resolve that situation, but it is too vague and typically too big for us to be able to do much about it directly. We need to reframe the situation into a problem, then uncover a root of that problem that we can do something about. After identifying the root problem, we need to craft a solution to that problem, plan the execution of our solution, and then implement that plan. The Innovation Pyramid reflects this approach by breaking down this pathway into the following four interconnected layers:

- Problem Identification
- Solution Formulation

- Plan Creation
- Plan Implementation

These four horizontal layers of The Innovation Pyramid are stacked top to bottom. These slices represent distinct levels of The Pyramid. Level 1, Problem Identification, is the top level, the broadest portion of The Pyramid. Level 4, Plan Implementation, is at the point of The Pyramid, the bottom level of the inverted pyramid. As noted in Chapter 1, there are two general parts to developing anything: its design and its execution. The top half of The Pyramid represents the innovation's design stages, while the bottom half represents the innovation's execution stages. The design and execution portions of The Pyramid are further bifurcated. Problem Identification (Level 1) is treated separately from Solution Formulation (Level 2). The execution portion is similarly additionally subdivided into Planning (Level 3) and Implementation (Level 4). These divisions accomplish two major goals. The first is that this structure increases the method's repeatability and learnability. Secondly, this segmentation immensely aids in diagnosing what may have gone wrong, so that we can make the adjustments necessary to hone in on our original desired outcome. This is especially important when we may be traversing The Pyramid structure multiple times, once for say, prototype development, and a second time for the final product launch – or once for a pilot program and the second time for its global launch. The motivation for the pilot program or the prototype is to increase our understanding. The Innovation Pyramid is a learning system. It is designed to incorporate new knowledge, as we obtain it, to refine our decisions and will improve the overall project's outcome.

The Pyramid has three faces or sections. Every Pyramid slice, therefore, has three segments, one on each Pyramid face. Each segment, of a particular slice, is connected to every other two segments on that level. The three Pyramid sections address three different aspects of designing and executing impactful solutions: the What, the How, and the Who.

What: What is the desired outcome at that level?

How: How will this be accomplished or enabled?

Who: Who will lead the activities and/or is impacted by the outcome of this level?

Slicing The Pyramid between the "Who" and the "How" sections and laying it flat produces the view shown in Figure 2.1.

Starting from the top, in the first design stage of The Pyramid, the "What" sections narrow from the original general situation to a specific, situation-causing problem (Level 1). In Level 2, the second design stage, that specific problem is transformed into unmet or undermet needs, wants, and/or desires of a narrowly identified adopter. A solution is crafted in this level that creates value for this adopter through the connection of the attributes of the solution to the needs/wants/desires of the proposed adopter. Continuing to descend down to Level 3, the focus switches from design to execution. The desired outcome for the "What" section of Level 3 is an actionable plan that both creates the innovation and delivers it to its targeted adopter. Level 4 is focused on successfully carrying out that plan.

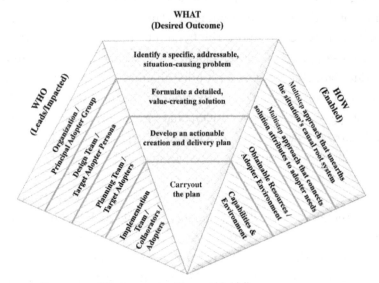

FIGURE 2.1 The Innovation Pyramid laid flat.

The "Who" section of The Pyramid encompasses several different points of view (POVs). At least two different people, or more typically two different groups of people, are always directly involved in innovations: those creating the potentially impactful solution (the innovator) and those who adopt that solution because they have a problem that they long to resolve (the adopter). There is no problem if no one is affected by it. The adopter description sharpens considerably as we traverse through the two design levels. In Level 1, the adopter is the broadly defined group affected by the issue. In Level 2, the adopter is narrowed to a very specific description of an arch-type adopter: an adopter persona with specific needs, wants, and/or desires. The creator of the innovation may have also have outside partners, or collaborators, who support the creation and delivery of the innovation to the adopter. The POVs of these collaborators are also important and must be taken into account.

There are times when the adopter and the innovator are the same person. This occurs, for example, when we are solving a problem for ourselves. However, we too often project ourselves as the solution adopter when we are not actually the ones directly affected by the issue; we will not be the ones adopting the solution we are creating. When this occurs, instead of creating impactful solutions that get adopted, we instead create solutions that we think we would like. Empathy is the key to creating impactful solutions. We must feel for and identify with those who are negatively affected. It is easy to view situations from our own POV, but significantly more challenging to develop empathy for others. Such empathy, however, is exactly what is required if we are to create true innovations, as a solution is only impactful if it is adopted.

The "How" section of each level outlines how the desired outcomes of each level will be accomplished or enabled. For the design portion of The Pyramid, this section contains the approach or guidelines for accomplishing the tasks necessary to lead us to the desired outcome of that section. For the execution levels, Pyramid Levels 3 and 4, this section describes the factors that will enable and/or hinder the would-be innovation's creation and adoption. The "environments" of both Levels 3 and 4 refer to conditions both inside and outside the innovation-creating organization as well as externalities beyond anyone's control.

The Innovation Pyramid is a solid, and not a hollow, structure. In addition to the components of the three faces, The Pyramid's core represents assessment. If we are not assessing, we are guessing. Assessment is the filling that binds the pyramid faces to each other. An assessment is applied to each level of The Pyramid. The level-specific assessments will ensure that we are making rational and reasonable choices at each Pyramid level, but will not guarantee the long-term outcome. Making the best decisions we can at each level with the information available to us at the time (local optimization) will simply not guarantee that our innovation will ultimately produce the desired impact (global optimization).

The Pyramid is also a learning methodology that enables our continuous improvement through the application of our past learnings to every subsequent innovation project. The more times we apply this repeatable method, the more we will learn and the better our judgment will become. Better judgment leads to better choices, better choices lead to better outcomes. The overarching assessment, in addition to specific-level assessments, aids us in determining why the target was missed and how to improve the next time.

OVERALL METHODOLOGY DESCRIPTION

One of the challenges of a nonlinear methodology is that there is no absolute "starting" point. There is no "It's always best to start at the beginning" (The Wizard of Oz, 1939) counsel that applies here. It is not uncommon to start at any point on the first two levels. Regardless of where we start, we will need to ensure that every segment of The Innovation Pyramid is eventually completed. Doing so requires that, regardless of where we start, we work our way back to Level 1 and resolve all three segments of that level before heading back down toward The Pyramid's point.

The Innovation Pyramid separates the innovation design from its execution. It also separates the POV of the innovator from that of the innovation's adopter. The method further separates the solution from the problem. It is actually quite common to confuse solutions with problems. Problem-solvers often argue over the best solution to implement when they have yet to define the specific problem they are attempting to resolve! We actually arrive at that situation honestly. We are action-oriented beings; this stems from our "fight-or-flight" heritage. If our ancestors would have deeply contemplated the root cause of why that saber-toothed tiger was charging them, we would not be here today! It is actually uncomfortable for us to stay in the problem-examination space, and so we have to fight the urge to jump to the solution mode. When we visit our physician, however, we want her to fully understand and properly diagnose our problem before prescribing a treatment. The same applies to innovation development.

The typical starting point for producing an innovation is the original situation or an initially identified issue. That situation is often fairly high level. We want better roads, our sales are dropping, or perhaps we are feeling unsatisfied with our current job. While we typically believe that the situation is a problem statement, it often comes disguised as a proposed solution. Notice that "better roads" is actually a solution. What problem does "better roads" actually resolve? The more we can train our minds to separate problems from solutions, the better innovators we will become.

The first layer of The Innovation Pyramid, detailed in Chapter 3, is Problem Identification. This layer describes an approach for identifying and defining root causes of larger situations. Like The Innovation Pyramid itself, this five-step procedure for Problem Identification is a nonlinear and iterative process of discovery. Steps may be skipped or repeated depending on where we start or how the process of discovery unfolds. The five-step procedure is, therefore, more of a guideline than a rigorous process. One of the characteristics of The Pyramid is that we always diverge before converging. Problem Identification ensures that we will not miss diagnosing the disease by focusing too narrowly on its symptoms. The goal for this level is to identify an issue we can affect, but also be assured that that the issue is firmly connected to the original situation that we desire to impact. The five-step guideline detailed in Chapter 3 is as follows:

Step 1: Clearly state the starting situation or issue.
Step 2: Zoom out to define the General Problem.
Step 3: Draft a neutral problem statement.
Step 4: Zoom in, layer by layer, to a root cause.
Step 5: Identify the Principal Adopter.

The first step in the Problem Identification guideline is to describe the original situation or initially identified issue. We may have started with a solution concept, but if that was the case, we need to flip that perspective and describe the problem we are facing. The second step is to zoom out and broaden our purview. This allows us to see the problem in a bigger context, which ensures that we are not initially focusing too sharply on a symptom of a larger issue. We do not want to miss the forest for focusing on a particular tree. The third step is to create a neutral General Problem statement. Our problem descriptions can be biased. Those biases infer certain solution approaches while eliminating others. As we are not searching for solutions at this Pyramid level, it is important not to eliminate some.

The fourth step in the guideline is to narrow from the General Problem to a root cause that we will attempt to resolve in the second stage of the design, Level 2 (Chapter 4). We want to methodically and purposefully dig down from the General Problem, layer by layer. We are not simply seeking a smaller problem to solve; we are searching for a smaller problem that has a strong connection to the General Problem. We want to create a domino effect such that when we resolve the root-cause problem, the impact of that resolution cascades all the way up to impact the General Problem. The stronger the root system we identify as we dig down, the bigger the domino effect will be as the impact cascades back up. We also want to avoid any logical leaps as they represent disconnections in the root system. With an intuitive leap we no longer know how the root system is interconnected; we simply randomly jumped to another issue at another level of the root system, that is a situation we need to avoid.

The fifth and final step of the Problem Identification guideline is an assessment of whether or not we have completed the previous step. When digging down, layer by layer, uncovering the interconnection of the roots of the General Problem, we need to know when to stop. We have reached that endpoint in our archaeological dig when we can clearly name the Principal Adopters of our innovation, not only those affected by the issue we have identified.

At the end of Level 1 of The Innovation Pyramid methodology, we have:

- defined a General Problem from our initial situation;
- determined a root cause of that General Problem that our organization is able and willing to resolve;
- determined the connections between the root cause and the General Problem; and
- identified an adopter group that is both impacted by the root-cause issue and will be the general group for whom we are creating the innovation.

Level 2 of The Innovation Pyramid is Solution Formulation. It is not uncommon to iterate between Levels 1 and 2 multiple times, as the two design stages of The Innovation Pyramid work together to ensure that a complete and detailed design is crafted before any implementation is attempted. This second design stage focuses on Solution Formulation. At the end of Pyramid Level 2, we will have identified a

- specific new solution (detailed and fully designed);
- specific Target Adopter persona with clearly identified unmet or undermet needs, wants, and/or desires; will also have quantified the size of this group (even if it is only a rough estimate); and

- distinct value proposition: a clear connection between the features of the new solution with the needs/wants/desires of the target persona.

The entire pathway through Level 2 requires multiple steps. These steps are a guide to reaching the objectives of this level and are not a prescription. Iteration among these steps is not uncommon. It is also recommended that Step 5 *not* be completed until that specific information is needed to perform the assessment in Level 3. The rationale for keeping the first two design stages as qualitative as possible for as long as possible is that this encourages flexibility. Qualitative descriptions of problems and solutions can easily change, but detailed quantification of adopter group sizes cannot. Once innovation teams have performed the quantitative work, they are less likely to pivot from the identified target persona or their solution concept. Given this is a process of discovery, we want to stay as flexible as possible. A ballpark estimate of the adopter group will be helpful and is recommended, but creating a detailed estimate before completing Level 3 could derail the discovery process. The five steps of the guideline for this second design stage are as follows:

Step 1: Describe a specific Target Adopter persona.
- Identify the Principal Adopter's current BATNO (i.e. their Best Alternative To a New Option).
- Perform open-ended interviews to obtain insight.
- Craft personas from the unmet or undermet needs, wants, and/or desires uncovered during the interviews.
- Select a Target Adopter persona.

Step 2: Determine a solution approach.
Step 3: Craft a detailed solution.
Step 4: Establish a clear value proposition.
Step 5: Quantify the Target Adopter group size (ballpark estimate, initially).

The first step in creating our final design is to transform the root cause and Principal Adopter group that we identified in Level 1, Chapter 3, into a Target Adopter persona with a defined set of unmet or undermet needs, wants, and/or desires. This requires obtaining tacit knowledge from the Principal Adopters. Open-ended Interviews for Insight (IFIs), described in Appendix A, are used to obtain decision and motivational insights from the interviewees. The information gathered from those IFIs are first categorized and then connected to a set of personas. These personas represent arch-type adopters who make choices based on a common set of needs, wants, and/or desires. From that set of personas, our Target Adopter persona, the subgroup for whom we are creating the innovation, is selected. Details on conducting IFIs and the subsequent persona development from this information are elaborated in Appendix A.

Once we have a clear Target Adopter for our innovation, we begin to think about the high-level approaches we can take to create a solution. It is important not to confuse our approach to resolving the Target Adopter's issues with the actual solution. That solution, which we craft in Step 3, is detailed and specific. That solution's specific features should satisfy the primary needs/wants/desires of our Target Adopter. It is also important not to include product or solution features that are of no value to the adopter, as they will increase the cost of the innovation without generating an increased benefit.

The fourth step of the innovation design stages is an assessment of how we have created value for the Target Adopter. This step validates that the specific features of our proposed innovation benefit the Target Adopter by connecting to their specific needs/wants/desires through the linkages as illustrated in Figure 2.2.

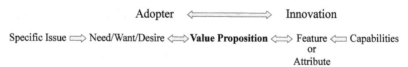

FIGURE 2.2 Value proposition creation.

As mentioned, it is recommended that the fifth step, quantification of the size of the Target Adopter group, be left until the assessment stage of Level 3 or only be roughly estimated at this point. That means we will be moving on to the first stage of execution and iterating back to this design stage to complete the quantification only when we need to do so.

Once the innovation design is complete, at least qualitatively, The Innovation Pyramid shifts to the execution levels (Levels 3 and 4). Planning is the first of the two execution stages. The aim of this level is to develop a creation and delivery plan. The plan must include how the innovation will actually be created, of course. But the plan must also articulate how that created innovation will be delivered to the adopter. Without adoption of our innovation, we cannot generate impact.

There are four components to the plan. A plan will vary in detail, depending on the complexity of the innovation, but it must always contain the following four components:

- Operations. How the innovation will be created?
- Delivery. How the innovation will be delivered to and acquired by the adopter?
- Resources. What resources, inside and outside our organization, will be needed to complete creation and delivery of this innovation?
- Risk. Description of the risks associated with the creation and delivery of this innovation.

If a detailed plan cannot be crafted or the resources cannot be committed to the project, then the design must be altered. That means returning to Level 2 (Solution Formulation), the second design stage. Depending on the reason for the failure of the design, we may have to iterate all the way back to Level 1 (Problem Identification). Failure is not terminal. It is merely part of the learning process. Our increased understanding that we obtained from the planning level will be incorporated into the selection criteria of the choices we make in Level 2. If those new criteria do not lead us to a new solution, we will need to iterate back to Level 1 and choose a different cause on which to focus.

The plan we create in this level must be detailed enough to be executable. That plan is also a way to communicate and sell the project to potential supporters, collaborators, and detractors. The value of the innovation project is not self-evident to all that we need to involve. We must communicate its value to them. However, we do not want to introduce our project by dropping a 1,000-page tome on our audience. Chapter 5 also outlines varied levels of pitching the innovation project: core concept opener, the elevator pitch, and the resource pitch. We need to use all three to transfer our enthusiasm for the project to those who can aid us in creating its ultimate impact.

Carrying out the innovation creation and delivery plan that was created in the first execution stage (Level 3) is the aim of this final level of The Innovation Pyramid. This is a project-management challenge. Launching new innovations have challenges beyond those of a typical internal-company project in that they generally involve collaborators and adopters outside the innovation-creating organization. This means that multiple environments and multiple POVs, in addition to the innovation creator's internal environment and POV, must be appraised.

Volumes have been written on project management. Rather than being a substitute for those writings, this chapter introduced a modification of Drucker's core Management-by-Objective framework, Figure 2.3. This framework is particularly useful in managing complex innovation projects that may be outside the normal operations of the firm as it focuses on the alignment of all the people and activities associated with the plan's successful implementation. The framework is also useful as a postimplementation review guide as it forces us to reconsider all the components, inside and outside our organization, necessary to accomplish such a project.

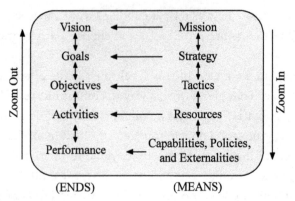

FIGURE 2.3 Extension of Drucker's Management-by-Objective framework.

The remainder of the chapter focuses on performing a postexecution variance evaluation of the plan's implementation in order to better understand what can be learned from carrying out the plan developed in Level 3. All four aspects of the plan are reviewed: Operations, Delivery, Resources, and Risks. A poor plan execution does not automatically mean the implementation team underperformed. The issue may lie with people or environments well beyond the core team.

In the end, the usefulness of The Innovation Pyramid, like any tool, comes down to how well we learn to use it. The more we learn about its application to our organization and our innovations, the more useful it becomes. Chapter 7 lays out a systematic process for reviewing the entire Innovation Pyramid, revealing how choices made at each layer may have factored into the nondesired outcome. That assessment process is illustrated in Figure 2.4. Once the root-cause issue is uncovered via this process, we will need to iterate back to the appropriate Pyramid level, alter our original choice, and proceed again from that point. The goal is learning, not witch-hunting; learning how to better design and execute innovations.

The Innovation Pyramid is not only a learnable strategic methodology for producing innovations but it is also intended to create

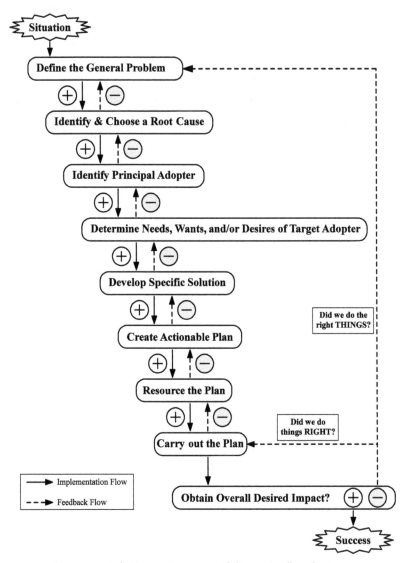

FIGURE 2.4 The Innovation Pyramid diagnostic flowchart.

serial innovators and increase the innovative capacity of organizations by providing a learnable, repeatable methodology to transform general situations into specific solutions that generate impact. The design thinking–based Innovation Pyramid, which is detailed in Part I of this book, describes this overarching methodology. The second section of the book (Part II) details the creativity-based DOC Process, a tool used repeatedly in implementing The Innovation Pyramid methodology. The appendices highlight detailed techniques that support the use of the DOC Process in both Problem Identification and Solution Formulation.

3 Level 1
Problem Identification

One of the challenges of a nonlinear methodology is that there is no absolute "starting" point. There is no "it is always best to start at the beginning" (The Wizard of Oz, 1939) counsel that applies. Impactful solutions can be successfully created without starting at Level 1 of The Innovation Pyramid. Indeed, it not uncommon to start at any point on the first two levels. Chapter 4 will provide more details about starting from Level 2.

Focusing on the design first forces us to think about what we are creating before immersing ourselves into the details of how we are creating it. This is one of the critical tenets of The Innovation Pyramid. Another foundational component of the methodology is the separation of the problem from the solution, or to put it another way, the opportunity from the desired outcome. The Innovation Pyramid Level 1, Design Stage 1, forces us to think about the problem before diving into its solution.

Clearly identifying the problem before considering the solution is more difficult than it sounds. We are hardwired as human beings to think in terms of "actions" – what will we do. It is therefore easy to think about these proposed solutions as the problems we need to resolve. Better solutions, however, come from more clearly defined problems. When a friend starts the conversation with this typical advice, "The problem is that you need to do..." we must recognize that the advice may or may not even be germane to the real, underlying cause of our situation. The power of separating problems and solutions is that it allows us to fundamentally understand both better. Deeper understanding of the problem expands and significantly improves the solution possibilities. As Albert Einstein is quoted as saying, "If I were given one hour to save the planet, I would spend 59 minutes defining the problem and one minute resolving it." We would do well to heed Einstein's advice and spend quality time on the problem before moving on to its solution.

Innovation teams, however, are often reluctant to spend time exploring and identifying the problem. There are two primary reasons for this reluctance. First, we are solution-oriented beings after all. We are much more comfortable in the solution space than in the problem space. This orientation is also corporately rewarded. When was the last time you heard of someone being recognized for identifying a problem? Probably never. We are recognized for our unique, creative, and impactful solutions. But if we solve the wrong problem, a problem that has little consequence to the bigger picture, we will not create the impact we long for.

The second reason innovation teams avoid spending time exploring the problem space is that they are too often "assigned" the problem they are charged with resolving. As a result, our supervisors are looking to see evidence of our progress toward a solution. Reporting that we are "assessing the issue," sounds like we have yet to start the project. That perception will not put us on the promotional fast track! But applying a new coat of paint on a structurally unsound bridge will not win us any points in the long run, regardless of how good the bridge looks during its collapse. We owe it to ourselves, our team, our organization, and particularly to those who are directly affected by it to first get the problem correctly determined.

The overall aim of Level 1 is to ensure that we have clearly defined the problem, by delving down into the circumstance we are facing to uncover a root cause to which we can apply ourselves. That root cause problem definition must be specific. It must be sufficiently narrow to allow us to act upon it, yet firmly connected to the initially identified issues as it is the strength of those linkages that creates impact well beyond the resolution of the narrowly identified problem. This is the "What" face of Level 1 of The Innovation Pyramid, as shown in Figure 3.1. The "Who" face is the identification of the individuals or group who are most directly affected by the specific cause we have

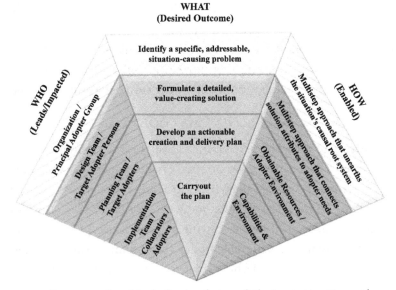

FIGURE 3.1 Level 1 of a flattened view of The Innovation Pyramid.

identified, those Principal Adopters who will ultimately utilize our innovation. The third face of The Pyramid is the "How" we will reach these desired outcomes of identifying a root cause of our circumstance and Principal Adopters of our future innovation. That "how" is a five-step methodology that is detailed in the next section that will unearth the causal root system of our situation. However, one of the common flaws of Problem Identification is to get too specific too soon. One of the themes of this book is to always take a step back before moving forward. For this level, that means that we will initially broaden our purview, before narrowing in on a root cause. Doing so ensures that we are addressing the actual disease and not just one of its symptoms.

As with each of The Pyramid levels, we will be making decisions based on the best information available to us at the time. Those judgments we make throughout the methodology will impact the ultimate outcome of the innovation project. The advantage of using a repeatable methodology like the archer having a consistent way of firing their arrow, as discussed in Chapter 2, is that a consistent method eliminates some of the variability of the shooting process.

A consistent method, combined with a consistent review of the outcome of the shot, allows the archer to improve their judgment. While making rational and reasonable judgments will not guarantee the overall results we desire, they provide us a solid place to pivot from should the ultimate innovation impact not turn out as we had hoped.

PROBLEM IDENTIFICATION METHOD

The ultimate objective of Pyramid Level 1, Design Stage 1, is to determine a root cause of our original circumstance that we (or our organization) are capable and willing to address. The precise pathway for getting to that desired outcome will vary depending on where we start. Independent of the starting point, however, realizing this objective will not be achievable from a single brainstorming session. Uncovering root causes of a broad issue is a multistep research project. This section offers a general step-by-step guide for reaching Level 1's objectives. The steps represent guidelines for proceeding through this level and are not a checklist of procedural boxes to tick off.

Starting Point

There are multiple places from which to start an innovation. None of them are "wrong." It is simply the nature of a nonlinear system. There are times when we will start with a specific solution concept. There are other times when we think we know the "real" issue and will want to start there and yet other times when we will start with an overwhelmingly broad perspective – such as a desire for world peace. All of these are legitimate starting points. But none are ending points for this stage of the design process.

The ability to adopt multiple points-of-view (POVs) and perspectives will be necessary as we move through this level. Both the innovator's and the potential adopter's POVs are extremely important to the design process. Most of the time, however, our predominate initial view is self-centric. That's actually okay. We want our organization to grow. We want better lives for our children. We want our parents' final years to be comfortable and worry free.

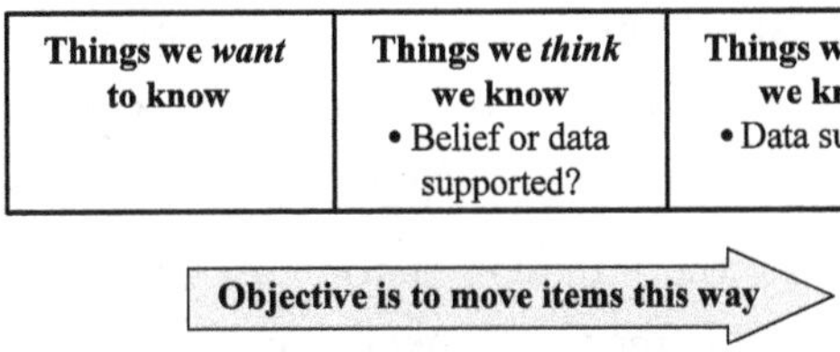

Things we *want* to know	Things we *think* we know	Things we *know* we know
	• Belief or data supported?	• Data supported

> Objective is to move items this way

FIGURE 3.2 Hypothesis-directed discovery.

Those self-centric POVs are a natural place to start the process. We simply need to ensure that we do not get stuck there and can take on alternate POVs and perspectives as we proceed.

The Innovation Pyramid is a hypothesis-directed discovery process, as illustrated in Figure 3.2. We may *think* we know the real issue or even the perfect solution. At this point, these are nothing more than hypotheses. We need to do more research to move these and other items from the *"think* we know" column or the *"want* to know" column of Figure 3.2, to the data-supported *"know* we know" column on the far right.

Endpoint

Before delving into the specifics of the navigating guidelines for this level, we should be very clear about where we want to end up. At the end of Level 1, the first design stage, our aim is to:

- identify a well-articulated General Problem from our initial situation;
- determine root cause(s) that, through an understood system of links, connect to the General Problem;
- select one root cause of the General Problem which the organization is willing and able to address; and
- identify an adopter group, the Principal Adopters, that is both impacted by the identified root cause and will be the broad group for whom we are creating the innovation.

In between the starting point and endpoint is a five-step, nonlinear, iterative process of discovery. The five steps are only a guideline and not a rigorous list of steps to check off. Steps may be skipped or repeated depending on where we start or how the process of discovery unfolds. That five-step guideline is as follows:

- Step 1: Clearly state the starting situation or issue.
- Step 2: Zoom out to define the General Problem.
- Step 3: Draft a neutral problem statement.
- Step 4: Zoom in, layer-by-layer, to a root cause.
- Step 5: Identify the Principal Adopters.

Step 1: Clearly State the Starting Situation or Issue

Whenever we are traveling across uncharted territory, it is wise to mark our point of departure. That embarkation point is our initial statement of the situation we desire to address or the initially identified issue we desire to resolve. Depending on where we start, this step may be achieved by merely documenting our initial understanding of the issue.

If, however, we are starting with a solution idea, which means we are starting at Level 2 of The Innovation Pyramid, then we need to return to Level 1, flip our perspective, and define the problem for which that proposed innovation is a solution. People adopt solutions to their problems. If there is no problem, there will be no adoption. If there is no adoption, there will be no impact. We may *think* we know the problem; we may even *think* we have the solution, but we likely do not have either. If we are starting with a solution concept, we need to ask ourselves "what problem does this solution resolve?"

Let us say that it has been proposed that we increase our product marketing. From this initial solution concept, we need to do two things. First, we have to recognize that this is a solution and not a problem definition. Secondly, we need to transition this solution concept into a problem by asking ourselves "why do we want to do this?" Why do we need more marketing? What would that do for us? The answers to these questions are the problems that this proposed solution is addressing. That problem is our starting point.

Stay alert for solutions that come disguised as problem descriptions. These so-called problems often have action verbs like "increase" or "decrease" or adjectives like "more" or "less" in their description. Our "increase marketing" was one example. "The potholes in community roads need fixing" is a solution. Why is this a problem? The answer is the problem statement: "The community roads are unsafe and make driving difficult." We must also realize that the answers to our initial "why" questions may also be solutions. We may desire "more marketing" to help us "increase sales." Unfortunately, "increasing sales" is also a solution (the action verb gives it away). Whenever the initial answer to our "why is this a problem?" question results in another answer, we will have to repeat the "why" question process until a problem is uncovered. Answering the "why do we need our sales to increase?" may bring us closer to the real issue that needs addressing as we shall see in the example later in this chapter.

If we think about the problem at all, we tend to think of it too narrowly, "I need a faster horse," or too broadly, "I want world peace." One perspective is focused on a feature of a current solution, while the other end of the purview spectrum is focused on a societal-scale issue. Either is an acceptable starting point. Neither is an acceptable ending point. Beyond restating these desired outcomes as problems, both initially identified issues will need refinement before we start thinking about developing solutions. If the starting problem is very broadly defined, skip this step and proceed to Step 3. If our initial issue's scope is narrow, then we first need to broaden our purview.

Given that at the end of this level, we want to uncover a root cause of our original situation or initially identified issue, it might seem odd that we would want to begin by broadening our purview. A fundamental tenet of The Innovation Pyramid is "diverge before converge"; we broaden our perspective before narrowing it. Doing so ensures that we do not overlook the disease by focusing on a symptom. Treating diseases is impactful, but treating symptoms is not.

Too often the situation we are facing and reacting to is nothing more than a symptom or component of a bigger, systemic issue. While symptoms are often important warning lights, those broader issues need to be defined before moving forward. Stopping that red warning light from blinking is not the objective; addressing the issue that the light is warning us about is. Focusing on the problem, as Einstein advised, while unnatural, is critical to creating impactful innovations.

To broaden our purview from our original situation or initially identified issue, we will need to change our perspective by zooming out. Just as we zoom out on Google Maps, we gain perspective, but lose detail. For many, this is a very uncomfortable step, given our aim to create a very specific and detailed innovation. We need to work through that discomfort to see the bigger picture.

To broaden our perspective from our initially identified issue, as illustrated in the left half of Figure 3.3, we need to ask "why" questions. Why is this an issue? Are their broader consequences resulting from this issue? Later, in Step 4, when we zoom in, we will be looking for factors or causes of the stated problem by asking "what" questions, as illustrated on the right-hand side of Figure 3.3. Zooming out within the problem space is holism, attempting to piece together a larger issue from the identified components. Zooming in, on the other hand, is reductionism, which attempts to break down the problem into components that contribute or cause it. Together, the two processes engage both sides of our brains.

Zooming out forces us to consider whether the issue we initially identified in Step 1 is but a portion of a larger problem by considering the broader consequences of this identified issue. Why do we care about absenteeism? It is a factor of a larger issue, namely,

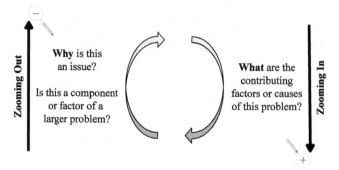

FIGURE 3.3 Zooming in/out within the problem space.

productivity. Why do we care about productivity? Because it impacts costs. Why do we care about costs? Because it impacts our ability to compete in the marketplace. Each time we ask "why," it zooms us out one level; incrementally broadening our purview. Continuing to pose "why" questions to the previous question's answer continues that broadening. As our purview broadens, both the problem definition and the group most affected by the problem change. That POV shift is important to track as we shift our perspective. While our initial problem may have been stated from a self-centric POV, that will likely shift as we zoom out.

This incremental zooming-out process to broaden our purview can seemingly continue without end. When is our purview broad enough? We want to create a "big picture" view but we also want the problem to fall within the scope of our organization. Identifying a problem that our organization is unable or unwilling to address is not useful. We need to zoom out "far enough," to broaden our purview, but not "too far" for the problem to become intractable from our organization's POV. Fortunately, we have assessment guidelines for determining this balance.

Given we want to define a problem that we or our organization can do something about, we need to ensure that we zoom out only as far as to identify a General Problem that the organization still sees as part of who it is and what it does – this is the vision or purpose level of the organization. Drucker (1954) defined the company's vision as a description of an organization-influenced future state. It is not "world peace," but for a psychotherapy, company may be a "world of self-actualized individuals." Alternatively, we can think of a problem falling within the scope of the organization's core purpose. Collins and Porras (1996) defined this core purpose as the company's reason for being. For Disney, it is "to make people happy." For Mary Kay, it is "to give unlimited opportunities for women." Both the vision and the core purpose take on a POV beyond the organization, yet one that the organization can influence. We therefore want to zoom out from our initially identified issue far enough that it comes close to, but does not go beyond, the organization's vision or core purpose.

Zooming out in the problem space is less familiar than zooming in. We are far more comfortable with reductionism, breaking down a bigger problem into parts. Holism or integrating parts into a bigger picture is less familiar and therefore less comfortable. As a result, the following example will first illustrate zooming in from the vision level and then show how we could approach the problem in reverse. In this example, we will use Drucker's Management-by-Objective framework to identify the purview levels. In this example, we initially derive a proposed new program by working down from the most zoomed-out vision-level to the most zoomed-in activity-level.

Vision – organization-influenced future state description.

Our vision is to assist in the creation of a robust, diversified regional economy.

Goal – long-term desired outcome.

Our long-term goal is to increase the rate of formation by local founders of traded-cluster firms (companies who primarily serve markets outside the region).

Objective – tangible step toward goal, often SMART (Specific, Measurable, Achievable, Results-focused, and Time-bound).

In the next sixteen months, we will create and launch a training program that will train twenty regional entrepreneurs per year providing them with the skills necessary to found traded-cluster firms in the area.

Activities – Specific tasks and/or programs implemented to accomplish the objective.

Specific program elements:

- Twelve-month founders boot camp where the candidates will
  - gain exposure to intellectual property from which they can start a company;
  - have networking opportunities with investors and other high-tech entrepreneurs; and

- be able to build relationships with successful entrepreneurs globally.

Innovations, however, tend to work in the opposite direction, from the bottom up. This is why learning to zoom out is so important. Often, we start with a program idea. One day one of our team members says, "hey, we need a founder's training program in the region." Someone then says, "that's a great idea," and what typically happens next is that we are off and running detailing the program elements. While that is the typical process, the resulting outcome is typically ineffective. Why? Because we have generated a solution in search of a problem.

What *should* happen next after an idea is proposed, a company-founder's training program in this case, is that we go to Step 1 and define what problem that program would address. That answer could be as simple as "develop more regional entrepreneurs with the skill set to found high-growth businesses." Now as we have an initial problem statement, but as it is a pretty narrow perspective, the process should then move to Step 2.

Step 2: Zoom Out to Define the General Problem

Step 2 of the Problem Identification process zooms out on the identified issue by asking "why" questions. Why would we want to do this? Answer: We need local founders to start more local firms. Why? Answer: The local economy is in decline. Now we are at the "vision/purpose" level. We are no longer limited to think about training founders of new companies. There are other ways to support the growth of a regional economy; ways we would have missed thinking about if we had not zoomed out and broadened our purview.

Zooming out to the vision/purpose level is ideal, but may be overly intimidating for an innovation team. Any zooming out from the initial starting point will improve the potential for an impactful solution. If our organization will not buy-in to zooming out all the way to the organization's "vision/purpose" level, try to at least zoom out to the organization's "goal level" – develop a problem definition that falls within the realm of the organization's long-term desired outcomes.

Once we have broadened the purview by zooming out from the initially identified issue, we have defined the General Problem that we intend to address. It is recommended that we do one more thing before starting to zoom back in to define a specific root cause of that General Problem. That is to craft a neutral General Problem statement, a neutral, fact-based, zoomed-out problem statement. That is Step 3 of Problem Identification.

Step 3: Draft a Neutral General Problem Statement

How a problem is framed is important in identifying its solution. Given we want to not overlook any potential solutions, we need to craft the problem statement that does not bias us toward a specific solution approach. We need a fact-based, balanced problem described with neutral language. A "neutral" problem statement is a statement of facts not desires. Being neutral, it is void of any solution implications. Crafting a pure problem statement – one that is completely neutral – is more challenging than one would think due to our propensity toward action (i.e. solutions). An "energy shortage" is not neutral, as it implies the need to increase supplies, but ignores the potential solution of reducing demand through conservation. A better, more neutral, problem statement would be "energy demand exceeds supply." It contains the facts and only the facts.

Continue to be alert to solution-biased problem statements. These disguised problem statements typically have action verbs attached to them like "increase" or "decrease." These so-called problem statements have already set us on a solution pathway. A problem statement like "we need to reduce absenteeism" is a solution disguising itself as a problem. Again, the "reduce" is our hint that something is amiss. Reducing absenteeism is a means to what end? What problem does that proposed solution address? It will be a challenge to craft a neutral, specific, fact-based problem statement, but is worth the effort as it will open up solution possibilities.

In Step 2 of this example, we defined the problem as "the local economy is in decline." That description of the problem is OK, but it could be more fact-based, as "in decline" is a bit ambiguous. How would we measure that? Gross domestic product (GDP)? Income per capita? Unemployment rate? If we created an innovation to address this problem, how would we know if it was impactful? How would we measure the impact we have made? We could reframe the problem statement this way: The regional GDP has dropped nearly 20 percent in the last decade. That statement is a neutral, fact-based description of the situation. We are measuring the results in terms of GDP, so if we craft an impactful solution, we should be able to see the results in the region's GDP. Is training regional entrepreneurs the only way to address this problem? Of course not. There are lots of ways to address this issue. That's the power of broadening our perspective. Now that our perspective has been broadened, it is time to move to Step 4 and zoom in and uncover a root cause of this General Problem that we will choose to address.

Step 4: Zoom In, Layer-by-Layer, to a Root Cause

We now have a broad purview of the problem we want to address. We have a neutral General Problem description that originated from the initially identified issue. The neutral General Problem description is not biased toward a specific solution approach – yet it is powerful in that we now know how to measure the effect of our future innovation. The General Problem statement is, however, too large for us to address directly. It is at the "vision" level and not the "objective" or "activity" level of the organization, to use Drucker's framework. We purposefully broadened it from our initially identified issue to make sure we did not overlook any aspect of the problem, and as a result, any potential solution: diverge before converge. Now it is time to converge. We are now ready to break the General Problem down into something we can directly affect with our innovation. What we want to identify is a root cause of this General Problem. In this step, we will drive down to a specific root cause that we will resolve with our innovation. Resolving that root cause should be like toppling that first domino in a series; when it falls, it will knock down subsequent dominos creating a chain reaction. Our aim is to identify a root cause that when resolved, will create a domino effect that will ultimately impact the General Problem.

There will likely be many root causes of the General Problem we have described. Ideally, we would like to find the root-of-the-root. The root cause of the root causes; identify that single domino that, when toppled, causes all the others to fall. While ideal, it is not likely to occur. First, it may not exist. Second, we have constraints; our organization does not have the capabilities nor the resources to do everything. We therefore want to identify a root cause that our organization is capable and willing to address. One that, if we resolve it, will create a positive chain reaction that will ultimately impact the General Problem we have identified.

Layer-by-Layer Archaeological Dig
When archaeologists excavate a site, they do it meticulously and methodically. They painstakingly remove dirt, layer by layer. A similar approach is necessary to carefully zoom in and uncover the factors and causes that extend from the General Problem that we formed in Step 3 to the root cause we will attempt to resolve with our innovation. For it is not simply a root cause we seek, but one through which we can create a domino effect that ultimately positively impacts our General Problem.

This archaeological de-layering that will uncover, layer by layer, all the connections that exist between our General Problem and its root causes is a research project; it will take secondary and some primary research. As we work down through the layers, starting from the General Problem, we are not seeking the consequence of having the problem, that was zooming out, the left-hand side of Figure 3.3. What we are now focused on is the right-hand side of Figure 3.3, seeking to uncover contributing factors of the General Problem. Zooming out was understanding the consequences of us having the flu, but now we seek to identify the factors that could have contributed to us contracting it.

At this stage we are mainly seeking explicit knowledge. The primary research portion of this investigation will include interviewing experts for facts regarding causes and relationships. This is not the Interviewing for Insights that we will need to perform when we seek tacit knowledge in Chapter 4. The research required here is more straightforward; we are seeking to understand known causes and relationships. Our aim is to not to identify causes we *believe* connect to the General Problem, but instead to understand how those causes actually do link to the General Problem. For it is only through those links that our innovation will create a significant impact; not by simply resolving a small cause, but through the resulting domino effect that ultimately impacts the General Problem.

We zoom in starting from the General Problem statement, as illustrated in Figure 3.4. For this first layer, we are seeking contributing factors to the General Problem. What factors contribute to this problem situation? What factors might be causing it? This research will result in the acquisition of a number of pieces of information: some ideas, some facts, and some factoids. Research is a divergent process; the initial step of the Diverge–Organize–Converge (DOC) Process is described in Part II of this book. We will need to organize this divergent information

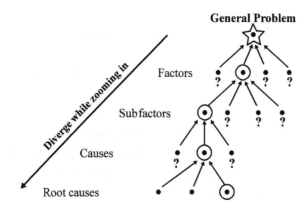

FIGURE 3.4 Problem Identification Root System.

into categories – this is the first part of the "organize" step of the DOC Process. The second part of the "organize" step is to find the connections between the categories. In this case, we are specifically seeking the connections between the categories of information we uncovered and the General Problem. The first row of dots, or nodes, on Figure 3.4 (the "Factors" level) represents the categories of factors that we determined directly cause or contribute to the General Problem.

The "factors" level is but the first layer of our archaeological dig. We will now repeat the process, digging a second layer down, by looking for contributing factors or causes of the primary factors that we identified as directly causing or contributing to the General Problem. Note that the root system of Figure 3.4 is expanding as we zoom in layer by layer. We are diversifying as we zoom in. We started with one General Problem, then identified factors to that problem. As we continue to dig, we will uncover subfactors of the factors, causes of the subfactors, causes of the causes, and eventually root causes. We will not, however, be able to explore the entire root system of the General Problem statement of Step 3. We would never have time to create an innovation if we did that. Some nodes will naturally terminate on their own, while others we will choose to ignore. We are making choices.

As we zoom in from the General Problem, layer by layer, we will be making choices as to which node to follow. We will find many factors of the General Problem, as Figure 3.4 illustrates, and then we will choose one of those factors and ignore the rest. We will then find subfactors that contribute to or cause the primary factor we chose. We will then choose one of those subfactors. Eventually, we will reach a group of root causes from which we will choose one to pursue. We are making rational and reasonable choices. These choices must also be conscious. It is important to eliminate intuitive logic leaps. For if we based our innovation on an intuitive logic leap and it did produce the impact we had hoped, we have no basis on which to pivot to an alternative choice, but are instead left with making a second intuitive logic leap. This random "throwing spaghetti against the wall" in hopes of finding something that may stick is not a successful approach to becoming a serial innovator.

That layer-by-layer discovery and selection process result in the Problem Identification Root System of Figure 3.4. We uncover several primary factors of our General Problem, and then choose one. We discover several subfactors of the primary factor we choose and select one. We continue this process until we get down to a root cause. We are typically ignoring the unchosen nodes at each level. We are making an imperfect choice based on limited information. Would it be ideal, for example, to explore all the subfactors to all the factors we discovered before selecting a factor to pursue? Sure. Is it practical to do so? Typically not. The choice we make will be the best choice that we can make based on the information we have at the time we are making the choice. But that choice will be imperfect. We need to document our criteria for making each choice so that we can subsequently review them when we review the entire project in Chapter 7. That review is an important part of the learning system which will ultimately help the organization make increasingly better choices as it gains experience with the innovation system.

As careful as we might be not to dig too deeply too quickly, we will inevitably uncover information that lies below the layer we are exploring; we will find information relating to the factors of the factors, for example, when we are seeking primary factors of the General Problem. We need to be disciplined about documenting the links between layers and not creating "phantom links." Phantom links are individual pieces of information or entire categories of information that have unknown linkages to the General Problem. We might intuit that they connect, but that is not enough, we need to know. If we have uncovered information layers down from the layer we are currently connecting, simply set it aside and see how it might connect as we continue the dig.

The following is an example of how phantom links, particularly when supported by false or misleading data, can derail an innovation. In this extreme example, we will say that we are trying to determine why students leave the university. As we start to establish the primary factors, someone says "the classroom chairs are too uncomfortable. We need to upgrade the furniture, that would solve the problem." This is a clear "logical leap" as student comfort in the class is a long way from the more common primary factors of "being homesick," "poor performance," or "deciding college is not for them." But when pushed, our eager colleague creates some "phantom links" to support their claim. "They are leaving because they are flunking out of the university. They are flunking out because they are doing poorly in their classes. They are doing poorly in their classes because it is impossible to concentrate when sitting on uncomfortable chairs." These are "phantom links" as there is no data or research to support them. There could be supporting data, but at the moment this is pure conjecture. In frustration, our eager colleague states he can "prove" this is true. He goes and talks to a group of students leaving a classroom. "Don't you think the seats are uncomfortable in this classroom?" he asks them. "Yes," the students compliantly reply. "Doesn't that make it hard to concentrate on the lecture?" he adds. "Yes," again the students comply.

This is "misleading data" at best. Instead of performing exit interviews on students who are leaving the university and asking them open-ended questions to explore their reasons for doing so (i.e. perform interviews for insight, as discussed in Appendix A), the direct questions were asked. Asking in such a direct manner will often lead to misleading results. People will typically agree just to be polite. Even if the seats were uncomfortable, there is no established link between leaving the university and these uncomfortable chairs. Before millions are spent on new lecture hall furniture, much more work must be done.

Yes, this is an exaggerated example, but this type of approach occurs too often in large organizations. Someone gets their personal idea supported by offering phantom links and false data. It all starts by taking "logical leaps." Be wary of these. Go slow to go fast. Dig carefully, layer by layer, to uncover the actual problem root system.

Step 5: Identify the Principal Adopters

The final challenge in our archaeological dig is to know when to stop digging. This is the opposite question to the one we had in Step 2, which was when do we know we zoomed out far enough. Now we need to know when to stop digging, as "root causes" simply do not appear tattooed with those clear labels. As we did in Step 2, we need to set parameters on how zoomed in is zoomed in enough. That assessment will combine all three sides of The Innovation Pyramid.

In the end, our aim is to clearly define a specific issue that we want to resolve. That clarity requires that all three faces of The Innovation Pyramid are specifically described. The three sides of The Pyramid represent the "what," the "how," and the "who" for each level. "What" we want to accomplish in Problem Identification is to uncover the interconnected root system that exists between the zoomed-out General Problem and the root cause which we will directly address. The "how" was the prior four steps of the process of zooming out, then zooming back in to a root cause that is both connected to the General Problem and one which our organization is willing and able to address. We are "done," meaning we can stop digging, when we can also define the "who" – which is the fifth step.

The "who" is the group directly affected by the issue. They are also the group that will adopt our innovation in order to resolve their present condition. They are the Principal Adopters of the innovation we aim to create. We must be able to specifically identify this group. It must be more specific than "our customers" or "our students." Which ones? Who, specifically, would we go talk to in order to obtain their POV on this issue? That's the level of Principal Adopters identification that we need, as that is precisely what we will be doing in Chapter 4. This assessment step is important enough to warrant its own step, Step 5, of the Problem Identification.

It is important to be aware that as we excavate down from the General Problem to its root causes, the POV shifts. We likely started with a self-centric POV. But we will have to shift our POV as we progress down, node-by-node, layer-by-layer, to our root system. Each node of our Problem Identification Root System will likely require a different primary POV that is important to hear and appreciate. That is why empathy is so critically important to the problem discovery process. We need to be able to get out of our own way, to see and feel the issue from the perspective of those directly affected by it. The child is hungry. Why? The parents' have insufficient resources to provide for them. And on it goes. At each level, indeed at each node, the POV of the group primarily affected is shifting. Empathy for the group at each node is critical in uncovering the next level of issues.

The Primary Adopters are the group that represent those directly affected by the root cause we have identified. They are also the general group for which we will be innovating. They are not quite yet our specific target group for which we will be innovating, that target group will be identified in Level 2. This target group is a subgroup of the Primary Adopters, so it is important to get a clear picture of the Primary Adopters before proceeding.

Our archaeological dig is concluded once the Primary Adopters of our innovation have been identified. We have uncovered a root cause of the General Problem we identified in Step 2 and neutrally described in Step 3. That root cause is an issue that our organization is able and willing to address. We understand how that root cause is connected to the General Problem. We have additionally clearly described the Primary Adopter group that is primarily affected by the root cause. We have completed Level 1, Design Stage 1, of The Innovation Pyramid and are ready to move to Level 2, where we design our innovation. But first, this chapter will provide a comprehensive example that works through all five steps of Level 1.

DESIGN EXAMPLE, LEVEL I

To illustrate how the two design levels of The Innovation Pyramid work together, a specific design-problem example will begin in this chapter and conclude in Chapter 4. Let us say that we are part of a for-profit company. The sales of our lead product are stagnating. The product sales had been growing steadily, but have recently leveled off. This is of great concern to our firm, as the sales growth of that product has been instrumental to the firm's profitability. There are now calls to "increase the marketing budget" to address this situation.

Step 1: State the Starting Issue

We need to immediately recognize that we do not currently truly understand the underlying issues at this point. All we have thus far is a situation. The "call for more marketing" is a proposed solution. But to address what problem? The "more marketing" is a solution aimed to resolve the "languishing sales of our primary product." It is therefore the stagnation of primary product sales that is the initially identified issue.

Step 2: Zoom Out to Define the General Problem

We want to ensure, at this level, that our vantage point is broad enough that we are not overlooking any potential problems or solution approaches. To broaden our purview from this particular situation, we ask a zoom-out question like, "why is flattening sales of our primary product a problem?" The answer is that it impacts our revenue. Why is stagnating revenue a problem? Because it impacts the organization's profitability. This is zoomed out enough. Have we zoomed out to "vision level"? No, we have definitely reached the goal level from the organization's POV with the aim of maintaining profitability. The main matter this zooming out accomplishes is to shift our purview beyond the product. Too many organizations are so focused on their current offerings that they cannot see beyond them. They fixate on tweaking their offering's features or market positioning when the real issue is that the market for the product may have simply matured and is on the decline. The market for buggy whips will never be what it was in the preautomobile era no matter how we may try to dress up the product's features. The power of this step is that it forces us to zoom out past our fixations and consider broader issues.

Step 3: Create a Neutral General Problem Statement

This step ensures that we have stated the problem in neutral language so as not to bias us toward any particular solution. Our initial "stagnating sales" issue was generalized to "stagnating profitability," which is actually a pretty neutral statement. We should refine it by adding, "as measured by earnings per share" or some other specific metric, so we know how to measure how we have impacted that issue. Our neutral General Problem statement is therefore "The Organization's profitability, as measured by earnings per share, has stagnated."

Step 4: Zoom In to a Root Cause

We now have a neutral problem statement for which we now seek to uncover root causes. We will begin our journey toward those root causes by zooming back in. We will be diverging as we zoom in, layer by layer. The zoom-in/diverge process will create a Problem Identification Root System whose branches irregularly divaricate as we zoom in. We will be using this developing root system to make choices; choosing to pursue a specific branch, and at least temporarily, ignoring the others. The Problem Identification Root System, illustrated generally in Figure 3.4, will be crafted in detail for this example. As we proceed we will be making choices, selecting certain nodes to pursue while consciously choosing to ignore others. It is important to explicitly document the criteria for choosing one branch over another, even if it seems obvious at the time. Postproject review of such decisions is how organizations improve upon their corporate judgment.

For this example, we must first identify the primary factors that could lead to stagnating or decreasing profits, which is our General Problem. The root system will irregularly diverge as we dig deeper. This is a research project. We will say, for this example, that we could organize our initial research findings into two categories that directly impact profits. Stagnating profits are either caused by (1) flattening revenues or (2) increasing costs. We now need to make a choice, to converge, and choose to pursue one branch. Before choosing, we do some exploration of the increasing cost branch. We check with our accounting department and find out that for the costs to be increasing, either the direct product cost and/or the general indirect costs must be increasing. These become the two branches under the "Costs Increasing" node of Figure 3.5. We discover that neither is increasing, so we therefore eliminate that branch from further pursuit. We will

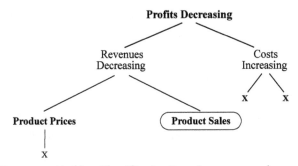

FIGURE 3.5 Problem Identification Root System example, part 1.

pursue the "Revenues Flattening" branch of Figure 3.5 as we have eliminated the other pathway.

Next, we zoom in on the "Revenues Decreasing" node by asking "what could be causing this result?" Our research yields the causes for decreasing revenues could be that product prices are falling or product sales have flattened or fallen. We quickly check with our sales department to see if the product prices have dropped. It turns out that they have not, so we can eliminate this branch. We therefore continue down "product sales" branch of Figure 3.5. Yes, we are back to our originally stated problem that product sales have stagnated. However, we have returned there knowing that other possibilities have been properly examined and eliminated.

Step 5: Identify the Principal Adopters

We have successfully broadly surveyed before narrowing to a specific point of attack. It seems as though we have found our "root cause" of our stagnating profits which is "stagnating sales." We may be tempted to jump to the "we need more marketing" solution with a glib "I told you so" kicker. But before we begin working on solutions (Chapter 4), we need to assess whether we have dug "deep enough." That assessment requires asking ourselves about the adopters. Can we identify a specific Principal Adopter group? Who is the adopter for a "stagnating sales" issue? Who would be the Principal Adopters of our innovation? The adopters are directly impacted by the issue, but there is more. It is for them that we are crafting a solution for the problem. People have problems. It is people who adopt solutions to their problems. Certainly, our organization is affected by stagnating sales. But is our organization doing something, or not doing something, to inadvertently limit those sales? Why has our customer's purchasing leveled off? We actually do not know the answers to either issue yet. As a result, we do not yet have enough information to determine for whom we would be creating an innovation to resolve this issue. We need to dig a bit further to understand the root of the stagnating sales issue and the "who" associated with it. Failing the assessment, not being able to clearly identify the Principal Adopters at this level, means that we are still at too high of a level and need to return to Step 4 to continue to dig down deeper into the root system of our General Problem. Having to occasionally jump back a step is the nature of a nonlinear, iterative methodology.

Step 4: Continued

Stagnating product sales could be a supply-side problem or a demand-side problem. These are the next level of nodes below the "product sales" node of our root system as shown in Figure 3.6. Are our sales

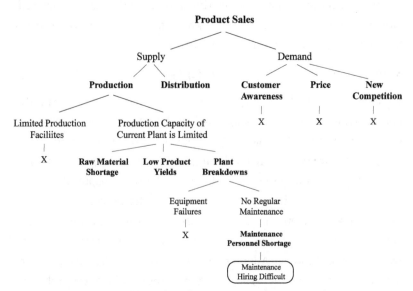

FIGURE 3.6 Problem Identification Root System example, part 2.

limited by the quantity of the product we can produce or are the sales limited by the current market demand? To determine which branch to pursue, we need to obtain a better understanding of both branches.

On the supply side, the production bottlenecks could be the production of the product itself or its distribution. In the latter case, we could be making enough product to satisfy increasing demand, but our supply chain is inadequate to deliver that volume of supply to the customer. On the demand side, the issues could be a price issue, a customer awareness issue (they simply do not know how wonderful our product is), or something else in the marketplace has changed to dampen demand, like the appearance of new competition for our product. If the issue is on the supply side, then the adopters are our own organization or our distributors. If the issue is on the demand side, then the adopters will be our customers or potential customers. Identifying our Principal Adopters, in this example, requires more research. Note how, as we dig deeper in the root system of our General Problem, the POV changes and narrows. At the General Problem level, the POV was from that of our organization as a whole. As we dug down, it shifted to accounting and sales departments. Now it is again shifting to our production department, our distributors, or our customers. It is important to consciously track these shifts as we continue to dive deeper into the root system of the General Problem.

Further research, which leverages the hypothesis-directed discovery process illustrated in Figure 3.2, reveals that our customers are aware and would like to obtain more of our product, but they just cannot get additional quantities. This fact discloses that the need for "more marketing" is incorrect. In fact, if we would have pursued that option from the beginning, we would have made the problem (flattening profitability) even worse by increasing costs!

On the supply side, we discover that it is not a distribution issue, but one of production. Our research focus shifts to the POV of those in production. We discover two factors contributing to our limited product production. One is we have only one facility within the firm that can produce this product. Second is that production capacity of this facility is limited. Figure 3.6 shows this next branching of the Problem Identification Root System. Conversations with the organization's financial planning group reveal that there is no immediate plan for the organization to build a new manufacturing plant. We therefore choose not to pursue this line and instead focus on uncovering the factors that limit the capacity of our current facility.

Conversations with the production department reveal three predominate issues: (1) production yields are low, (2) one of the key raw materials is in short supply, and (3) current plants have frequent breakdowns that cause them to unexpectedly go off-line.

From follow-up conversations with the plant equipment suppliers and our research chemists, we determine that our yields are as good as they are likely to get in the short run. We therefore decide not to pursue this branch.

Subsequent conversations with our purchasing personnel confirm that the shortage of raw materials is worldwide. They have tried alternate suppliers to no avail. They tell us that a couple of companies are contemplating expanding their production capabilities, but any increase is "years away." Given we are seeking more immediate impact, we choose not to pursue this branch.

Since we have eliminated the other branches, we are choosing to attack the problem of "frequent plant breakdowns." Again, it is important to document why we are choosing this path. We may have considered the production yield problem a long-term issue we may tackle, but we are looking for more immediate results, which is why we chose the "breakdown" issue. Whatever our logic for selection (the Converge step) it must be clear and conscious.

We are now chasing down answers to the question "why are the current production facilities frequently breaking down?" Discussions with facility managers may lead to several issues, including the fact that the facility's equipment often unexpectedly fails. Why is this happening? Discussions with plant maintenance personnel may lead to several revelations; such as there are no scheduled preventative maintenance programs for the plant's major equipment which leaves plant maintenance personnel continuously dealing with the breakdown-of-the-day. Our further research indicates a causal connection between the lack of preventative maintenance and the unexpected equipment breakdowns. We therefore choose to pursue the "maintenance" path forward.

In our pursuit to understanding why there is no regularly scheduled maintenance, we surprisingly discover that our firm has a shortage of maintenance personnel, which is the underlying cause of no scheduled maintenance program. Pushing further, we discover from personnel that there are a number of unfilled open maintenance positions that HR is trying to fill by hiring people from outside the firm. Meanwhile, we discover there are folks inside the firm who would like to transfer to the maintenance department for a variety of reasons, but are unable to do so. The root cause of our limited production issue is the difficulty in hiring maintenance workers at our facilities.

It is important to notice the items that may have been on our list of issues but, through our research, turned out not to be causal issues. Our interview of plant maintenance personnel may have revealed their opinion that the firm was unwilling to spend money hiring maintenance workers. That turned out not to be true, as we discovered the firm is advertising for several open maintenance positions. Some might have suspected "low pay" as an issue. If we cannot hire enough maintenance workers, we must not be paying them enough. That also turned out not to be true, as HR receives many applicants for those positions, only to deem them unqualified. These are examples of items that started on the things we would "like to know" or even the things "think we know" column of Figure 3.2. They never move to the "things we know" column as there was either no evidence to support them or there was evidence contrary to those hypotheses.

Step 5: Reprise

We now have a root cause of our production problem and, surprisingly, it is a lack of qualified maintenance workers. As before we need to test to see if we have "dug deep enough" by assessing whether or not we can identify the adopter of any solution we may create. That adopter is not our HR Department nor our production facilities, although both will benefit from our solution to this issue. Our Adopter group are those would-be plant maintenance personnel who are interested in the open positions but are currently deemed unqualified for them.

Example Summary

We have now completed Level 1 of The Innovation Pyramid for this example.

- We have a clearly stated initial situation.
  - Our lead product sales have stagnated.
- We have zoomed out and created a neutral General Problem statement.
  - The Organization's profitability, as measured by earnings per share, has stagnated.
- A root cause of the General Problem has been identified that the organization is able and willing to address.
  - The root cause of our stagnating company profits lies in our inability to hire qualified maintenance workers.
- The Primary Adopter group is clearly described.
  - The Primary Adopter group for our potential innovation are those would-be plant maintenance personnel who are interested in the open positions but are currently deemed unqualified for them.

COMMON MISTAKES

The biggest mistake is to skip this level entirely. Often, we are so convinced that we either absolutely know what we need to do or we know the issue we need to resolve that we consider going through the broad exploration of Level 1 a waste of time. Taking either position is a huge mistake. Our initial solution concept, as we saw with the initial "more marketing" proposal in this example, would have made the problem worse. Too often groups start by brainstorming solution ideas for the wrong problem. They do so *believing* they know the problem. Solving a problem that is not worth solving is costly and unproductive. Bottlenecks are found at the top of the bottle. Our assumptions about the problem are often those bottlenecks. When we put what we "know" into the three columns of Figure 3.2, we will find very few items that actually make it into the "know we know" column; if we are honest, most will fall in the "want to know" or "think we know" columns.

The second significant mistake made on Level 1 is to start with a solution concept (e.g., "open a restaurant") and then define the issue as a reflection of this solution – "There are not enough restaurant choices in this town." Like any mirror image, that problem definition has no depth. It is also prematurely narrowed. We need to zoom out to broaden our purview to truly understand the issue we want to impact.

Remaining too zoomed out is also an issue. Too many fruitless brainstorming sessions have been spent trying to come up with specific solutions to resolve "world peace" level issues. While zooming out to a General Problem is a good step, it is far from the last step required before starting on a solution. Innovation is not a one-and-done; the two design stages alone have many steps to perform.

Logic leaps, phantom links, and false or misleading supporting "data" are to be avoided. Our aim is to identify a root cause that has known connections to our zoomed out General Problem. The linkages of the Problem Identification Root System (Figure 3.4) must be understood and data-supported. Imaging links between items is not good enough. The links must be supported with data; not misleading data that is contrived to support the conjecture. Crafting the Problem Identification Root System is a research effort that, if done correctly and methodically, will pay dividends in the end.

The final major issue when implementing this level is that no other POV, beyond that of the would-be innovator, is ever considered. The rationale is that this can be left until later, as the identification of the Primary Adopter group feels like a "marketing issue" that we do not need to address until we are ready to sell our innovation. The "marketing issue" that is usually referenced is promotion, which is communicating our value proposition to our potential customers. This is design, where we are *creating* a value proposition for a specific group of people. If we do not know who we are innovating for, how can we possibly know if we are creating value for them? Therefore, identify the Principal Adopter group, create value for them in design, and then communicate that value proposition when promoting the innovation.

Go slow to go fast. A methodical approach saves time in the long run. This first design stage forces us to ask the right questions, which will in turn lead us to the root causes of our General Problem. Once we have the right problem with the right adopter group identified, finding a solution becomes much more straightforward as we will see in Chapter 4.

SUMMARY

The Innovation Pyramid segments the innovation's design from its execution. The design stage is further segmented into Problem Identification and Solution Formulation. The first level of The Pyramid, which is the first stage of the innovation's design, describes a procedure for identifying and defining root causes of larger situations. Similar to The Innovation Pyramid, this five-step procedure for Problem Identification is a nonlinear and iterative process of discovery. Steps may be skipped or repeated depending on where we start or how the process of discovery unfolds. The five-step procedure is therefore more of a guideline than a rigorous process. That five-step guideline is as follows:

Step 1: Clearly state the starting situation or issue.
Step 2: Zoom out to define the General Problem.
Step 3: Draft a neutral problem statement.
Step 4: Zoom in, layer by layer, to a root cause.
Step 5: Identify the Principal Adopters.

The first step in the Problem Identification guideline is to describe the original situation or initially identified issue. We may have started with a solution concept, but if that was the case, we need to flip that perspective and describe the problem we are facing. The second step is to zoom out and broaden our purview, which allows us to see the problem in a bigger context and ensures that we are not initially focusing too sharply on a symptom of a larger issue. We do not want to miss the forest for focusing on a particular tree. Broadening our perspective will ensure that no problem, and therefore no potential solution, is overlooked. The General Problem that we identify by this zooming out process may be very different from our initial problem description. The POV of the problem, whose eyes through which we see the problem, will also likely change. If we started our search with a very wide purview, this second step is skipped.

The third step is to create a neutral General Problem statement. Our problem descriptions can be biased. Those biases infer a certain solution approach while eliminating others. An "energy shortage" infers that we need to produce more energy and is biased against the conservation solution pathway. As we are not searching for solutions at this Pyramid level, it is important not to eliminate some. Broadening our problem perspective while inadvertently sabotaging the scope of our potential solutions is to be avoided. Doing so requires us to pay conscious attention to the descriptive language of the General Problem.

The fourth step in the guideline is to narrow from the General Problem to a root cause which we will attempt to resolve in the second stage of the design, Level 2 of The Innovation Pyramid (Chapter 4). We want to methodically and rationally dig down from the General Problem, layer by layer. We are not simply seeking a smaller problem to solve; we are searching for a smaller problem that has a strong connection to the General Problem. We want to create a domino effect such that when we resolve the root cause problem, the impact of that resolution cascades all the way up to impact the General Problem. The stronger the root system we identify as we dig down, the bigger the domino effect will be as the impact cascades back up. As we descend from the General Problem to its root causes, we will be exposing the root system of the General Problem. The POV necessary to truly understand each node of that root system will also change.

We also want to avoid any logical leap as they represent disconnections in the root system. With an intuitive leap we no longer know how the root system is interconnected, we simply randomly jumped to another issue at another level of the root system. Losing those linkages makes it impossible to obtain any meaningful feedback on our decisions at the end of the project; no way to determine how an alternate choice may have made a difference in the outcome of the innovation project.

We will not have the time nor the energy to trace the entire root system. We will be making choices, deciding which branch of the root system to follow as we proceed. We will have to choose as we descend down the root system, which contributing factor of the General Problem to pursue, then which contributing cause of one of those factors to pursue, etc., until we reach the root cause level of the root system. At each juncture, in addition to the strength of the subissues' ties to the problem, we are assessing whether or not the organization is willing or able to address this subissue.

The fifth and final step of the Problem Identification guideline is an assessment of whether or not we have completed the previous step. When digging down, layer by layer, uncovering the interconnection of the roots of the General Problem, we need to know when to stop. We need to know we have excavated deep enough to stop identifying the problem and begin to move on to the problem's resolution. We have reached that endpoint in our archaeological dig when we can clearly name the Principal Adopters of our innovation, not simply the groups affected by the issue we have identified.

At the end Level 1 of The Innovation Pyramid methodology, we have:

- defined a General Problem from our initial situation;
- determined a root cause of that General Problem for which our organization is able and willing to resolve;

- determined the connections between the root cause and the General Problem; and
- identified an adopter group that is both impacted by the root cause issue and will be the general group for whom we are creating the innovation.

Now it is time to create a solution for this clearly identified problem. We are now ready to begin the Solution Formulation stage of The Innovation Pyramid that will be detailed in Chapter 4.

4 **Level 2**
Solution Formulation

It is quite common to start the innovation process with a solution idea. That seems to be how our brains work; we are action-oriented beings, those "fight-or-flight" approaches to problems run deep. It is perfectly fine to start there. The Innovation Pyramid is a nonlinear system, it does not matter where we start. In fact, trying to not initially think about solutions will likely stifle our creative thinking. It is the next step that is the critical one. Instead of delving further into the details of that initial solution idea, we need to train ourselves to switch our perspective from that solution to the problem it addresses. This requires moving from Level 2 back to Level 1 of The Pyramid. Once that design stage is complete, we will return to this level.

In addition to being nonlinear, The Innovation Pyramid is also an iterative method. In Chapter 3, we saw how we could iterate among the steps within Level 1. The same holds true for this level too. We can also iterate between levels. The previous discussion regarding starting in Level 2 is but one example of the iterations that can occur between levels of The Pyramid. We may also iterate through the entire Pyramid multiple times; proceeding through The Pyramid once for prototype development and then a second time for the final innovation development is but one example of this class of iteration. While the overall innovation method does not change for prototype development, the amount of information we have at each decision point will very likely be less for the development of a prototype. There will also be occasions where we will create a less-than-full-featured prototype to test a particular aspect of the innovation's design. While the project's scope may narrow, that does not change the objectives of each Pyramid level. While it is important to document decisions made throughout The Pyramid generally, it is particularly important that we document decisions made during prototype development, as it is guaranteed that we will be assessing the overall outcome, as described in Chapter 7, and iterating back through The Pyramid a second time.

The first innovation design stage, Level 1 of The Innovation Pyramid, is focused on Problem Identification. That stage uncovered a root cause of our original situation that we (or our organization) are capable and willing to address. The objective of this second design stage is to craft a solution that addresses that root cause. The solution design must be specific and detailed. We are not simply building a "house"; that level of description is nothing more than a solution concept. Instead, we are designing a specific dwelling for which we will need to create detailed blueprints. What's more, that specific solution must create value for the precisely described adopters of our solution. Doing so requires that we understand how our innovation's attributes satisfy the unmet or under-met needs, wants, and/or desires of those adopters. Solution Formulation integrates all these aspects of the solution design.

The desired outcome for this level, as was the case for Level 1, represents the "What" face of The Innovation Pyramid, as illustrated in Figure 4.1. That desired outcome is to craft a detailed solution that

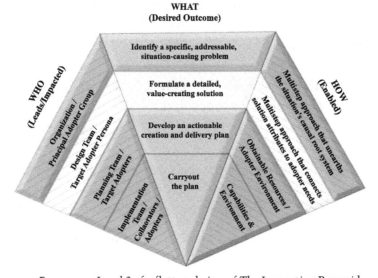

FIGURE 4.1 Level 2 of a flattened view of The Innovation Pyramid.

creates value for a specific Target Adopter. The "Who" again takes on two points-of-view, the innovator's and the adopter's; both of which are narrowed at this level. The adopter is narrowed in this level from the broad Principal Adopter group identified in Level 1 to a specific Target Adopter persona with known unmet or under-met needs, wants, and/or desires. The innovation creator is narrowed from the organization that will create the innovation to its design team. The "How" segment at this level is again a multistep process which will be detailed in the next section. These steps will detail how to transition from the identified root cause to a precise adopter, with specific unmet or under-met needs, wants, and/or desires, and then craft a solution whose attributes create value by directly connecting to those need/wants/desires.

SOLUTION FORMULATION METHOD

At the end of this level, we will have a specific new solution design. That design must be detailed enough to execute it in the next two levels of The Pyramid. This solution must also create impact, which means we will need to understand why the adopter would embrace it, and how it is better than, from the adopter's point-of-view, the adopter's current alternatives. The precise pathway to that desired outcome will vary depending on where we start. This section offers a general step-by-step guide for reaching Level 2's objectives. Similar to the Problem Identification steps, the Solution Formulation steps represent guidelines for proceeding through this level and are not a checklist of procedural boxes to tick off.

Starting Point

Level 2 of The Innovation Pyramid is the second stage of the design process. The starting point for Level 2 is the endpoint of Level 1. At the end of Level 1 of The Innovation Pyramid methodology, we had:

- defined a General Problem from our initial situation;
- determined a root cause of that General Problem for which our organization is able and willing to resolve;

- understood the connections between the root cause and the General Problem; and
- identified an adopter group, the Principal Adopters, that is both impacted by the root cause issue and will be the broad group for whom we are creating the innovation.

Endpoint

Beginning with the end in mind, before undertaking the second leg of our design journey, it is prudent to articulate our destination. By the completion of Level 2, our aim is to have a:

- specific new solution (detailed and fully designed);
- specific Target Adopter persona with clearly identified unmet or under-met needs, wants, and/or desires; and
- distinct value proposition: clear connection between the features of the new solution with the need/wants/desires of the target persona.

While the ultimate outcome of this design stage is the detailed design of an impactful solution, we simply cannot get there without first further narrowing the identification of our problem; specifically, the adopter we will target with our innovation. The Principal Adopter, which we defined in Level 1, sets the direction for our aim, but is not the precise target on which we need to focus.

Whether we are creating a solution as an initial prototype or the final product, we need to begin with the adopter. People have issues and will adopt solutions to resolve them. We cannot innovate without first identifying the specific people for which our innovation is intended to benefit. In Level 1, we identified a Principal Adopter group. This is a starting point for developing our innovation, but it is, unfortunately, not detailed enough to design the impactful innovation we seek. A professional golfer does not aim their approach shot at the green, but at a specific point on the green. A bowler does not aim at the pins, in general, but at a specific pin or spot on the lane. The Principal Adopter describes the general direction of our aim. We first need to transform that into a specific target before we begin crafting solutions. This specific target is our Target Adopter. This Target Adopter will have identifiable wants, needs, and/or desires that are currently unmet or under-met by their present solution choices. Converting the root cause and the Principal Adopter that we identified in Level 1 to the Target Adopter with specific needs/wants/desires is the final transformation on the Problem Identification side of Figure 4.2.

Once the Target Adopter is well defined, including their unmet or under-met needs, wants, and/or desires, we can begin to craft a specific solution for them. In Level 1, one of our selection criteria for the root causes was one that our organization was willing and able to address. That is the starting point for Solution Formulation, as represented on the extreme right-hand side of Figure 4.2. The fact that the organization is willing and able to address the cause means that the problem falls within their capabilities. The term "capability" is very specifically defined in this book and includes both competencies as well as aspirations (Faley, 2015a). The vertical bubbles in Figure 4.3 represent the "hard" capabilities of assets and know-how, while the horizontal bubbles represent the "soft" capabilities of relationships and aspirations.

The Problem Identification and Solution Formulation aspects of the design must converge to a single point. That point is the previously stated end point of this level. The entire pathway through Level 2 will require multiple steps. As was the case in Level 1, this section offers a general step-by-step guide for reaching Level 2's objectives. These

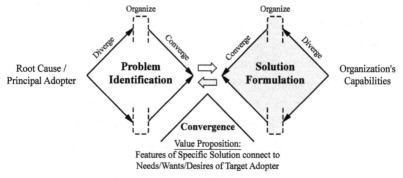

FIGURE 4.2 The Innovation Pyramid Design Level 2.

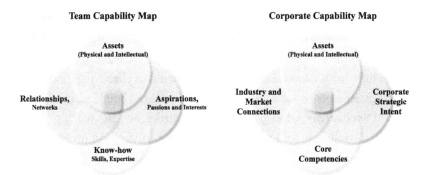

FIGURE 4.3 Team and corporation Capability Map.

steps are a guide and not a prescription. The guidelines for proceeding through this level are not a checklist of procedural boxes to tick off. There will be times when, as in the subsequent example, where we will choose to move forward to the next step before the current one is absolutely "complete." That is perfectly acceptable as long as each step is eventually completed.

Step 1: Describe a Specific Target Adopter Persona

We need to refine the innovation target. That target needs to be a person, as it is people who adopt innovations to resolve their issues. The Principal Adopter sets the direction of our innovation, but is not specific enough to define its target. The Target Adopter is that target. We will be developing a persona to represent our Target Adopter. That personification of our target will allow us to move beyond a dispassionate list of unmet or under-met needs, wants, and/ or desires and embody that list in an archtype adopter, a persona. This Target Adopter persona will be specific. It will be an aggregation of individuals with similar decision-driving needs, wants, and/or desires. These personas will *not* be solely based on a demographic description of a person (sex, race, age, etc.), although those characteristics may be a part of the persona description. Instead, these persona descriptions focus on how this group thinks and chooses. Specifically, we will concentrate on creating personas that make choices based on common needs/wants/desires. We want to build a picture of the representative archtype person that is our Target Adopter. How do they make choices? What desired outcomes do they value? We want to make sure to include both rational and emotional facets of these questions – it saves them time, it saves them money, it makes them feel good, etc.

Discovering what people think and know, uncovering their tacit knowledge, is an important part of the innovation process. We will be interviewing members of the Principal Adopter group to refine that group into segments, one of which we will choose to be our Target Adopter. To make sure our purview is complete, we will additionally include interviews 360-degrees around these Principal Adopters. That group will vary with the specific innovation project, but could include coworkers, supervisors, and/or subordinates for those in a work environment.

In Chapter 3, our primary research was aimed at obtaining "facts." In this level, we will be performing a special type of interview as we are not interviewing for facts, but insights. The details of this Interviewing for Insight (IFI) technique is detailed in Appendix A. People cannot generally tell you how and why they make decisions the way they do. Sure, we each can rationalize every decision we have ever made after the fact, but we typically cannot identify the general algorithm we would use to make future decisions. We are humans after all, not machines with known decision-making instruction sets. As a result, we, as the interviewers, have to draw those conclusions, or insights, based on the information gathered during the interviews. The information we gather is the foundation and support for the insights we reach. Instead of asking pointed questions aimed at obtaining facts, we will be asking open-ended questions that, through their answers, will allow us to get to know the interviewee and provide us insight into their motivations and how they make choices relative to the issue we are trying to resolve for them. This is why being empathetic is so important to the process. We simply cannot commit to the level of listening required to obtain these insights if we are not empathetic with our adopters.

We are definitely *not* asking our interviewees to comment on any premature solution ideas we may be thinking about. We want to diagnose the situation before prescribing a solution. Before crafting any innovation, we want to understand our target's decision-making needs/wants/desires. Those identified wants/needs/desires, combined with our knowledge of their current solution options, will allow us to develop an innovation that creates a specific value proposition for them. This is detective work; we are seeking to uncover evidence.

This final phase in the development of our Target Adopter persona is yet another application of the Diverge Organize Converge (DOC) Process, detailed in the second half of this book. The "Diverge" step of the process, as illustrated in Figure 4.4, is a result of our open-ended IFIs. We will, as a result of these interviews, uncover a wide range of unmet and under-met needs/wants/desires of the Principal Adopters affected by our identified root-cause issue. We will organize these needs/wants/desires and then craft personas from combinations of these need/want/desire categories. Finally, in the "Converge" step of the DOC Process, we will select one of the crafted personas, our Target Adopter, which will be defined by a specific subset of needs/wants/desires categories we uncovered. We will, of course, need explicit criteria for choosing the Target Adopter persona for which we will be innovating. It will also prove helpful to name the personas to help give them "life" and make them less abstract. It is much easier to see how "Unmotivated Uma" approaches her job, for example, than a list of need/wants/desires would do so. This entire process is detailed in Appendix A.

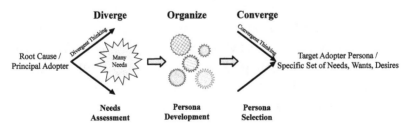

FIGURE 4.4 DOC Process application to Target Adopter persona creation and selection.

It is always important to remind ourselves that every issue has an existing solution. It may not be a very good solution, but people cope somehow. At the very least we want to identify, during our interview process, our potential adopter's point-of-view regarding their current solution options and determine why they are choosing the one solution they are currently utilizing. The solution they are currently using to resolve the issue we are pursuing is their Best Alternative to a New Option (BATNO). We want to understand, from their point-of-view, what about it they like and do not like. While these responses will provide us with some insight as to their unmet and under-met needs, wants, and/or desires, we also seek broader insights. A narrow discussion limited to the adopter's current BATNO will only lead to solution ideas that are incremental improvements of the adopter's current solution; to put it in Henry Ford's parlance, it will only lead us to that proverbial "faster horse." To broaden the potential innovations, we need to take a step back from their BATNO, once we have identified it and broadened our purview.

The type of innovation (incremental to radical) that we will eventually design is an outcome determined, in part, by how we identify and define the problem we are seeking to resolve. The narrower the scope of our interview, the more likely the innovation will be incremental. If we ask people what they like and do not like about their cell phone, their answers will help us innovate at the feature level. But it will not lead us to anything other than a "better" cell phone. The result will be, at best, an incremental innovation. If, on the other hand, we push the interviewees to answer broader questions like "what is working and not working for them regarding staying connected to their globally distributed business team?," it will provide us insights that will enable us to develop a more radical innovation. Either way, the potential innovation is partially dependent on how narrow or broadly we engage our interviewees.

Unless we are only interested in improving on today's solution features, we need to broaden our questions from specific questions about our potential adopter's likes and dislikes of their current

BATNO. To broaden our purview, we need to ask, "what issue does the BATNO resolve for them, generally speaking?" What does their BATNO allow them to accomplish? If their current BATNO is a mobile phone, the more general issue is communication. If they frequent a certain restaurant, what are they getting out of it? Is it a convenient means to get a quick bite to eat or is it a place to meet up with friends and family? A narrowly scoped IFI will lead to an incrementally improved solution. Broadening the scope of the IFI will provide us broader insights which will, in turn, lead us to more diverse solutions.

Step 2: Determine a Solution Approach

Once our target persona is clearly articulated, we can begin working the right-hand side of Figure 4.2. Before delving deep into solution features, however, it is beneficial to first think about the approach we want to take. An approach sets the direction for the solution we will eventually pursue in more detail. If you lost your car keys and need to drive to the store, for example, you can search for the lost keys, use the spare set (assuming one exists), or obtain a duplicate key. These are different approaches to resolving the problem. If you choose the approach of searching for your lost keys, you will only pursue a path forward that is related to that approach, unless and until you consciously circle back and change that approach decision. These switches occur very quickly in our lives; so fast in fact, that we may not be aware of them. The last time you misplaced your car keys right before you were heading out you likely looked for them for a while, but when that search did not immediately pan out, you grabbed the spare keys and left. Before grabbing the spare keys, however, you had to change your approach, at least for the moment, to resolving that issue. As Robert Frost said in his poem "The Road Not Taken" (Lathem, 1969), the path is chosen far before the destination is in sight. We will still have a long way to go before reaching a fully designed solution to a precisely defined problem, but many potential avenues are being eliminated by the initial solution direction we choose.

Considering the solution approach warrants its own step for two reasons. The first is that we often, unconsciously, get locked into an approach. We often get so locked into our approach that we forget that the approach is not the problem we are attempting to resolve, it is only an approach to resolving it. During the 2008 US Presidential campaign, for example, the two opposing campaigns had very different approaches to resolving the United States' desire to become more energy independent. The slogan of the McCain campaign was "drill baby drill" ("Drill"), which represented their approach to tapping more US-sourced oil and gas supplies. The solution approach for the Obama campaign, on the other hand, was to increase renewable energy supplies through investments in wind and solar. The two political camps became so embroiled in their approaches that any discussion of the real issue, American energy independence, was lost.

Whenever we find ourselves struggling between two choices, look for a third alternative, as the root of our struggle is likely a false dichotomy. Alternatives can be discovered, but only if we first get out of the solution space and refocus on the issue we are trying to resolve. It takes a mindset shift. Part of that mindset shift is altering our approach.

The second reason thinking about the approach warrants its own steps is that the approach we choose is often mistaken for a solution to the issue. Solution approaches include solution categories or common classifications of solutions. "Opening a restaurant" is a solution category, as is "creating an online degree program." Solution approaches include "increasing product marketing" or "debottlenecking manufacturing." None of these categories or approaches are detailed enough to implement, yet each significantly narrows how we will address the issue. Too often innovation teams fail by jumping from the solution category directly to execution. A solution category or approach is a start toward designing a detailed solution that we can execute. It is not an executable solution.

An approach lies at a higher level, has a broader purview, than the detailed solution. This higher level thinking requires that we shift our thinking above that of the product or service. We should first think about what desired outcome we seek, as illustrated in the McCain/Obama energy positioning, then ask ourselves "what are all the ways…" to get us there. Creating high-level challenge statements with "How to…," "what are all the ways…," "How might we…," or "How can we…" reach that desired outcome we seek should challenge us to focus, not just on a detailed product-feature level, but also on a function and system level.

Completing Step 2 should not take much time. The emphasis on this step is to ensure the approach is, as in all choices made during The Innovation Pyramid methodology, made consciously. The approach should be recognized as nothing more than what it is. It is not the issue we are attempting to resolve. It is not the solution that will resolve that issue. It is only an approach. That approach is nothing but a direction. To pursue solutions outside of this approach, we will first have to shift our mindset away from this approach and toward another.

Step 3: Craft a Detailed Solution

Before we leave the design stages of The Innovation Pyramid, our final design must be detailed enough to implement. We need to drill down on our approach set in Step 2 and create a detailed solution. That solution must contain descriptions of precise features or attributes. Those specific attributes must create value for the Target Adopter by connecting to that adopter's list of unmet or under-met needs, wants, and/or desires. This is the value proposition we are generating that is described in Step 4 and is the completion assessment of this second design stage. As superfluous solution features have no connection to our Target Adopter, we do not need them.

While this is a narrowing step, a consistent theme of The Innovation Pyramid methodology is that we always broaden before we narrow, always diverge before converging. As the right-hand side of Figure 4.2 illustrates, this detailed solution development will involve the DOC Process. Very likely it will take several applications of the DOC Process before we reach our final design.

When divergently considering potential solutions to align with the identified wants, needs, and/or desires of the Target Adopter, we will want to consider multiple levels of thinking. Groups often get fixated on the feature level of potential solutions. They tend to only consider how they could improve features of the potential adopter's current BATNO. While it is perfectly fine to start at this thinking level, all three levels of Figure 4.5 need to be considered.

The feature level represents "me too" solution ideas. A "me too" product or service is something that is currently available, although we will try to spice it up by tweaking the features. A smartphone with a slightly better camera is still a smartphone. The new feature has some advantages, but represents an incremental improvement versus a significant change. A less-expensive USB drive or one that has more storage capacity is an improvement over existing options, but it is still a USB drive.

Zooming out one layer up from the current BATNO, our broadened purview is now at the function level of Figure 4.5. At this level, we are not creating a "me too" offering, but a substitute. A substitute is quite different from the incumbent BATNO; it simply performs the same function. An MP3 player performs the same function as a CD player – they play music. The iPad performs many of the same functions as a laptop computer. Functional equivalents

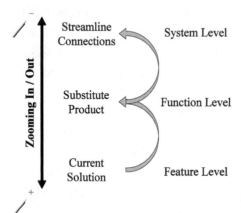

FIGURE 4.5 Divergent solution formulation techniques.

typically have many inherent advantages (smaller, more convenient, etc.). They also typically incorporate new or emerging technology. Substitute products can also be better at addressing an emerging or previously underserved market versus the incumbent product. Cell phones are a much more convenient way for a mobile society to stay connected than landlines and pay phones, for example.

Figure 4.5 shows that one more zoomed-out layer up from the function level, this final broadening of our purview, puts us at the system level. This purview requires system-level thinking; assesses all the linkages in a system, and asks if these can be enhanced or even eliminated. If so, how? Consider the "system" of selling our used stuff via a traditional garage or yard sale. We would gather up all our treasures, price them, put them on a table in our garage or the end of our driveway, and wait for someone to come by and see if they are interested. We may have even gone one step further by putting information about our "sale" in the newspaper or on a bulletin board at our workplace. Customer acquisition is limited to our region. Now consider eBay. Did eBay "invent" selling used goods to others? Absolutely not. But what it did was consider the entire system and realize that the weak link in the system was connecting buyers and sellers. After eBay, the geographic reach of miscellaneous goods sellers dramatically increased – eventually becoming international. Most smartphone apps make the connection and transaction between buyer and seller or between information gatherers and data sources more convenient. We will not ever get to these possibilities by limiting our divergent thinking to the feature level. Feature-level, function-level, and system-level alternatives must all be considered. It will very likely take several iterations of Solution Formulation to craft a solution that creates the desired value proposition for the Target Adopter.

Step 4: Establish a Clear Value Proposition

The convergence of Problem Identification and Solution Formulation, as illustrated in Figure 4.2, is the creation of a clear value proposition for the Target Adopter. That value proposition is constructed through

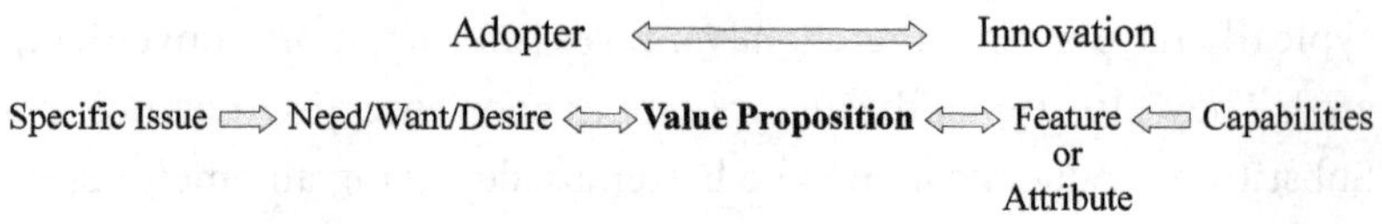

Adopter $\Longleftrightarrow$ Innovation

Specific Issue $\Longrightarrow$ Need/Want/Desire $\Longleftrightarrow$ **Value Proposition** $\Longleftrightarrow$ Feature $\Longleftarrow$ Capabilities
or
Attribute

FIGURE 4.6 Value proposition creation.

the connection of the features of our specific solution to the unmet or under-met needs, wants, and/or desires of the Target Adopter. Those fundamental connections between the innovation and the adopter is illustrated in Figure 4.6. Those solution attributes are, in turn, derived from the innovator's capabilities. The needs/wants/desires of the Target Adopter are a subset of those who were struggling with the specific root cause issue identified in Level 1.

The ability to clearly articulate the value proposition that the proposed new solution creates for the Target Adopter is the assessment step for Level 2. During this assessment step, we are examining whether the features of our proposed solution align with the needs/wants/desires of our Target Adopter. If not, then we will have to return to Step 3 and alter our solution. We also do not want to put extra unnecessary features into our solution as they will only increase that solution's cost without creating additional value for the adopter.

Step 5: Quantify the Target Adopter Group Size

This step will not always be performed and if it is, it is recommended that it not be completed until the quantitative financial assessments of Level 3 need to be completed. Up until this point, our design has been descriptive. This has been purposeful, as once we begin investing time into the numbers, we become increasingly resistant to changing our design. Human nature is that we will resist pivoting from our initial design after we have spent significant time and effort determining the adopter volumes and solution costs. During those hours, we will have convinced ourselves that our Target Adopter choice and our design are perfect. To avoid being prematurely locked into a specific design, it is recommended that we proceed to Level 3, the planning stage of execution stage, before completing Step 5. This is yet another example of the nonlinearity of the methodology. Once we have progressed through Level 3 far enough to warrant detailed numbers, we will return here to obtain them.

We will be seeking two quantitative values: the size of the Target Adopter group and the segment of that group that we feel will be the early or most likely adopters of our innovation (i.e. the Target Adopter segment). These groups can be sized from the bottom up or the top down. The determination of the size of these groups will leverage both primary and secondary research. Fortunately, we are starting with a very precise Target Adopter persona description.

Bottom-Up Quantitative Sizing Method

In the bottom-up approach, our aim is to quantify the size of the Target Adopter group by starting from a very zoomed-in perspective. Surveys and other primary research methods are one way to address the size question this way. While we used IFIs to obtain the Target Adopter description in the first place, surveys are a useful tool to quantify their numbers. Surveys were *not* applicable to defining the Target Adopter, as we were seeking tacit knowledge. But now that we definitively know our Target Adopter persona description, we know precisely what questions to ask on our survey. An example of this approach is included in the example that began in Chapter 3 and concludes in this chapter.

Top-Down Quantitative Sizing Method

The alternative to building up the target size from a bottom-up approach is to take the top-down approach. In the top-down approach, we begin from a zoomed-out perspective. We quantify the size of our Target Adopter group by winnowing away at the aggregate data we uncovered. The top-down approach, while popular, is also the most erroneously used. This is due to the fact that market research reports tend to report group sizes from an end-user aggregate perspective, such as saying that the smartphone market for 2018 was $522 billion representing 1.44 billion units ("Global"). Innovators often make the mistake that this number is the quantification of their Principal Adopter group described in both terms of sales and monetary value. That is not correct as the Principal Adopter group's size will depend on where in the value system the innovation lies.

Let us look at a simplistic example to illustrate how these sizes are often erroneously overestimated. Let us say that our team is creating software that would augment a smartphone's Android operating system. Let's say our research informs us that that 85 percent of the smartphones sold in 2018 contained Android operating system. We therefore estimate the size of the Principal Adopter group as 85 percent of $522 billion or $443.7 billion. That is not correct. The number of units for our Principal Adopter group is indeed 85 percent of 1.44 billion units or 1.22 billion units because we could, in theory, sell one unit of our software innovations per phone sold. The monetary value we calculated is, however, the market value of Android-based smartphones, not the value of our improvement. The monetary value of our innovation is much, much less.

One way to get at the potential value of our improvement is to determine the value of the operating system relative to the phone, and then the value of our augmented software to the operating system. For the sake of this example, let's say that the operating system represents 10 percent of the value of the phone and that our improvement represents 2 percent of the value of the operating system for a smartphone. The potential value of our innovation is therefore ($522 billion)*(85%)*(10%)*(2%) or = $0.89 billion. That's a far cry from $443.7 billion initially calculated. We would then need to determine the fraction of the Principal Adopter group that our Target Adopter represents, but you can now see where we need to be careful with this approach.

DESIGN EXAMPLE, LEVEL 2

In order to illustrate how the two design stages of The Innovation Pyramid work together, this example will continue the one started in Chapter 3. Recall that in that example we are part of a for-profit company. The sales of our lead product is stagnating. That stagnation is negatively impacting the profitability of the firm as a whole. At the end of the example in Chapter 3, we discovered that a root cause of this issue was, surprisingly, our inability to hire qualified maintenance workers for the production facility of this lead product. The Primary Adopter group for our potential innovation are those who are interested in the open maintenance positions but ones that our human resources (HR) department are currently deeming unqualified for these positions.

Step 1: Describe a Specific Target Adopter Persona

From the organization's point-of-view, we learn that the maintenance personnel need certification to work on the production plant's equipment. Without that certification, the warranty of the plant's expensive equipment is voided. The firm does not want those warranties to be voided, as the equipment is too expensive to replace. We also learn that the firm has other needs. It needs the maintenance people to be aware of the plant hazards and materials that are part and parcel to the production process. We learned that all plant employees, other than administrative personnel, receive this in-house training before they start working at the firm.

With the help of the HR department, we learn that we can categorize the maintenance applicant pool into three groups. One is existing plant personnel that would like to move to the maintenance department. While this group does have the required training on plant hazards and material handling and maintenance acumen, they have no formal maintenance experience. As a result, they would have difficulty obtaining equipment-specific certification on their own. The outside applicants fall into two groups. One has maintenance experience, but lacks the firm's plant safety and materials training. They also do not have the specific equipment maintenance certification that the job requires. The second group of outside hires are career starters. They are seeking their first maintenance job. They have an overall lack of job experience in addition to the same issues of the other outside applicant group. We can personify these three groups based on their unique needs. These needs are what they are lacking in order to be hired for the open maintenance positions. For convenience, and to give them some life, we will name these three personas, "Transfer Tom," "Maintenance Mike," and "Green Greg," respectively.

In this organization, we see that the common need of all three personas is the lack of specific equipment maintenance certification for the equipment that our plant utilizes. Maintenance Mike and Green Greg have additional needs. Maintenance Mike lacks company-specific experience including the production plant's safety and material training. Green Greg has all of Mike's needs plus lacks general work experience. We choose to focus on the "Transfer Tom" persona as that persona only has the need to obtain equipment-specific maintenance certification, while the other personas have that need plus additional ones. "Tom" has experience in our plants, maintenance acumen, but lacks equipment-specific certification. We have now driven down the general situation of company revenue stagnation to the need of Transfer Tom to qualify for a maintenance job in our firm by somehow obtaining equipment-specific certification. Whatever solution we develop for "Transfer Tom" could also likely be useful to "Maintenance Mike," the outside applicant with maintenance experience. For now, however, we are focused on Transfer Tom.

We could continue with Step 1 at this point and dive deeper into their needs/wants/desires by assessing the adopter's BATNO. Instead, since we have at least a start on our Target Adopter persona description, we will jump ahead to Step 2 (Solution Approach) and return to Step 1 to fill in the details later. This is another example of the nonlinearity of the approach; there is no single order in which to accomplish the necessary tasks.

Step 2: Determine a Solution Approach

Having done the hard work of Problem Identification, the Solution Formulation work would seem trivial. It appears all that we need to do is to create a training session for would-be applicants to address their lack of certification. This could be a path forward, but before we lock in on that approach, we need to do some more research. We need to know what BATNO exists, and why it is not working for our applicants. In other words, we need to get more details about the "needs" of our applicants beyond the general "they need certification." We will temporarily set "provide training" as the approach and return to Step 1 to uncover more detailed needs.

Step 1: Reprise

At this point, the research will become more personal. We will need to perform one-on-one IFIs (Appendix A) to obtain the next level of detail we need. We have the general needs of "Transfer Tom" in that he needs certification, but we do not know the specific issues he may have in obtaining that certification. Those barriers will likely apply to our other two personas, so we will interview all three (the entire Principal Adopter group) regarding this issue.

We also need to consider all three solution levels of Figure 4.5. To do that we will need to uncover more about the applicant's current BATNO for obtaining equipment-specific maintenance certification and then expand from there. Is there training available to obtain this equipment-specific maintenance certification? Why are these applicants not pursuing that option, if it is available? Perhaps it is a system-level issue, the training exists, but is somehow unavailable? We need to do more research. We will use the IFI technique detailed in Appendix A to perform 360-degree interviews around our applicants. We will interview the applicants, HR personnel, the head of maintenance for our firm, and our current maintenance people. In doing so, we create a large list of needs, wants, and/or desires related to certification. This is the "Diverge" step of the final DOC Process application of Problem Identification.

What's the applicant's current BATNO? Is there any equipment-specific training available? If so, why is this inadequate? Is the curricula of this training insufficient for the applicants to pass the certification exam? This is feature-level exploration, as we are thinking only about the specific elements of a training program. If we start thinking on a higher level, a system level, we start thinking of the training as an element of a bigger picture. Is training, if it exists, somehow inaccessible to the applicants? Is it too expensive? Is it only offered in a location far from our facilities? These are system-level issues. We also need to think about function-level issues. On a function level, the training provides a means for maintenance workers to obtain certification on our equipment. Perhaps this can be accomplished in another way. Something that is not a training class, but perhaps an apprentice program that would get our candidates the experience they need to obtain certification. If it is training, is this a problem just for our firm or is it a regional issue? If regional, should we partner with other regional firms or the local chamber of commerce or university in developing the training? Should we partner with the equipment manufacturer?

We will need to perform the follow-up interviews. Given we are focused on the BATNO, we need to expand the interview pool beyond the Principal Adopters. We need to include existing plant maintenance personnel to see how they obtained certification. Given that the equipment manufacturer is the one who is certifying the candidates, we need to have a conversation with them about potential training they may offer or recommend.

We will say, for this example, that the manufacturer does have a training program. It is only available online. The certification exam, which the equipment manufacturer administrates, is given twice a year and only at the manufacturer's facility in a city 1,000 miles away from our plant's location. The exam is a combination of written and practice. The written exam is an online exam. The practice portion must be done face-to-face. During the practicum portion of the exam, the examinee must perform maintenance on the equipment while being observed and assessed by an examiner. The existing plant maintenance personnel tell us the practicum is the most difficult part of the exam. The available online course does not adequately prepare them, in their opinion, for this portion of the exam. We learn from the Principal Adopters that the time and cost of the exam, including the travel to the examination site, is too much for them to risk when they do not even know if they would be offered the job if they passed the tests.

Step 3: Craft a Detailed Solution

Now we have a much better idea of the underlying needs/wants/desires and are therefore ready to dive in and craft a solution that fits our Target Persona's need. Our solution may or may not also work for "Maintenance Mike," but for now he is not included in our target. We break the issue down and work on each part. In the first brainstorming session, we focus on the online preparation training offered by the equipment manufacturer. We ask, "How might we make this more accessible to would-be applicants?" This accessibility also needs to cover the training's cost barrier.

We then tackle the practicum training. "What are all the ways we could offer practicum training?" Finally, we brainstorm on the exam itself by brainstorming around the question, "How might we reduce the barriers (including cost) of taking the certification exam?"

We may have to do some follow-up research to augment our brainstorming session. We may want, for example, to have follow-up conversations with the equipment manufacturer to see how they may collaborate with us, especially given that we buy both the equipment and parts from them.

In the end, the equipment manufacturer is willing to provide, at their site, a "train the trainer" program for both practicum trainers and examiners. They agree that if our personnel successfully completes this in-person course, that they will accept the use of our own personnel as trainers and examiners. After more internal discussion, we craft a training program with the following features.

- We will create a space at our facility where our employees can take the equipment manufacturer's online training. This facility will be open extended hours so that our personnel who are working the day shift will be able to access this facility during their nonwork hours. Our firm will pay our equipment provider with an annual license fee so that up to twenty of our employees per year can take this training free of charge to the employee.

- The equipment manufacturer will work with us to create a hands-on training for preparation for the practicum portion of the exam.
- Two of our senior plant maintenance personnel will be sent, at our firm's expense, to the equipment manufacture's site to be trained to teach this practicum course and trained in giving the practicum exam.
- We will offer the practicum training course on an as-needed basis for those who have passed the written exam. The training will be offered at least monthly. The time of the training will change from month to month so that personnel working on every shift will have the opportunity to participate. That practicum training course will be free to our employees.
- The practicum exam will be administered, at the end of the training course, at our facility. Our own examiners will be trained and approved by the equipment manufacturer.

Step 4: Establish a Clear Value Proposition

We have eliminated the barriers that "Transfer Tom" had for receiving adequate training and obtaining certification. We have eliminated the costs for him, provided him with a place to train, and made it more convenient by having both available at our own facility. It is also important to notice what the program does not include. It does not include any incentive for our employees to study for or take the maintenance certification exam. Our identified Principal Adopters were self-motivated and did not express this as a need.

While the program covers the needs for "Transfer Tom," the same cannot be said for "Maintenance Mike," which was the other persona we were considering. Given that our online training facility will be open at off-hours, we would have to decide as a company if we were okay with allowing such access to nonemployees. We are also covering a lot of costs for the online training, practicum training, and examinations. Do we want to extend those to nonemployees or have them pay a fee? These are the types of additional questions that would have to be answered if we were to extend the program. However, as designed, the program is targeted for our own internal candidates, "Transfer Tom." The proposed program *should* have the impact we desire, as long as the pool of "Transfer Tom" is large enough to satisfy our maintenance-hiring demand. If it is not, we will have to consider redesigning the program to also address the needs of "Maintenance Mike." But for now, doing so does not appear to be necessary.

Step 5: Quantify the Target Adopter Group Size

The question is how many potential "Transfer Toms" exist in our firm. That's our potential adopter group size. That certainly does not mean everyone who fits the "Transfer Tom" profile will adopt our proposed solution, it is the maximum number that could. We could talk to our HR department and see how many internal applications they have received, but that number may be a deceiving low representation of our "Transfer Toms." There may be those who have been discouraged from applying because they heard they would not be considered. We instead survey our employees to see how many may be "Tom." We know that "Transfer Tom" has experience working in our plants (i.e. is not an office worker) and has mechanical acumen. We can therefore ask in our survey of company employees who has these two qualifications. We can additionally ask who might be interested in transferring to the maintenance department. We will say that our company has 10,000 employees. Four percent of the survey results indicated all three criteria – has experience working in our plants, has mechanical acumen, and is interested in working in our maintenance department someday. That puts our Target Adopter group at 400 employees (4%*10,000) total. We cannot expect 400 potential adopters to the solution we will be creating, that is maximum adopters possible. We also want to get a sense of timing, so we also ask on the survey how many might be interested in making a job change in the next twelve months. That drops the responses down to 10 percent of the previous total, or forty employees. Forty employees is the maximum adopter group size we can anticipate for our training program.

No product gets 100 percent of a share of their market and our innovation will not either. It is likely that a significantly lesser number of those forty will not be interested going through the effort of getting themselves qualified to transfer to the maintenance department. People will say they want something if it is free, but as soon as it has some cost to them (monetary, time, etc.) the fraction that deem it worth it drops precipitously. Adding additional solution-specific questions to the survey would refine that number. Let's say for argument's sake, based on participation in other training our firm offers that we estimate that 50 percent of that Target Group will likely participate. That makes our Target Group segment twenty people, total. Geoffrey Moore, in his book *Crossing the Chasm* suggests that less than 15 percent of our attainable market will be early-adopters of a new offering. That would suggest that we can expect somewhere around three people to initially participate in our program. Could it be more? Sure? But it will not be a big number.

Given that everyone who begins the program may not finish, the fact that we may only have a handful of initial participants should make us reconsider our solution. What would be prudent to do at this point is to continue to Level 3, the plan stage, and flesh out the details and rough cost-estimates of the plan. We can then determine if that price is worth it for this few number of participants. We can then return to Level 2 and consider other solutions, such as paying the full cost of sending our candidates to the supplier firm to obtain their training and certification there. For in the end, we want a solution, in this example, that is both impactful and cost-effective.

COMMON MISTAKES

There are a number of common mistakes made at this level, but the most egregious is completely ignoring the adopter. Would-be innovators can get so enamored with their own creativity and ideas that they focus entirely on Solution Formulation. The adopter is essentially an after-thought that will perhaps be addressed when "marketing" the innovation. The Level 2 assessment – ensuring that the features of the innovation connect to the needs/wants/desires of the innovation – is never performed.

The other common mistake is not getting detailed enough in the solution design. The so-called design stops at the solution approach. The Principal Adopter is not narrowed to a Target Adopter with specific needs/wants/desires. The current BATNO is not identified nor are its shortcomings from the point-of-view of the adopters. These shortcomings reveal detailed unmet under-met needs/wants/desires that are the foundation upon which an impactful solution is based. No specific solution features can be developed to address these unmet needs/wants/desires if they are never uncovered in the first place. The result is that a detailed solution is never created and, as a result, no assessment performed at this step. No check to examine if, let alone how, the proposed innovation creates value for the Target Adopter.

If the solution is considered more precisely, the divergent thinking is performed too narrowly utilizing only feature-level divergent thinking. Envisioning substitutes (function-level thinking or system-level solutions) is rarely performed, which is a shame as these are the thinking levels where truly impactful innovations tend to occur.

SUMMARY

The two design stages of The Innovation Pyramid work together to ensure that a complete and detailed design is crafted before any implementation is attempted. The design methodology separates the problem from the solution. The first design stage, Level 1, focuses on Problem Identification. This stage ensures that the problem is considered broadly enough so that no problem or solution possibility is overlooked. At the end of Level 1, the first design stage of The Innovation Pyramid, we had:

- defined a General Problem from our initial situation;
- determined a root cause of that General Problem for which our organization is able and willing to resolve;

- determined the connections between the root cause we are choosing to act on and the General Problem; and
- identified an adopter group that is both impacted by the root cause issue and will be the general group for whom we are creating the innovation.

The second design stage focuses on Solution Formulation. At the end of Pyramid Level 2, we will have identified a:

- specific new solution (detailed and fully designed);
- specific Target Adopter persona with clearly identified unmet or under-met needs, wants, and/or desires; and
- distinct value proposition: clear connection between the features of the new solution with the need/wants/desires of the target persona.

The entire pathway through Level 2 requires multiple steps. These steps are a guide to reaching the objectives of this level and are not a prescription. Iteration between steps is not uncommon. This five-step guideline is as follows:

Step 1: Describe a specific Target Adopter persona.
- Identify Principal Adopter's current BATNO.
- Perform open-ended interviews to obtain insight.
- Craft personas from the unmet or under-met needs, wants, and/or desires uncovered during the interviews.
- Select a Target Adopter persona.

Step 2: Determine a solution approach.
Step 3: Craft a detailed solution.
Step 4: Establish a clear value proposition.
Step 5: Quantify the Target Adopter group size.

The first step in creating our final design is to transform the root cause and Principal Adopter group that we identified in Level 1, Chapter 3, into a Target Adopter persona with a specific set of unmet or under-met needs, want, and/or desires. This requires obtaining tacit knowledge from the Principal Adopters. Open-ended IFIs, described in Appendix A, are used to obtain decision and motivational insights from the interviewees. The information gathered from those IFIs are first categorized and then connected to a set of personas. These personas represent archtype adopters that make choices based on a common set of needs, wants, and/or desires. From that set of personas, our Target Adopter persona, the subgroup for whom we are creating the innovation, is selected.

Once we have a clear target adopter for our innovation, we begin to think about the high-level approaches we can take to create a solution. It is important not to confuse our approach to resolving the Target Adopter's issues with the actual solution. That solution, which we craft in Step 3, is detailed and specific. That solution's specific features should satisfy the primary needs/wants/desires of our Target Adopter. It is also important not to include product or solution features that are of no value to the adopter, as they will increase the cost of the innovation without generating an increased benefit.

The fourth and final step of the innovation design stages is an assessment; to assess how we have created value for the Target Adopter. This step validates that the specific features of our proposed innovation benefit the target adopter by connecting to their specific needs/wants/desires.

Crafting impactful solutions takes more than one creative problem-solving session. It is a knowledge-discovery process that separates design from execution. The entire innovation design methodology extends over two levels of The Innovation Pyramid and separates problems from their solutions. Each of the two design stages requires multiple steps to complete. Throughout the method, we are making choices. We need to document our decisions, the judgments we made given the information we had at the time. Doing so will allow us to review those choices versus the final innovation's outcome and incorporate that learning into future innovation iterations. This is important for all innovation projects, but is particularly critical when developing a prototype. In prototype development, we know the final product will be different, we are just not sure how different. Being able to review the assumptions and decisions we made during the design, combined with the customer feedback from the prototype, will provide us with significant more information when we go back through The Innovation Pyramid levels a second time to craft the final product.

Upon the completion of Level 2, our design is now complete. It is time to transform our design into reality, which starts with a plan to implement the design, Level 3 of The Innovation Pyramid, the first stage of the two execution stages.

5 Level 3
Plan

INTRODUCTION

One of the dominant characteristics of The Innovation Pyramid is the separation of components of the method. Adopter and creator are considered separately. Design and Execution are considered separately. Within the design, the problem and solution are treated separately. This bifurcation of elements continues now that we transition to the execution levels of The Pyramid. The execution portion separates the development of the plan from its implementation. The importance of separating the implementation from the plan is that it allows us to focus on the primary issues of each step at the appropriate time. This makes for a much more efficient development process. It is also of significant benefit when diagnosing where things may have strayed in the review of the entire project (see Chapter 7 for details).

With this chapter, we are moving from the innovation's design to its execution. This is not to imply that we are "done" with the design levels. Depending on how the implementation plan develops, we may have to cycle back and alter details of the design. If we cannot create the innovation, obtain the resources to implement our innovation–creation plan, or there is no pathway for its adoption, that is, no way for the innovation to reach the adopter, then we will need to redesign. Redesign means returning to Level 2 and completing that level again. That may, in turn, require a return to Level 1, the first design stage. As a design cannot be "fixed" in the execution stages, it must be altered in the design stages. If we need to return to the design stages, we will be doing so with additional insight: insight regarding implementation or adoption. Insight that will add or alter the selection criteria we previously applied during the design stages.

The potential need to redesign is yet another example of the nonlinear nature of The Innovation Pyramid.

The second and final design stage, Level 2, concluded with a final design which was specific, detailed, and executable with:

- a specific new solution (detailed and fully designed);
- a specific target persona with clearly identified unmet or under-met needs, wants, and/or desires; and
- a value proposition: a clear connection between the features of the new offering and the needs/wants/desires of the target persona.

In this first stage of the project's execution phase, we are creating an actionable plan. But not just a plan to create the innovation, but also one to deliver it to the adopter. This is a "creation and delivery" plan. The innovation implementation plan will be created by the project's planning team that may or may not be the same as the project's implementation team, although there will probably be some overlap between the two. That plan will require the identification of the acquirable resources necessary to execute the plan. The plan's needed resources are identified and committed at this stage, but not yet acquired; hence, "acquirable" resources, as some proof of their obtainment, are necessary at this stage. While this level is primarily assessed from the innovator's point-of-view (POV), it cannot be the only POV assessed. It is all too easy to focus purely on the innovation "creation" plan and forget the plan's "delivery" component. That "delivery" perspective requires understanding the adopter's POV. The adopter's environment, in particular, must be explored at this level to ensure a pathway exists for their adoption of the proposed innovation. Without a "delivery" component, this plan will produce no impact as the delivery of the innovation to the adopter is vital to its impact. Figure 5.1 highlights The Innovation Pyramid segments of Level 3.

Every project will have a plan. The plan may be simple or complex. It may be well documented or exist only in the implementer's

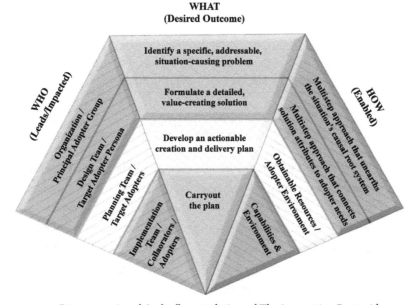

FIGURE 5.1 Level 3 of a flattened view of The Innovation Pyramid.

head, but there will always be a plan. Even innovators who "never had a plan" had a plan. They simply did not write that plan down. When an experienced carpenter is asked to frame a doorway in a new house, they do not have to have a written plan to know how to proceed. They are experienced and the outcome is predictable. They have a plan, but one that is primarily in their heads and grounded in their experience. New innovators are not experienced, and the outcome of their plan is not predictable. We have designed the innovation; now we need to document a plan for its implementation to keep everyone on the same page during the launch and through the inevitable adjustments that will come as new information is discovered.

The amount of detail in the plan depends on the innovation's complexity and the complexity of its delivery to the adopter. For some innovations, a high-level, general plan will be enough. For the implementation of a large-scale commercial innovation, however, significantly more detail and specificity will be necessary. Both will be discussed.

Table 5.1 *Innovation plan components*

	Operations	Delivery	Resources	Risk
General	Scope	Pathway to adopter	Resource commitments	Identification
Specific	Gantt chart	Marketing plan	Financial analysis	Mitigation strategies

There are four basic components of the innovation implementation plan: operations, delivery, resources, and risk. Too often the innovation's plan only covers the creation of the innovation – the "operations" component of the implementation plan. The other three components are equally important. The delivery component focuses on the delivery of the innovation to the adopter. The third component, resources, concentrates on the resources required to successfully implement both the operations and delivery components. Risk is the fourth component. This component puts everyone on the same page with respect to the risk of creating and delivering the innovation. Many of the risks arise directly from the discussion of the three other components of the plan. But there are those that extend beyond those components must also be considered, such as long-term political or relationship implications.

For complex innovations that involve a lot of people or in other ways have a lot of moving parts, the plan needs to be specific and detailed. The planning team will often create a general plan first before creating the specific plan. In these cases, the general plan is an "outline" or overarching guide of the specific, detailed, plan. Table 5.1 presents the desired outcome for each of the four components for both the "general" and "specific" versions of the innovation implementation plan. The remainder of this chapter will detail the development of each component of the plan, for both the general and specific cases.

PROJECT OVERVIEW

Every project innovation plan should begin with a project overview that generally describes and justifies the project. Descriptions of the four components, listed in Table 5.1, will follow this overview. While "overviews" range from 250 words (half a page) to 10 pages, the true "executive" summary is short, in the order of 250 words.

The executive summary will be the most-read portion of the plan and is, as a result, the most important section of the plan. It is therefore essential that it accurately summarizes as well as sells the innovation project. Given its capstone nature, it is highly recommended that it be the last plan element written since it is based on the details provided in the rest of the plan. It should include the "why," "what," "who," and "when" elements of the project. That said, this summary should be very readable and compelling.

Why

Why are we doing this? What is the overall situation that we are trying to resolve? Demonstrate how this project connects to that situation. Why is it important to both the innovating organization and the innovation's potential adopter? The information to support this work was completed in the design stages, particularly Level 1, but needs to be verbally summarized here.

What

This section addresses the project's scope. Describe the innovation. What are the tasks necessary to complete this project? Equally important, what are the tasks NOT being done as part of the project? What are the project's deliverables? How will they be measured? How do these deliverables relate to the project's success? What are the assumptions being made? Which internal or external environment aids in or complicates the execution of this plan? How will the innovation be delivered to the Target Adopter? Some of this necessary information at this point will come from the design levels; some will need to be created at this execution level. What are the resources, beyond the "who" described in the following section, required to accomplish these tasks? What commitment do we have to obtain these resources? How will they be acquired when the time comes?

Who

Who is the Target Adopter? Describe this persona. What are their unmet or under-met needs, wants, and/or desires? How were these determined? How do these needs align with the features or attributes of the innovation? Who is included in the implementation team? How will the team be organized? Who is the communication point person? What are the team's individual responsibilities during the project? How do the team's capabilities align with the needs of the project?

When

Timing is everything. When will the tasks outlined in the "what" element be accomplished? When will the overall outcome be obtained? What could cause delays in this timing? "Operations" section will provide timing on the specific elements of the project. The overview should contain the final timing, major milestones discussed in the "what" section, and the general risks related to meeting this schedule.

OPERATIONS

The "operations" component of the actionable innovation implementation plan focuses solely on the creation of the innovation itself. This is what most teams think of as "the plan." It is, in reality, half of "the plan." "Delivery" section details how the innovation will end up in the hands of our Target Adopter. Both halves are equally important. This section is written primarily from the POV of the innovation's creator, while the "delivery" portion extends that POV to the adopter. There are additional POVs in between the two that must also be considered as additional parties will be involved in the creation and delivery of the innovation to the adopter.

This section starts with a description of the innovation. That description has been crafted, in detail, in the second design stage. The remainder of this section elaborates on how the innovation will be created. If, for any reason, the innovation cannot be crafted – the design is not manufacturable, the necessary resources cannot be acquired, etc. – the innovation will have to be redesigned. That means returning to Level 2 of The Innovation Pyramid as a design cannot be "fixed" in the execution levels of The Pyramid. A faulty design should never be "corrected" during implementation.

General

A high-level operation plan is a description of the innovation development's scope. That scope (Larson, n.d.) at its essence is a list of the tasks and timing of the project's deliverables that is required to accomplish the completion of the innovation. For very straightforward projects, the timing may be for only one deliverable, the final project deliverable. Beyond the project deliverable, the scope forms the foundation for the remainder of the project's description. The scope describes the project and is used to obtain agreement among the stakeholders.

A general operation plan also includes roles and responsibilities. This segment of the plan identifies who is responsible for performing the activities that result in the operation's desired outcomes. Roles inside and outside the organization are delineated. A project point person is named. This allows communication to flow and be distributed through a single person.

Specific

A more detailed plan is required for more complex innovation projects: those that have a number of moving parts. A combination of elements both inside and outside the organization, for example, will require a more detailed operations component of the plan. The plan should connect its detailed activities to its short-term objectives. The short-term objective will then need to be tied to the long-term goal of the plan. The goal is in turn tied to the plan's vision of resolving the original situation. That strategy for meeting that goal is to resolve the case identified in Level 1. The objective is the creation of the innovation (Level 2) that addresses that cause. The activities are the specific tasks necessary to reach that objective.

The innovation team will, of course, be named as it was in the general version of the plan. For a complex innovation, however, there will likely be involvement of those beyond the implementation team. Those could be other groups within the innovation-development organization and/or groups outside that organization. The term "collaborators" is used to generically describe these groups that are beyond the implementation team. Consideration of the collaborators extends the POV beyond the implementation team to include all those collaborators who participate, directly or indirectly, in the innovation's creation. Those collaborators related to the innovation's delivery will be articulated in the "delivery" section of the project plan. These key operation-related collaborators could include suppliers, sub-component contract manufacturers, shippers, and other operation-related service providers. These collaborators need to be part of the action plan and their strategic relationship clearly described. Their commitment to participating in this project needs to be described by a letter of intent, memorandum of understanding (MOU), or some other less formal agreement. Whatever the supporting evidence of the collaborator's commitment to the plan, it should be documented as a part of the plan. This is an extension of documenting conscious choices that was applied to the design stages. These documents make the project review, and more important, the learnings from that review, less complicated.

The list of activities necessary to create the innovation is much more detailed in this specific version of the plan. It is not just the desired outcomes and who is responsible for them, but a delineation of the specific activities that will be necessary to obtain those outcomes along with their timing. The creation of a Gantt chart that clearly indicates the activity, timing, and resources committed to the activity is in order for this version of the operating plan. As previously stated, if the innovation cannot be crafted for any reason, including the lack of cooperation of outside collaborators, its implementation must be halted and the project returns to the design stage of The Innovation Pyramid.

DELIVERY

To create impact, the would-be innovation needs to be created and delivered to the adopter. If there is no adoption, there will be no impact. If there will be no impact, then there will be no innovation. In this section, the primary POV shifts from that of the innovation creator to that of the adopters. The POV is not exclusive to the adopter's, but must also include any third party distributors who may be involved, directly or indirectly, in the delivery of the innovation to the adopter.

General

In the general version of the implementation plan, it is necessary to include the adopter's environment. The exploration of that environment ensures that a pathway exists for the adoption of the proposed innovation. How will the adopter obtain our innovation? What is the mechanism and/or delivery system to the adopter? Who are the distributors involved? What is the distributor's motivation to participate? What commitments have been obtained for their participation? What documentation do we have to demonstrate that "we know we know" this commitment? Simply laying our innovation at the feet of our Target Adopter is not enough. Do the adopters have the resources they need to obtain the innovation, if it is available to them? If there is not a pathway to the adopter, then the innovation must be redesigned, it cannot be left to the implementation team to "figure it out." Redesigning the innovation will require us to return to Pyramid Level 2, the second design stage.

Specific

The specific version of the "delivery" component of the implementation plan is much more specific. We will need to zoom in beyond the general pathway of adoption to the specific details necessary to ensure that adoption occurs. Key collaborators for this component of the plan include distributors and other marketing-related service providers. These marketing-related service providers could include website developers, advertising agencies, and others.

These organizations, like in the "operations" component, could be within the innovation creation organization or outside of it. Either way, they are beyond the control of the implementation team, and their commitment to participating in the project needs to be clearly described and supported by some formal or informal documentation.

A specific marketing plan is developed and added to the Gantt chart developed in the "operations" component for the implementation plan. Much of the background of the marketing plan was developed in the second design stage and includes:

- Description of the Target Adopter persona.
  - The target's current Best Alternative to a New Option (BATNO).
- Value proposition of the innovation to the Target Adopter.
  - Connection of the features/attributes of the innovation to the unmet or under-met needs, wants, and/or desires of the Target Adopter persona.

In addition to this background information, the marketing plan should include the remaining elements of the marketing mix.

- Promotion
  - How will the value proposition be communicated to Target Adopter?
  - How will that message reach the target?
- Place
  - How will the target obtain access to the innovation?
    - Directly or through distributors?
    - Physical or virtual access?
- Price
  - If the firm is to put a price on the innovation, what will that price be?
    - How does the value creation articulated in the design state translate to price?
    - What are the total costs to the adopter of obtaining and using the current BATNO?

RESOURCES

This next component of the plan focuses on all the resources necessary to create the proposed innovation and deliver it to the Target Adopter. Each critical resource must be identified, and acquirable, but not ultimately obtained at this level of execution. The key resources required, beyond the implementation team and those resources that team may have direct control over, could be financial or other assets. Access to specialized assets – be it unique equipment (physical assets) or right to practice certain patents (intellectual assets) – must be included in the plan. How will this access be gained? What commitments exist for this access? What documentation supports this commitment? And, of course, what is the source of the money needed for the innovation? How much is required – what is the project's budget? Who is committed to supplying these funds?

General

Beyond those resources described in the "operations" component, the general description of this component of the plan identifies the additional key resources that are required to implement this plan – both from operations and delivery perspectives. What is the approximate budget for the plan? How will that money be obtained? Will we need pledges or other commitments for the required resources? If we cannot obtain that financial or other resource commitment, the design of the innovation will have to be recrafted. In moving back to the design stage, we will now have new selection criteria for selecting the "best" design in Level 2. Those criteria will now include the resource constraints we discovered in this execution stage.

Many nonprofits fall into the trap of simply saying "donors" will provide the required funding. Which donors? Why will they provide money to the cause? It is not simply soliciting "people with money," but those that are aligned with the cause we are pursuing. How does resolving the identified situation relate to the donor's passion, purpose, or POV? Have they been involved with our organization in the past? Do they trust that we can deliver on the promises we are making? If not, how can we get them comfortable with our commitment to this project?

If a revenue stream to the innovation development organization (which could be a for-profit or not-for-profit organization) is anticipated, then, at the very least, a Potential for Value Capture (PVC) qualitative analysis should be performed. Even when plans need to include a more detailed financial analysis (see "Specific" section), the PVC should be performed as a financial assessment screen before diving deeper into detailed numbers. The aim is to identify issues in the design earlier than later. That way the process can return to the design stage before the time investment of a detailed financial review is made.

The PVC is a qualitative assessment of the innovation creator's ability to capture the lion's share of the value the innovation creates for the adopter. It is a straightforward 2×2, as shown in Figure 5.2. The vertical axis is a qualitative measure of the possibility that the would-be innovation could be imitated. Are there barriers that would prevent others from creating such an innovation? Patents? Trade secrets? Unique know-how that is possessed only by the innovation creation organization? A "low" ranking would suggest that there are significant barriers to replicating or imitating the innovation, putting

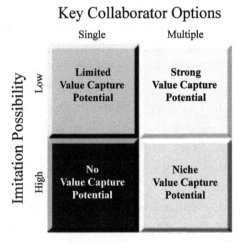

FIGURE 5.2 Innovator organization's Potential for Value Capture.

the project in the top row of the PVC. A "high" rating would indicate that it would be fairly straightforward for another organization to replicate or in other ways to imitate the innovation resulting in the project being in the bottom row of the PVC.

The horizontal axis of the PVC is related to the key outside collaborators. They were defined as those outside the organization whose participation is required to create and/or deliver the innovation to the adopter. They include suppliers, contract manufacturers, distributors, and service providers of all sorts (from advertising firms to legal counsel). Being in the right-hand column of the PVC suggests that the innovation creation organization has multiple options for each category of key collaborator. Several ad agencies are available, several distributer options exist, etc. We will likely have commitments from only one, but we had options in selecting that one. On the other hand, being in the left-hand column of the PVC suggests that at least one of the collaborator categories has only a single option. We may have many advertising agencies we could use, but there is only one contract manufacturer who is capable of creating a critical component of our innovation.

The combination of being in the right-hand column (multiple collaborator options) and the top row (low probably if imitation) puts us in the top right-hand quadrant. This quadrant suggests that the innovation creation organization is in a strong position to capture the value it has created with its innovation. Being in the right-hand column, but in the bottom row puts us in the lower right-hand quadrant. This quadrant suggests that we could capture value if we competed only locally or in a niche market. The limited size of our Target Adopter market is the barrier to attracting additional competition.

Being in the left-hand column suggests that we are at the mercy of a single key collaborator. If we are in the top row (low imitation possibility), we will have to negotiate a split in the captured value with them. If we are in the left-hand column and the bottom row, we have no chance of capturing any value as the sole collaborator could likely reproduce this innovation on their own as they could create it without us, but we are not in a position to create and deliver the innovation without them.

Specific

The resource component assessment of the general plan should include the qualitative PVC analysis described in "General" section. The rationale for doing so is to avoid time spent performing detailed financial analysis if the qualitative assessment demonstrates the innovation needs to be redesigned.

If the qualitative project assessment is positive, then the project can move on to increasingly rigorous financial analysis. The first would be a margin analysis. The analysis here is a steady-state look, sometime after the start-up phase. "Long term" in this case means after the start-up phase, however long that may be. What do we expect the innovation creation and delivery costs to be in the long term on a per unit basis? What price do we think we can obtain for this innovation in the long term? Is that an acceptable margin for the organization? If not, then we will have to return to the design stage. But in doing so, we will now have a new selection criterion for choosing the "best" design in Level 2, which can be developed at a cost sufficiently less than the price we believe we can obtain for it.

If the margin analysis is positive, then we can move forward with a project cash flow analysis or return on invested capital, or any other financial project assessment our firm typically performs. To calculate the project's net present value (NPV), we will need adoption estimate numbers, from Step 5 of Level 2. It was recommended that Level 2, Step 5 not be completed until absolutely necessary to avoid prematurely getting emotionally locked into a Target Adopter and a proposed solution. Once the number-crunching starts, a team's desire to change either the design or the plan diminishes significantly. It is a pitfall of innovators and entrepreneurs; the more we spend time pursuing a specific idea, the deeper we fall in love with that idea. It is therefore best to keep things qualitative as long as possible to expedite our progress of the process. At this point, in order to calculate the project's NPV, it is now necessary that these quantitative values be determined. We should now return to Step 5 of Level 2, determine those quantitative values, and then return to this point in Level 3. With these quantitative sizing of the Target Adopter group and the Target Adopter segment (the fraction of the Target Adopters who will be interested in acquiring our solution to their issues) complete, the NPVs can be estimated. Is this NPV an acceptable return on investment for the organization? If not, then we will have to return to the design stage. But in doing so, we will now have additional new selection criteria for selecting the "best" design in Level 2, which can be developed for a lesser start-up cost or higher margin or both.

RISK

General

Specific innovation project risks have been identified in the development of each of the other three components of the innovation implementation plan. There is one additional risk category that may not have arisen in the development of the other sections that should also be considered. It is what generally called Political, Economic, Social, and Technological (PEST) risks ("Understanding PEST," 2013). Each project should consider and identify key risks from this group, in addition to the other three component sections. What if there were changes in the political climate (inside or outside the innovation-developing organization)? Is this a "pet project" that the organization's CEO is championing? If she suddenly retires, is it still a viable project? Is there an impending legislation that could enhance or deter the need for this innovation? Is there technology on the horizon that would render our proposed solution obsolete? Each PEST category should be considered and identified if it presents a significant risk to the proposed project. For the general version of the plan, the identification of these risks is all that is required.

Specific

In addition to the identification of key risks, including PEST risks, the specific version of the plan calls for a mitigation strategy to be articulated for each key risk identified. Risks cannot be eliminated, but they can be managed. What is the approach to managing each risk should it arise? How would the plan be adjusted?

The previous sections laid out the element of an actional implementation plan for the creation of the innovation and its delivery to the adopter. The overview section briefly touched on the motivation for the project. While it is important to mention it in the overview, the motivation also needs to be more clearly articulated as is described in section "Sales Document".

SALES DOCUMENT

The implementation plan typically has two functions. It is most obviously a plan for creating the innovation and delivering that innovation to the adopter. Like a business plan, however, this implementation plan has another purpose – that of a sales document. A "sales" document necessary to pitch this concept to potential supporters or detractors. For supporters, the pitch is generally to obtain commitments of support. For detractors, the aim of the pitch is to nullify their future potential blocking of the project. That means describing the motivational impact of the innovation; adding context to the creation and delivery of the innovation. What is the bigger problem we are attempting to resolve? How is this innovation, targeting this particular adopter, going to impact that larger issue? This context, in many ways, is a summary of the previous design stages.

The plan's "sales pitch" component should be achievable at different levels, consistent with the overall zoom-in, zoom-out philosophy of The Pyramid methodology. Each of these levels will, in turn, be detailed. These project advocation pitches essentially fall into three categories:

1. Core concept opener. One or two sentences that describe the essence of the project. This ends with an invitation to discuss the new venture in more detail.
2. Elevator pitch. One- to three-minute monolog that provides a brief overview of the aspects of the project: the situation, the specific issue the innovation is addressing, the specific solution, and the size of the potential impact. The elevator pitch typically ends with a "happy to tell you more" offer.
3. Resource pitch. This is a fifteen- to thirty-minute presentation with visual aids that details the opportunity, the innovation, and the team. This pitch typically ends with a specific ask for resources or a call to action.

Core Concept Opener

This is the introduction of the innovation. It is also an invitation for the audience to inquire about it in more detail. This is one or two sentences of the innovation that can ideally be expressed in one breath. It should always end with an invitation to discuss the innovation in more detail. The trick is to make it compelling without getting into too much detail. Context is the key; provide the audience with the big picture with a hint of detail into its resolution.

> When people ask what I do, I say:
>
> I teach courses and create experiential learning programs that accelerate the development of the next generation of serial innovators, entrepreneurs, and venture investors. I'd be happy to tell you more, if you are interested.

We want to make it easy for our audience to ask a question. These are the hooks. If our summary is complete, there is simply no place from which the conversation can begin. One of the hooks in my opening sentence is "experiential learning." Many people outside academia are not familiar with "experiential learning." I do not define it in my one sentence, but it creates a natural opening for many people to ask their first question – "what is experiential learning?" Then the conversation is begun.

Elevator Pitch

The elevator pitch derives its names from an elevator ride. It is as if a person asked us to tell them about the innovation as we both were stepping onto an elevator. We would need to finish the presentation before we exited the elevator. The elevator pitch is generally considered to be one to three minutes in length.

To have a very tight, yet very complete elevator pitch, it is useful to first write it down. Some guidelines are helpful. The first guideline is that that average speech rate in the United States is about 150 words per minute. If we are excited about what we are talking about, that rate might increase to 200 words per minute. That means the 3-minute pitch cannot be more than 600 words. Of course, we can talk faster, but our audience will not be able to absorb all we say if we talk that briskly. They will either pick parts of our talk out as important or miss our message entirely in the verbal onslaught. We are in a much better position than our audience to pull out the important aspects of our innovation, so do that work for them.

On one hand, putting all the individual aspects of the innovation into a 600-word description is a challenge. On the other hand, three minutes is a long time to hold an audiences' complete attention. Begin the pitch with a reason why they should pay attention to the rest of the two and a half minutes or so. As was the case with the executive summary, we could capture this compelling connection by zooming out – putting our innovation in the context of a larger picture, the original situation. We could also make this connection by zooming in – personalizing the impact the innovation. The following example is crafted by first zooming in, personalizing the message, before zooming out.

We have all been touched by a cancer death. My first loss came when I was seven and my grandmother died of breast cancer.

She was my card-playing buddy – that loss was devastating to me. The statistics – 7.6 million who die of cancer every year – do not begin to capture the pain and loss felt by those left behind. Where are the new cures? Lost in the research labs. Our innovation is the development of a unique device that will allow medical researchers to quickly, accurately, and inexpensively sort out the promising drug candidates from the thousands being evaluated; a task that is expensive and painfully slow today.

That short introduction is 109 words, or about 33 seconds at 200 words per minute. It zooms in by personalizing the problem in a way that every audience member can understand. It then zooms out to capture the scope of the problem, followed by a brief introduction of the innovation. Now that our audience has some context, it is more likely to be receptive to hearing the details of the innovation. The best feedback for an elevator pitch, as it was for the core concept pitch, is "tell me more." The worst is not understanding why the innovation is being proposed to be created in the first place.

Beyond the introduction of the opportunity, the elevator pitch should cover an overview of the innovation. While the key elements of the innovation plan should be included, the order will be that which best fits the particular project's story. These elements include:

- Adopters:
  - o Who is the Target Adopter persona?
  - o What is their compelling need/desire? Value proposition?
  - o Willingness to pay?
  - o Size the opportunity (number of buyers, units sold, currency value of sales).
- Innovation:
  - o What precisely is the proposed product/service?
  - o How much will it cost to produce?
  - o Uniqueness? How will the innovation stay differentiated?

- Key collaborators:
  - o Which outside agents are critical to the development and delivery of the innovation?
  - o Why will they collaborate with us in this development?
- Resource needs:
  - o What is the value proposition for the innovation-developing firm?
  - o How much money or access to other key assets is required?

Resource Pitch

After having prepared a three-minute elevator pitch, preparing for a thirteen- to thirty-minute investor pitch may seem easy. After all, we have so much more time! That is the downfall of many teams – trying to tell their *entire* story. Even if we are given thirty minutes to present to the organization's CEO, we should plan on twenty minutes. Something will go wrong. The principals will be late or need to leave early, the projector will malfunction, our carefully planned demonstration will lock up, we will be interrupted by questions, etc. Something will happen. We want to make sure we complete our presentation. There is nothing worse than being on slide eighteen of a fifty-two-slide deck when the meeting ends. (Of course, we should NEVER have a fifty-two-slide deck, but we will get to that.)

The first thing we need to know to prepare our presentation is how long we will have to present. Honor that time. Do not be that innovator who thinks the time limit does not apply to them. Guy Kawasaki, of Garage.com, has written and talked extensively about investor pitches. While his work is aimed at entrepreneurs pitching venture capitalists, most of it applies equally to pitching the CEO or our organization for support. It is definitely worth reviewing some of his materials before the presentation, particularly his 2012 blog entry that includes an example slide deck – eleven slides (Kawasaki, 2013)! That's right, it is not the thirty slides most think it is. Also think minutes of presentation per slide, not slides per minute. Remember frames per second is how they describe movie projection rates. We do not want our slide show to be a continuous blur of slides to our audience. Instead, make it a series of captivating still photos; we want each frame to be memorable.

The content of our resource pitch will be the entire innovation, from the general situation through the delivery of the innovation to the Target Adopter. Of course, we cannot review our entire plan in that time and certainly not the entire design method. We will need to tailor that presentation to the audience. What do we want from them? What is our ask?: Support? Access to assets? Money? We need the right message for the right audience clearly articulated and delivered with passion!

The Presentation

Like theater productions, presentations generally have three acts: the introduction, the body, and the conclusion. The introduction should only take 10 percent of our speaking time and the conclusion only 5 percent. That's one or two slides (maximum) for the introduction and one for the conclusion. The remainder is dedicated to the body of our presentation. This presentation approach is sometimes described as "tell them what you are going to tell them," "tell them," "tell them what you told them." Simple but effective. Most importantly it contains the key element of persuasion – repetition.

Credibility is crucial. When the planning team enters the room, they are perceived to be experts in the creation and delivery of the innovation. Do not destroy that. Check the math on the presentation slides. Those slides will constantly be updated – market numbers, cost estimates, financial projections – it is far too easy to miss an update on one of the slides. Make sure these numbers all get transferred to the presentation so that there is not one market size value on one slide and a different value on another slide. Senior administrators and investors quickly pick up on math errors and inconsistencies. They will notice, and the team's credibility will drop when they do. Also stay away from phrases like "we hope," "we think," or "we believe." Make evidence-based arguments. "Our preliminary market research suggests..." is much stronger than a "we believe." Remember we are being tested on our ability to change if the data suggests our current hypothesis is incorrect. Senior administrators and investors are not looking for a leader who simply "believes they know," but ones that "know they know" by pointing to data to support their conclusions. When asked a question whose answer is currently undetermined, avoid these two common responses: (1) Answer a different question from the one that was asked, or (2) say, "We don't know." The first response seems like the team is being evasive, which is a credibility killer by making the team appear ignorant. Of course, the innovation team cannot know the answer to every question. It is certainly fine not to know. However, saying "We don't know" suggests that the team has not even considered the point or did not think the point was important. The asker thinks it is important. If the team needs clarification on the question, ask for it. If the team did look into the question, but has not reached a conclusion, say so. It is much more powerful to say, "That is a very important issue for the project and we are still in the process of collecting information to reach a definitive conclusion" than to simply say "We do not know."

Finally, when presenting, have fun. Be honest, be passionate, and be enthusiastic. Not everyone will connect with the innovation, but they will respect the passion and clarity of the message. Walk away from the meeting with that "win" even if the sought-after resources were not obtained ... this time.

COMMON MISTAKES

The biggest mistake is not to have a plan at all. This level of The Innovation Pyramid is skipped entirely, and the project moves from design to implementation. The implementation team is forced to make it up as they go. Yes, we all have to be flexible. No plan is perfect and we will have to pivot from that plan, but we need a pivot point: a defined plan from which we are adjusting.

The other significant error of this level is to focus solely on the "operations" component of the implementation plan and completely ignore the Target Adopter and how we will communicate with them. The planning team becomes too internally focused, only considering the innovation-developing organization's POV. That is a death knell for the project's success. There is no impact without the adopter. A "perfect" innovation that has no chance of reaching the adopter will have zero impact. This is a "creation and adoption" plan and both portions are equally important. In addition to the innovator's and adopter's POV, there will likely be many key collaborators to the success of the project. Their POVs and perspectives are also important to the project's success.

Another common mistake of this level is to not get detailed enough regarding the resources required to execute the plan. The specific resources are either not identified or obtaining them is not specified. In the latter case, the issue is simply pushed off to the implementation team. "Donors" will magically appear, or the company will "naturally" allow us access to the unique equipment we need at the specific time we need it; no need to follow up on these issues. Wrong! Specific commitments of resources must be made at this level.

The final mistake is to continue to push forward when the developed innovation design turns out not to be implementable. There could be any number of reasons for the failure of the design at this stage: It may not be manufacturable, it may have no pathway to the adopters, there may not be sufficient resources to create it, etc. Whatever the reason, the design failed. That is not the end of the project. There is no need to throw up our hands and quit. And certainly, there is no reason to simply put our head down and move forward. There is work left to do and put our head down to do it we must, but we need to move back to the design stages, and not forward, in order to accomplish the necessary changes. This is an iterative method. We learn and we adjust. We learned something in the planning stage that we did not originally recognize during our first pass in the design stages. We now need to take that new understanding and update the selection criteria for the choices we made during the design stages and remake those choices. This is another example why those choice criteria have to be conscious; we cannot update and improve choice criteria that we do not recognize we are applying in the first place.

The final mistake of the planning level is forgetting or not appreciating the fact that the innovation project must be sold – sold to its potential resource providers and to its potential detractors. One person in a key position in an organization can derail the best plan. We need to transfer our enthusiasm for the plan to them. Get them as excited as we are about achieving the innovation's potential impact.

SUMMARY

Planning is the first of two execution stages of The Innovation Pyramid. The aim of this level is to develop a creation and delivery plan. The plan must include how the innovation will actually be created, of course. But the plan must also articulate how that created innovation will be delivered to the adopter. Without adoption of our innovation, we cannot create impact.

As illustrated in Table 5.1, there are four components to the plan. That plan may vary in detail, depending on the complexity of the innovation, but it must always contain the following four components.

- Operations. How will the innovation be created?
- Delivery. How will the innovation be delivered to and acquired by the adopter?
- Resources. What resources, inside and outside our organization, will be needed to complete creation and delivery of this innovation?
- Risk. Description of the risks associated with the creation and delivery of this innovation.

If a detailed plan cannot be crafted or the resources cannot be committed to the project, then the design must be altered. That means returning to Level 2 (Solution Formulation) of The Innovation

Pyramid, the second design stage. Depending on the reason for the failure of the design, we may have to iterate all the way back to Level 1 (Problem Identification). Failure is not terminal. It is merely part of the learning process. Our increased understanding that we obtained in the planning level will be incorporated into the selection criteria of the choices we made in Level 2. If those new criteria do not lead us to a new solution, we will need to iterate back to Level 1 and choose a different cause on which to focus.

The plan we create in this level must be detailed enough to be executable. That plan is also a way to communicate and sell the project to potential supporters, collaborators, and detractors. The value of the innovation project is not self-evident to all that we need to involve. We must communicate its value to them. However, we do not want to introduce our project by dropping a 1,000-page tome on our audience. This section outlined various levels of pitching the innovation project: core concept opener, the elevator pitch, and the resource pitch. We need to use all three to transfer our enthusiasm for the project to those who can aid us in creating its ultimate impact.

6   **Level 4**
Perform

INTRODUCTION

This chapter is about implementation – getting it done. This is the second execution stage, Level 4 The Innovation Pyramid. The outcome of this level, as illustrated in Figure 6.1, is to carry out the plan. If the plan is not executable, then we will need to return to Level 3 and adjust the plan. This is the iterative nature of The Pyramid. Continued iteration further up The Pyramid may be warranted if the issue with the plan turns out to be innovation's design itself, as will be discussed in Chapter 7.

A vast number of books are dedicated to project execution and management. This chapter will not be a substitute for those. The chapter will review a structure for ensuring alignment; alignment of all the people and activities associated with the plan is critical to its timely success. The remainder of the chapter will concentrate on what can be learned via the implementation of the plan developed in Level 3.

ALIGNMENT

Alignment is the most reliable way to ensure things proceed as we desire. Yes, we can craft agreements that commit outside organizations to perform tasks contrary to their corporate goals, but that will only work for the short term. When two organizations' interests are aligned, cooperation and collaboration become much simpler. The same is true inside our organization. If a group's or individual's incentives are ill-aligned with the activities we need them to perform, we will encounter constant friction as we try to implement our project.

In the mid-1950s, Drucker (1954) created a framework to assist organizations in aligning their activities with their vision. The framework, although often criticized, continues as the backbone

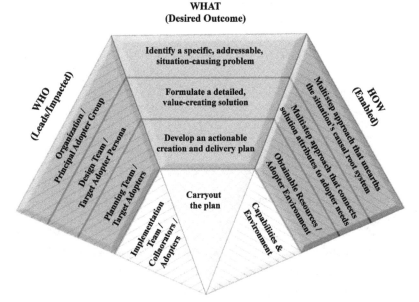

FIGURE 6.1 Level 4 of a flattened view of The Innovation Pyramid.

of the current business management standard. Many have added to or in other ways modified Drucker's original framework with the aim of eliminating its perceived shortcomings. Michaelides (2012), for example, published a visual version of Drucker's work, which clearly delineates an organization's ends (what they want to accomplish; the desired outcomes) from the means (how they intend to accomplish it; the approach). Figure 6.2 further extends Michaelides's framework by including the critical performance level and adding the associated means to the activities and performance levels. As the figure illustrates, there is a two-way alignment in this structure. The upper part of Figure 6.2 represents a zoomed-out view, one with a broad purview. As we descend down the figure, we are zooming in, increasing the detail we can observe, but narrowing our purview. Both vertical and horizontal alignments are necessary in this framework. Each of the means and ends columns must align vertically in addition to the means at each level aligning with that level's end.

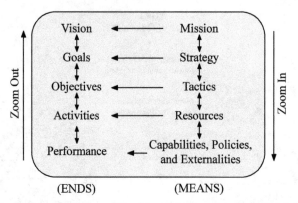

FIGURE 6.2 Extension of Drucker's Management-by-Objective.

As Figure 6.2 illustrates, every activity in which an organization engages should be aligned with a specific short-term desired outcome or objective. The performance is, in turn, aligned with these activities. These objectives, or tangible targets, are typically SMART: Specific, Measurable, Achievable, Result-oriented, and Time-bound. As we continue to zoom out, the objectives need to be aligned with the long-term and broad goals, which are, in turn, aligned with the organization's vision (organization-influenced future state). Institutions typically have a number of long-term goals that support their vision. Each goal is typically supported by a number of objectives, each objective supported by a number of activities, and each activity supported by the performance of a number of individuals or groups.

The "means" column of Figure 6.2 is similar. The organization's mission (who they are and what they value) supports the organization's vision and is consistent with the strategy. That strategy represents a general approach to accomplishing the goal. The tactics are the specific approach, or the game plan, to meeting the short-term objectives. The objectives should be consistent with the strategy. There must be the resources – physical, human, and financial – available to support the activities and enable the tactics. Finally, the team's Capabilities (assets, know-how, relationships, and aspirations), the organization's policies, and other externalities must enable, versus constrain, the performance. These three must also be consistent with the available resources. An organization, for example, cannot wirelessly deliver content (tactic) to their customers if they do not have or are not committing the necessary underlying resources to support that approach.

Drucker's framework can be applied to any organizational effort. It is particularly useful in managing complex innovation projects, which may be outside the normal operations of the firm, as it forces us to reconsider the alignment of all the organizational elements necessary to accomplish such a project. It is far too easy to blame the implementation team when the innovation creation and delivery plan are not carried out as constructed. Assuming the plan is appropriate, the real blame often comes down to misalignment: misalignment of unit operations, including reward systems, within and between organizations. If something is amiss with the innovation project's performance, the root cause can often be uncovered using the framework represented by Figure 6.2.

The remainder of this chapter will examine the plan's performance. Chapter 7 will extend that examination beyond performance to all the remaining levels of The Innovation Pyramid, as performance is far from the only element that can cause our innovation not to have the impact we desired and anticipated.

PERFORMANCE ASSESSMENT

The Innovation Pyramid is a knowledge-based process. Improvement in its use depends on insights gained from comparing how things actually turned out versus how things were predicted to turn out. Performance assessment, in the form of variance reports, is commonly used in finance to compare actual financial performance versus predicted performance. Such an analysis leads to understanding. Understanding leads to improved forecasts. Level 4 of The Pyramid is our first opportunity to generate a data-based variance report as the implementation is the first contact our innovation has with actual adopters. We have gathered as much information as possible and made the best decisions we could based on our understanding at the time. Now, at this level, we have real reactions from real people. We need to take advantage of that information. It is insights we seek, not blame. These insights are particularly useful as we may be traversing through The Pyramid multiple times – once for a pilot program, for example, and once for the innovation's global launch.

This chapter will assess the performance of the plan. This is certainly not the only cause for the variance between the predicted impact of our innovation and its actual impact. The remainder of the elements that impact that outcome, which covers all the remaining levels of The Pyramid, will be discussed in Chapter 7. Assessment of the plan's performance will manifest as a variance report of all four components of the implementation plan (Operations, Delivery, Resources, and Risk). Chapter 1 discussed the three primary elements necessary to become a serial innovator: people, environment, and methodology. For this level, the focus is on the "people" and the "environment" elements. Each of the four components of the plan developed in Level 3 will be assessed from these two perspectives. The "people" element will include an assessment of all of the people and relationships necessary to implement the plan. That includes the implementors, the adopters, and the key collaborators both inside and outside the innovation-developing organization.

Too often implementation focuses exclusively on the people; it must also examine the creator-organization's internal environment in addition to externalities that may impact the innovation's creators or its delivery to its adopters. The "environment" will therefore include the environments of the adopters, our external collaborators, and the innovation-developing organization in addition to externalities that may impact all of those environments. The innovation-developing organization's environment includes the work processes of the organization, as these formal and informal policies and procedures may directly or indirectly negatively impact the implementation of the innovation plan.

Operations

The "operations" component of the actionable innovation implementation plan focuses on the creation of the innovation itself. It is too often the sole focus on the plan's implementation review, although it is just one of its four components. The variance report for this component of the plan reviews the execution and timing of the activities called out in the plan. Were the activities executed as described in the plan? Was the timing of their execution consistent with that described in the plan? If not, why not? Was the variance caused by a resource issue (Figure 6.2) or a more fundamental Capabilities/policies/environmental issue?

People

In his book, *Good to Great*, Jim Collins' focus was "first who, then what." Get the right people on the bus is the concept he developed in this book. Plans are often created with people to execute them in mind. Those individuals do not always end up getting assigned to the project. That leads to the first question we should ask, was the implementation team identified in the plan's development actually retained for the project? Or to put in Collins' framework, did we indeed get the right people on the bus?

The implementation team is responsible for carrying out the plan and will achieve that outcome by leveraging its Capabilities (access to assets, know-how, relationships, and motivations – both intrinsic and extrinsic). Did this team that was actually assigned to carry out the innovation plan have the Capabilities (see Figure 6.3) necessary to implement the activities of the "operations" component

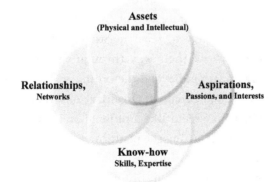

FIGURE 6.3 Team Capabilities Map.

of the plan? Was the team given access to the physical or intellectual assets as called for in the plan? If not, why not?

The next layer of the implementation team is the collaborators: both those inside and outside the organization who were identified in the plan as willing and able to assist in its execution. Did this occur? Did the collaborators identified in the plan (suppliers, contract manufacturers, etc.) participate as anticipated? Were the terms of their participation as anticipated? Were these collaborators able to deliver as anticipated? If not, why not? Did these collaborators have and assign the resources to achieve their component of the plan?

To what extent did the people, and more generally the extended team's Capabilities, impact the quality of the innovation produced? Was that quality as anticipated? Did it contain all the features of the original design? Were we able to scale the production according to the plan? Were the suppliers able to deliver the quality and quantity of raw materials for our innovation? If not, why not?

Environment

An organization's culture and work processes play a large role in shaping how people work and interact. Innovation projects often work against the grain of an organization's normal practices. The culture of the firm, for example, may be secretive; we simply do not tell our suppliers what we are working on. But the innovation plan may have called for a true collaboration with a supplier. Whenever activities beyond the cultural norm of an organization are required, the organization is likely to react negatively. Work will slow as approval decisions work their way through the decision-making layers of the organization. Beyond-the-ordinary agreements will be forced to be drafted and executed. Organizations, like people, do not like change. What may seem like a rational and reasonable request from an internal group during the planning stages may blow up to a major corporate decision during the execution stage.

Questions that reveal environmental issues include: Were there any project delays due to internal work processes? Were the external collaborator contracts developed and signed expeditiously? Were the payments to suppliers made as anticipated? Was the internal environment generally supportive of this project? Were the internal collaborators able to deliver as anticipated and on time? Was the organization's reward system aligned with the timely execution of the activities of the project for all involved? During the assessment of the execution of the plan, we need to not blame the implementation team for these delays, but to identify the true source of the challenges – the organization's environment.

These cultural holdups can inadvertently ruin an otherwise impactful innovation project. For example, many universities today offer their student's experiential learning opportunities. Instead of working for a grade, these programs often incent student participation by providing participants with cash supplied by outside donors. Several universities have had difficulties in their initial launch of such programs. Not because the programs were poorly designed. They were well designed. Not because the students were not interested. Their Target Adopter was well identified and initially well motivated. Not even because the program delivery was ineffective. The root cause reason for the initial struggle with some of these programs was the ability to get a payment check to their students upon completion of the program. Universities are designed to accept money from students, not the other way around. They are also well equipped to distribute monies to employees and vendors. But there is often no precedent for paying students who are not employees. This is beyond the cultural norm, which causes a holdup in the accounting/accounts-payable department. The students become disillusioned with the program as the promised reward is not delivered in a timely manner. That information passes quickly among the student population resulting in diminishing student participation. What is the root cause of this lack of participation and therefore a lack of program impact? Organizational work processes and culture. Seemingly little things can have huge ramifications on an innovation project's impact. Watch for them.

Delivery

This component of the plan addressed the delivery of the innovation to the Target Adopter. The points-of-view of the adopter, and any third party distributors that may be involved, are assessed as they may be different than what was anticipated from the research done during the design stages. Particular attention must be paid to the Target Adopter. Was their perception of the innovation versus their current Best Alternative to a New Option (BATNO) the same as our own perception? Did they value the innovation as anticipated? Did our communication of that value proposition reach them as anticipated? Was the quantity of adopters as anticipated? If not, why not?

People

It is easy, during design and planning, to underestimate the difficulty involved in delivering our innovation to the adopters. Our self-centric point-of-view would suggest that we are the ones doing the heavy lifting by creating the innovation. The delivery, however, could be equally challenging. Given that delivery involves multiple points-of-view beyond our own (the adopters and those of the key collaborators), there is a high probability that we might not have gotten it quite right. It is more than warranted to deeply explore the collaborator's and adopter's variance to the plan.

From the collaborator's side, were the subset of delivery-related tasks in the plan carried out as planned? Did the collaborators identified in the plan (web designers, advertising agencies, etc.) participate as anticipated? Were the terms of their participation as anticipated? Were these collaborators able to deliver as anticipated? Were there any distribution issues? Was the innovation damaged, for example, in the transition to the customer? Were the innovation-to-distributer-to-adopter delays longer than anticipated? Was the value sharing with the distributors as anticipated? If not, why not?

From the adopter point-of-view, did the adopters take up the innovation at the anticipated adoption rate? Were the initial discounts offered to entice the early adopters useful? Did we get the pricing right? Did those adopters require more follow-up counsel (customer service support, etc.) than anticipated? Any unanticipated adopter complaints? Did the advertising message resonate with the adopters? Were the channels used to reach them the right ones? Was the overall cost of customer acquisition as anticipated?

Environment

In addition to the difficulty we have managing within the known culture of our own organization, the delivery of the innovation typically requires managing across several lesser-understood cultures of our collaborator's organizations. Did any internal issues arise in our collaborator's organizations that prevented them from executing their portion of the innovation plan as expected? If so, what were they?

The adopter's environment is critical to assess as is the reaction from the current BATNO producer. These environments are dynamic. One change will produce another. If the current BATNO producer feels that their market share will be threatened by our new innovation, they will respond in some way. What was the reaction from the producer of the current BATNO? Did they lower their price? Launch a negative ad campaign? How did that impact our adopters? Was the reaction beyond what was anticipated in the plan? Were there any externalities that impacted the innovation launch that were not anticipated? A macro-economic slump? A terrorist attack? Global pandemic? New legislation? Launch of a new, unanticipated, innovation from another organization?

Environments are important, yet those beyond our own are impossible to directly manage. The best we can do is anticipate environmental changes and develop mitigation strategies for those anticipated shifts.

Resources

The "resources" component of the plan focused on all the resources necessary to create the proposed innovation and deliver it to the Target Adopter. These resources were both internal and external to the innovation creator's organization. Was the identified access to specialized assets – be it unique equipment (physical assets) or right to practice certain patents (intellectual assets) – acquired as anticipated? Was the plan's budget fully funded? Was the timing of that budget allocation as anticipated?

People

Did the implementation team have the relationships required to consummate the deals on all the required assets? It is not uncommon for people changes within the organization, yet outside the project's core implementation group, to have an impact on the project's implementation. One of the core team members, for example, could have had a friend in our organization's contract office. That friend agreed to spearhead the negotiation of a supplier contract for the project. Before the innovation project is launched, that friend takes another job in a different organization. Now, even though our core innovation team did not change, that team no longer has the relationships necessary to perform that aspect of the project. In Chapter 3, we sought root causes that, if resolved, would create a domino effect on the General Problem we wished to impact. In assessing performance, we need to again be attuned to domino effects, particularly concerning relationships.

Environment

Were the organization's internal work processes able to support said asset acquisition in a timely manner? As discussed in the "Delivery" section of this chapter, many organizations are challenged in performing any act in a timely manner that is outside its normal work processes and policies. If the plan calls for such activities, policies could well be at the heart of the performance issue (see Figure 6.2).

Risk

Risks have generally been identified in the variance analysis of the other three components of the innovation implementation plan. This category is for those "other" risks that may be internal or external to the organization that were simply not anticipated. Odd things can happen. This is the component of the variance report that captures these odd occurrences. They could be Political, Economic, Social, and Technological (PEST) risks or something that came up within our organization or with our Target Adopter or external collaborators. No matter what it is, this is a "miscellaneous" bucket to capture those unanticipated deviations from the original plan.

COMMON MISTAKES

The most common mistake when carrying out the plan is to blame the implementation team when it does not go as anticipated. That deviation from the plan could be caused by a number of issues beyond the control of the implementation team. Alignment issues are often the culprit. Use Figure 6.2 as a guide to ferret them out. Focus on creating a fact-based variance report to increase our understanding of the roll out of our innovation. A witch hunt to identify a scapegoat does not improve our ability to innovate. In addition, as we will see in Chapter 7, the deviation from the anticipated innovation impact may have its roots all the way back in the design stages.

The second most common mistake is to try to implement a plan even though the conditions around which the plan was created have changed. The plan may call for a $1million budget, but the implementation team is only allocated $500,000. The mistake is going ahead and implementing the plan, as is. What should occur is that the process should return to the plan development stage (Level 3), and a new plan be created that takes into account the resource change. It does not matter which resource or assumption of the plan changed, that plan must be properly adjusted before it is implemented. Doing anything less is setting up the implementation team for failure.

SUMMARY

Carrying out the innovation creation and delivery plan that were created in the first execution stage (Level 3) is the aim of this final level of The Innovation Pyramid. This is a project management challenge.

Launching new innovations has challenges beyond those of a typical internal-company project in that they generally involve collaborators and adopters outside the innovation-creating organization. This means that multiple environments and multiple points-of-view, in addition to the innovation creator's internal environment and point-of-view, must be appraised.

Volumes have been written on project management. Rather than being a substitute for those writings, this chapter introduced a modification of Drucker's core Management-by-Objective framework (Figure 6.2). This framework is particularly useful in managing complex innovation projects that may be outside the normal operations of the firm as it focuses on the alignment of all the people and activities associated with the plan's successful implementation. The framework is also useful as a postimplementation review guide as it forces us to reconsider all the components, inside and outside our organization, necessary to accomplish such a project.

The remainder of the chapter focuses on performing a postexecution variance evaluation of the plan's implementation. Such a review allows us to hone in on the learnings attained from carrying out the plan developed in Level 3. All four aspects of the plan were reviewed: Operations, Delivery, Resources, and Risks. A poor plan execution does not automatically mean the implementation team underperformed. The issue may lie with people or environments well beyond the core team.

In the end, the usefulness of The Innovation Pyramid, like any tool, comes down to how well we learn to use it. The more we learn about its application to our organization and our innovations, the more useful it becomes. As a result, what we ultimately seek in reviewing the plan's implementation is to determine where things got off track. This chapter limited that review to the implementation of the plan. A poor implementation team can certainly destroy a good plan, but a great implementation team may not be able to save a poor plan. The implementation team is, in the end, limited by the plan they are provided. Setting them up for failure and then blaming them for the results is just terrible management.

Chapter 7 will assess the remaining innovation project elements that could be associated with the variance between the actual and the forecasted impact of the innovation. Were there issues with the plan itself? Was it simply a poorly designed innovation? Did we mis-identify the problem or its root cause in the first place? All elements of the design and execution must be considered. Chapter 7 will provide a structured way of accomplishing that assessment. The goal is learning. Learning how to better design and execute innovations.

7   Systematic Pyramid Review

PART I SUMMARY

The Innovation Pyramid is a strategic methodology for developing impactful new solutions to real problems, or in other words, to create innovations. The design thinking-based Innovation Pyramid is a visual representation of a repeatable, nonlinear, iterative, learnable methodology. The methodology leverages the nonlinear Diverge–Organize–Converge (DOC) Process detailed in Part II of this book. The DOC Process is an effectual and flexible standalone process in its own right. Together the two elements provide both a systematic guide for innovation development and a means to actualize it.

    Distinguishing aspects of The Innovation Pyramid are that it separates the problem from its solution and the innovation's design from its execution, while simultaneously considering both the innovation creator's and adopter's points-of-view (POVs). The three-sided, inverted pyramid has four horizontal layers, sliced top to bottom. The top two levels represent the two stages of the innovation's design (Problem Identification and Solution Formulation). The bottom two levels guide the innovation's execution (plan, then perform). The three sides of The Pyramid represent the "Who," the "What," and the "How" components of the innovation development methodology. The "who" section of The Pyramid encompasses multiple POVs. The "what" face of The Pyramid represents the desired outcome for each level. The "how" face of The Pyramid describes "how" the desired outcome(s) of each level will be accomplished or enabled. The unviewable center of the solid pyramid represents assessment. Assessment is performed at each level to ensure that rational and reasonable decisions are being made at each step of the development process.

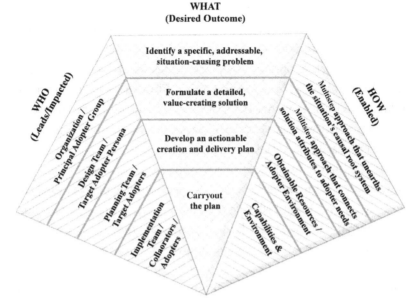

WHAT
(Desired Outcome)

Identify a specific, addressable,
situation-causing problem

Formulate a detailed,
value-creating solution

Develop an actionable
creation and delivery plan

Carryout
the plan

WHO
(Leads/Impacted)

Organization /
Principal Adopter Group

Design Team /
Target Adopter Persona

Planning Team /
Target Adopters

Implementation Team /
Collaborators /
Adopters

Multistep approach that unearths
the situation's causal root system

Multistep approach that connects
solution attributes to adopter needs

Obtainable Resources /
Adopter Environment

Capabilities &
Environment

HOW
(Enabled)

FIGURE 7.1 The Innovation Pyramid laid flat.

Slicing The Innovation Pyramid between the "Who" and the "How" sections and laying it flat produces the view of Figure 7.1. The first layer of The Innovation Pyramid, detailed in Chapter 3, is the first design stage, Problem Identification. The starting point for this stage is the original situation or the initially identified issue. A five-step guide for identifying and defining root causes with strong connections to the original situation is described. The Principal Adopters, the general group for whom the innovation is being created, are also identified at this level.

Chapter 4 delineates the detailed second stage of the innovation design process, Solution Formulation. During the multiple steps of this stage, our general Principal Adopter is narrowed to a specific Target Adopter persona with well-understood unmet or under-met needs, wants, and/or desires. A novel, detailed solution is created for the Target Adopters. The clear value proposition of this solution is generated through the connection of the attributes of the solution with the needs, wants, and/or desires of the Target Adopter.

The Innovation Pyramid then shifts from design to execution in Chapter 5. The first execution stage generates a creation and delivery plan for producing the solution designed in Level 2 and delivering it to the Target Adopters. The plan's necessary resources are also identified, but not acquired, at this stage. While this level is primarily taken from the innovator's POV, the would-be adopter's environment is also explored at this level to ensure a pathway exists for the adoption of the proposed innovation.

The final Pyramid level, the second execution stage, is detailed in Chapter 6. This execution stage focuses on implementing the plan created in Level 3. The "who" of this level is the implementation team, the external collaborators who will participate directly or indirectly in the creation and delivery of the innovation to the adopter, and the adopter. The "what" is the organization's ability to carry out the plan. The "how" this level is enabled is a combination of the capabilities and environments across the working groups, in addition to the environment of the adopter. Externalities, beyond the innovation team's control, that could significantly impact their ability to create and deliver the innovation to its adopters, are also examined at this level.

At the conclusion of the second execution level, a variance report is created which compares the forecasted implementation timing and impact to that which actually occurred, allowing us to learn from our experience at this level. A poor plan execution does not automatically mean the implementation team underperformed. The root cause of the variance issue may lie with the plan itself or all the way back to the innovation's design. In the end, all elements of the design and execution must be considered. The remainder of this chapter provides a structured way of accomplishing that review. The goal of this review is to learn. Learn how to better design and execute innovations, so that we can become better serial innovators.

OVERARCHING OUTCOME ASSESSMENT

The Innovation Pyramid is a methodology and not a recipe. The outcome of a precisely followed recipe is entirely predictable. This is not the case with a methodology. A methodology is a system of procedures and/or techniques that allows the accomplishment of a set of tasks without guarantee of a specific overall outcome. While the variability in the outcome cannot be eliminated, having a consistent method controls for a number of process variables makes the outcome variability conditional on the choices made during the design and execution stages. Those choices, in turn, are limited by the quality of the data we have at the time we make those choices and our judgment applied to making those choices. Neither that data nor our judgment can be perfect. Both can be improved with experience. By systematically reviewing each innovation project, comparing its actual impact versus its forecasted one, we can learn to improve both our judgment and our data-gathering skills.

Making conscious choices at each decision stage with clear and documented criteria is critical to being able to review the decisions made, layer by layer, throughout The Innovation Pyramid. It is nearly impossible to recognize, let alone change, a decision we made unconsciously, or intuitively. We often do not even recognize that we actually made a choice in those circumstances as it just "seems right" to proceed in a certain direction.

Ideally, a system-level review should be performed at the end of every innovation development project. This is true whether the desired outcome was achieved or not. Reviewing successful projects increases the organization's confidence and skill in implementing The Innovation Pyramid. The Pyramid is a knowledge process. Increasing the organization's understanding of its use increases the organization's ability to be repeat innovators. When reviewing less-than-successful projects, the implementation team, the group that carries out the execution plan, is often unfairly vilified when projects do not reach their overall, macro-level, desired outcome. The implementation team is only responsible for doing things right. Decisions made much earlier in the methodology could have inadvertently diverted the path away from that desired outcome; dooming the project from that point forward. Chastising the implementation team in those cases is not going to help the organization learn and grow. We need to learn from our hindsight to improve our foresight.

It is very common for an innovation design project to traverse through the entire Innovation Pyramid more than once. Any time a prototype is developed or a pilot program is crafted, the organization will traverse through The Innovation Pyramid at least twice – the first time through the prototype development and a second time through the final product development. In between, those two Pyramid applications should undergo a system-level review of The Pyramid's implementation. This chapter lays out such a review, revealing how choices made at each layer may have resulted in us falling short of our hoped-for impact. If the cause for the divergence from the ultimate impact can be uncovered, the innovator can then iterate back to the appropriate level, alter the original choice, and rework the innovation development from that point forward.

SYSTEMATIC PYRAMID REVIEW METHODOLOGY

This journey started with a situation we had hoped to impact. We designed and executed a would-be innovation with the goal of positively altering that situation. We designed an innovation. It was successfully created and delivered to our adopters. It just did not create the impact we desired. The measurement "needle," with respect to the original situation, did not significantly move. What went wrong?

In the previous chapter, we assessed everything that could have gone wrong during the implementation of the innovation's creation and delivery plan. We generated a variance report that, while limited to the plan's implementation, delineated the actual versus the anticipated elements of various aspects of the plan's implementation. There will always be variations between the actual versus the expected. That does not mean that these variations cause the innovation to not have the desired impact.

We must suppress our first impulse to blame the executers of the plan. We had, after all, done our research, created a thoughtful design, and crafted a solid plan. The only possible issue is that the plan was poorly performed, right? Probably wrong. That certainly *could* be the case. But before diving deep into an execution metrics discussion or complaining about how the project was clearly underresourced, we need to zoom out and broaden our perspective. "Did we do things right?" is a performance question. "Did we do the right things?" is a design question. Go ahead and ask if the plan's implementation was adequate. If it was, zoom all the way back to the top of the process, out to Level 1 of The Innovation Pyramid, as indicated in Figure 7.2. Alternatively, since we have already assessed the implementation of the plan, we could continue to work our way backward up through Figure 7.2, bottom to top. Every organization will develop its own preferences over time. This chapter proceeds, however, from the top down.

Starting from the Top

We made choices, often several, at each level of The Innovation Pyramid. During the design stages, we employed the DOC Process multiple times. Every DOC Process use ends with a choice. Was each choice the "right" one? We made rational and reasonable choices based on our understanding at the time, but were those choices ultimately the "right" ones? They were sound and reasonable choices at the time, but now we have additional insight. We now have actual experience that flows all the way through design to execution to an actual macro outcome; how much impact we generated. We no longer have to speculate how things *may* unfold, we have now experienced that unfolding. We need to take advantage of this new insight. We need to go back and review, layer by layer, the choices we made and assess how they did or could have led us to the macro outcome we actually did obtain. The Innovation Pyramid separates problem from solution and design from execution to streamline the innovation creation process, but those separations also simplify the postexecution analysis of the project.

Experienced process optimization specialists know that bottlenecks are often at the top of the bottle, so look there first. We started our innovation journey with a situation, so let us go all the

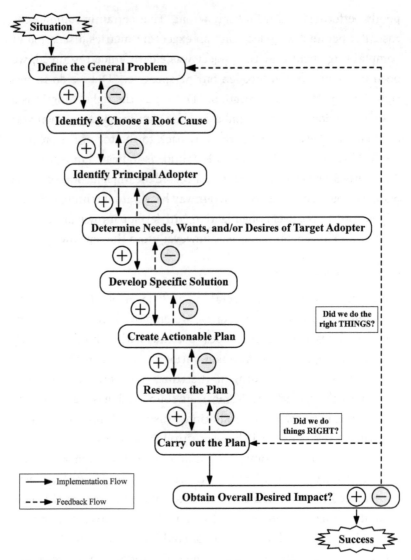

FIGURE 7.2 The Innovation Pyramid diagnostic flowchart.

way back there. Did we define the General Problem correctly? Did we
properly factor that General Problem, choosing the strongest linkages
of that root system to the right root cause? Did we initially choose the
right initial factor of the General Problem to address? If our innovation
impacted the chosen factor as anticipated, but we did not obtain the

overall impact we desired, then the factor we chose was not the rate-limiting one. Let's say our General Problem is decreasing profits. Our profits are impacted by two factors, our revenue and our costs. Say we choose to work on costs, and our implemented innovation had an effect at reducing our costs, yet our profits kept decreasing. That means we just chose the wrong factor; the costs were not the profit-limiting factor in this situation. We may have done everything else right after that choice, but none of it mattered as that choice was wrong. We now know two things we did not previously know. One is that our innovation *did* have an impact on the factor it was targeted to address (costs), and second is that it did not have an impact on our initial situation (decreasing profits). We need to now use our new knowledge to choose a different factor (revenue, in this simple example) and rework the entire Pyramid methodology from that point.

On the other hand, if we were not able to influence the factor as anticipated (our innovation, in this example, had no effect on the costs), perhaps we chose the wrong root of this factor to address. Or perhaps, we identified the unmet or under-met needs, wants, and/or desires incorrectly. Or we chose the wrong Target Adopter persona. We must follow our decision path back through the entire Pyramid, as illustrated in Figure 7.2, now armed with the knowledge of how our innovation impacted (or did not impact) each level.

For example, let's say the General Problem is the university's attrition rate. Given a number of students drop out of the university due to poor grades, the factor we choose to address is to help students get better grades. To address that specific issue, we decided to offer tutoring. Now it turns out that the increased tutoring had absolutely no impact on the university's attrition rate. We could question the tutors or how the plan was executed, or we could step back and ask ourselves if tutoring was the correct issue to address. We anticipated that the tutoring would help students get better grades and these better grades would, in turn, keep students at the university. Despite the increased availability of tutoring, the students are not getting better grades. The chosen factor may be right (the students need better grades), but the approach we took (increase tutoring) was wrong as it did not influence the factor in the way we desired. Why this is the case will take more research to uncover, likely additional Interviewing for Insights (IFIs). We have, however, more information than we had during our first pass through the design stages to aid us in this exploration. We now know, for example, that additional tutoring did not affect the situation. We had thought it would, but we now know that was not the case. Why not? Why was that new Best Alternative to a New Option (BATNO) inadequate? In pursuing that question, we discover that our students have little external financial support and, as a result, are working full-time, in addition to taking a full load of classes, to pay for their own educations. The lack of time to devote to their classes, not tutoring availability, is their root issue for poor class performance. The students are likely not engaging with the tutors for the same reason they do not always attend their classes: They are spending most of their time working at their for-pay jobs. The impact of this lack of time to devote to their classes is the root issue. Addressing any other issue will divert us from the path toward the ultimate desired impact.

A similar case can be made for slipping product revenues in the example of Chapters 3 and 4. As we saw in that example, "more marketing" was not going to help as customer awareness was not a root cause to stagnating sales; plant maintenance was that cause. In general, "more marketing" will never revive a product that is past its useful life in the marketplace. No one is buying VCRs today no matter how slick we craft the ads for them. If we had initially chosen to go with the "more marketing" approach in the example of Chapters 3 and 4, seeing that it did not have the impact we desired should force us to reevaluate the other three components of the marketing mix (product, place, and price). It is very likely that the product, not its promotion, is the culprit.

If the General Problem and root cause seem right, did we choose the wrong Target Adopter from the options derived from our identified root cause? This is a Pyramid layer-by-layer deconstruction that should examine every significant choice we made in each layer. If our Target

Adopter seemed right, perhaps it was just their numbers. Perhaps there simply were not as many as anticipated, which diminished the innovation's overall impact. If the Target Adopter definition and volume were correct, could it have been the design of our solution? Was the Target Adopter's perceived value obtained from our solution as we had conjectured? Did that solution's features connect with the adopter's needs/wants/desires as anticipated? If the solution seemed adequate, was the plan right? The solution design could have been great and the plan's execution flawless; the plan was simply off. We set up additional retail outlets in major cities across the United States in order to address our customer's desire for better access to our products. We had originally considered setting up these physical outlets along the main shopping thoroughfares of these target cities, but financial constraints led us to alter the plan by changing those locations. The stores were well staffed and operated, but their locations turned out to be wrong. That is an execution problem to be sure, but this is a problem with the plan, not its performance. It is dangerous to lump "plan" and "performance" together. They are both part of executing, but they not the same. This is why they are separated in The Pyramid methodology and why they should continue to be considered separately when diagnosing the project's lack of impact.

The layer-by-layer deconstruction of all the choices we made traversing through The Innovation Pyramid will take time and additional research (both primary and secondary). For each choice we made during this journey, we anticipated a micro-level outcome. Was that outcome obtained? If not why? If so, why did obtaining that outcome not lead to the macro-level outcome as we anticipated. Layer-by-layer analysis is the learning required to become better innovators.

ASSESSMENT REVIEW EXAMPLE

In this example, the local university desires to support the acceleration of a robust regional economy. Specifically, the university's aim is to support the creation of what Harvard's Michael Porter calls the formation of "Traded Clusters (TCs)." TCs are a collection of firms which primarily serve markets beyond their region. These companies export their products; maybe not across country boundaries, but across regional ones. TCs have been shown to have a significantly larger impact on local economies in terms of the creation of high-paying jobs, etc. (Porter, 2003). Local Cluster (LC) firms, the collection of businesses that primarily serve the local market, also benefit the local economy, but as Porter said, there should be no doubt which drives the local economy. In a talk given in September 2014, Porter said, "The Traded Cluster is the dog, and the Local Cluster is the tail" (Porter, 2014). While LC firms certainly add to the overall robustness of the regional economy, it is the TC businesses that drive the region's economic success. The university chose to support TC firm formation through the development of local entrepreneurs capable of founding such firms.

Now we will assume that the university obtained a grant to develop a founder-training program for TC founders. A detailed program was designed, planned, and launched. Five years later, there is no significant change to the regional economy. Was it poor execution? Possibly, but unlikely. How would we find out?

The rationalization for the training program contained a lot of information, but not well-structured information. This is not atypical of how "solutions" to problems are presented. We first need to break this down. What was the General Problem? It is desired that the regional economy be strengthened. What are the factors to this General Problem? There are only three, and none of them stated in the prior summary of the program and its rationale, so this may have been an intuitive logic leap in the original solution design that we now will have to perform some secondary research to rationalize. There are three approaches to increasing a regional economy: (1) launch new firms, (2) grow firms that already exist in the region, and (3) encourage successful firms that are currently operating outside the region to move to the region (i.e. "import" firms to the region). According to the initial analysis, these firms can be classified into two categories: TC firms (those with a customer base primarily outside the region) and LC firms (whose customers are primarily in the region).

FIGURE 7.3 Problem Identification Root System example.

The subfactor that the university focused on was forming new TC firms. There are likely lots of causes that limit the formation of such firms locally, but the university chose to focus on training, as that is an approach that aligns well with their education mission. Specifically, they are focusing "founder training," as shown in Figure 7.3.

Now we have a clearer picture of the design decisions that were made. Let us say that our postprogram review found no significant increase in the launch of TC firms in the region. The research further revealed, however, that there was indeed a significant increase in the number of people in the region that now had the skill set and relationships necessary to launch TC firms. They just were not launching them.

The program was "successful" in that it created more trained founders, but on a macro-level assessment, it was not impactful as it did not improve the regional economy. That suggests that the choices made during the design phase were incorrect. We still do not know if launching more TC firms would grow the local economy, but we do know that training founders for such firms did not increase the number of TC firms being launched. Why not? That is the research question we need to ask. Why is this new BATNO (founder training program) not working for these would-be founders? Our 360-degree IFIs may have revealed that other issues are limiting the launch of such firms. The lack of availability of intellectual property that could be used as a foundation to differentiate these firms was one factor uncovered. The lack of risk financing was another factor identified. Founder training was simply not the rate-limiting step in creating more TC firms in the region.

Normally in such circumstances, there is no follow-up research or program review. What typically occurs instead is that the program execution is blamed for the lack of impact. Worse, more money is often put into the failed program; the curriculum is changed, the program's promotion budget is increased, perhaps new instructors are brought in from other regions that have robust TC firms. The project review takes time. But it also saves time and further wasted effort spend on redesigning a training program that simply will not have any impact on the overall desired outcome. Instead, in this example, the university must decide if either of the other two identified factors fall within their circle of influence. If so, how would they approach addressing those issues.

COMMON MISTAKES

The biggest mistake is assuming execution of the innovation's creation and delivery plan was the cause of our lack of impact. The choice that took us off the path toward our macro-level desired outcome likely came in the design phase, long before the executed plan was ever developed. The fact is that things that do not work as they should are often poorly designed. Challenge the execution assumption and look at the top of the bottle for the bottleneck.

The other significant mistake is not to perform a critical analysis of the entire system. Dozens of micro-level decisions are made as we traverse through The Innovation Pyramid. Each decision sets a path forward, eliminating other options. Potential avenues forward are being eliminated by each decision we make during the two design stages. Those choices must be reviewed – not just at the design stages but at every Pyramid level – if we are truly going to create an impactful innovation.

The final mistake is not using the structure of The Innovation Pyramid in deconstructing the lack of impact. Even when The Innovation Pyramid methodology had been utilized in the original development of the innovation, the project's assessment is still occasionally performed viscerally. Becoming a serial innovator requires a consistent methodology, one that is utilized both in the development and in the deconstruction of its impact. What remains, beyond the method, is data and judgment. As both improve, so should the desired outcome. A good methodology is a knowledge process; one that promotes learning. We do not want to cheat ourselves out of important learning opportunities by failing to review our projects – both those that succeeded and especially those that failed. Failure is life's biggest learning opportunity. This is not a search for the guilty, but it is a system for organizational learning.

SUMMARY

The Innovation Pyramid is a strategic methodology for developing innovations. As a method, versus a recipe, the overarching desired outcome is not guaranteed. While every micro-level decision made during the advancement through The Pyramid assures the level-specific outcomes are attained, the overall, macro-level, desired outcome may or may not ultimately be realized. Despite the innovation project's overall outcome, it is valuable, from an organizational learning perspective, to review innovation design projects to better understand the linkages between the micro-decisions and the overall outcome. This is especially true given The Innovation Pyramid will often be traversed twice for any given innovation – once for the development of the prototype or pilot development and a second time for the final innovation development.

The Pyramid structure, fortunately, is equally useful in guiding the identification of which well-rationalized choice made during the design and execution of the innovation inadvertently caused us to veer away from our overall, macro-level, desired impact of the original situation. The distinguishing characteristics of The Innovation Pyramid – separation of the problem from its solution and the innovation's design from its execution while simultaneously considering both the innovation creator's and adopter's POVs – aid in its usefulness as an overall project assessment guide. The structured guidance that The Pyramid provides for a project's postexecution review must be augmented with additional research. Firms should consider this additional research an investment in their emerging core competency of serial innovation.

It is all too common to blame the innovation execution team when the macro-level desired change to the initial situation is not realized. Odds are it was not their fault. The reality is that this team's assessment is limited to whether they did things right. The remainder of The Pyramid levels determines if the right things were chosen to be done. Rather than searching for someone to blame for the project's failure, the organization should embrace this opportunity to search for deeper understanding. This deeper discernment requires a critical analysis of the entire innovation system – every decision taken between the initial situation and overall desired outcome must be reviewed. Fortunately, The Innovation Pyramid provides a streamlined approach for accomplishing that analysis.

PART II The Diverge–Organize–Converge Process

8 Diverge–Organize–Converge Process Overview

Impactful solutions are out there, but we have to hunt for them. It is myth that these clever thoughts just pop into the heads of naturally gifted innovative people. Those "naturally gifted innovative people" are intuitive. They follow an intuitive process that makes visceral sense to them. They typically cannot describe the process and sometimes do not even recognize that they are following one. To them it "seems" like the ideas just come. They do not. Their brain is working in a structured way; one that can be learned. The Diverge-Organize-Converge (DOC) Process is a creativity-based method to focus the hunt. Think of it as a multipurpose tool with many applications. Those three components of the DOC Process, which will be introduced in this chapter and detailed in Chapters 9–11, are "Diverge," "Organize," and "Converge."

A tool can be applied to many situations. Think of all the ways we use a hammer. Hammer nails into a board, sure. Flatten a piece of metal. "Fixing" our computer when we are frustrated with it ... okay, maybe not, but the point is made. Once we possess a tool, we will learn different ways to apply it. Learning the DOC Process alone will improve our innovation capabilities. It will not make us a complete innovator, but will move us in that direction. Parts of the DOC Process are familiar, particularly the "diverge" step. Applying only a piece of a tool, however, is like becoming familiar with the handle of a hammer. Good start, but without the rest of the hammer, nothing much is going get accomplished. At least not very well.

Learning a tool is a start. That is knowledge. For that knowledge to become a skill, we need to add our own technique to the tool, make it our own. To be a master at using the tool, we must learn techniques that work for us. The techniques we learn will turn our knowledge of the tool into a skill we possess. That will take practice and use. Simply reading this book will not make us an expert; we need to additionally practice the tools and techniques described in this book. Innovation, impactful problem-solving, is a skill. It takes both tools and techniques. The first time we tried something new and different, it very likely felt awkward. The same will be true for these tools. We need to allow ourselves the opportunity to grow past that stage. The rewards will be vast.

DIVERGE–ORGANIZE–CONVERGE PROCESS SUMMARY

Part I of this book describes an overall methodology, the design thinking-based Innovation Pyramid, used to design and execute impactful solutions to challenging problems. That, in itself, is also a learnable approach that many intuitive problem-solvers unconsciously already apply. It is certainly not the only way to solve complicated problems. It is, however, a repeatable, learnable method that can be applied to a vast array of business and life challenges. Within that overarching methodology are other tools and techniques that need to be mastered in order to become a successful serial innovator. Think of it like building a house. The overarching process lays out the most efficient order of things: site preparation, lay the foundation, frame the house, put up the roof, install the windows and doors, etc. Within each step, there are additional skills that are necessary to accomplish the tasks. The house framing step of our house-building methodology will be difficult if not impossible, for example, without knowing how to cut a piece of wood or hammer a nail. Think of those skills as subprocesses to the overarching "house-building" methodology. Those subprocesses can also be applied to a wide variety of projects and are certainly not limited to building a house. The same holds true for the DOC Process.

The DOC Process is an important subprocess necessary to reduce The Innovation Design to practice. It will be applied multiple times during the innovation design stages. The DOC Process can also be applied to a multitude of other noninnovative challenges, like diagnosing why the refrigerator stopped working or to help decide where a group of friends should go out to dinner. We use it all the time subconsciously. Making the process conscious allows us to improve its use.

There are three distinct components to the DOC Process. One or more of those is likely already familiar. It is the combination of all three that makes the method powerful. Skipping portions of the method significantly reduces its overall effectiveness; like generally knowing how to drive, but not being able to make left-hand turns. These limitations significantly reduce the impact and application of the overall technique.

The application of the DOC Process to both problems and solutions is a skill that can be developed over time by repeatedly using its three components. The aim here is to demonstrate how all three components come together to both identify underlying causes of issues we observe and create impactful solutions to those causes. It takes all three components working together to accomplish this aspiration. Yes, the DOC Process is applicable to both Problem Identification and the Solution Formulation, although our experience with all or part of the process will likely have been limited to its applications in deriving new solutions.

The Diverge step expands from the original solution idea or problem situation. It is too easy to get locked into our initial concept. We need to make sure that we have not inadvertently missed a "better" idea or problem description by being too focused too soon. The second step of the process, as illustrated in Figure 8.1, is the Organize step. This is an important but often ignored step in the overall process. This step actually has elements of both the Converge and Diverge Steps. As we organize the information developed in the Diverge step, we are naturally starting to narrow the concepts. This is part of Converge. However, the organization may make it clear that an entire class of ideas is missing. If a class of ideas is missing, then we will need to Diverge again, to include elements of this new class. Once the Organize step is completed, the process moves onto the Converge step. Converge narrows all the concepts down to the "best." Of course, we will need to define our criteria for choosing the "best" before we converge.

Before we can formulate a solution, we must first identify the problem we are trying to solve, or in other words, the opportunity we are addressing. This section will refer to the Problem Identification

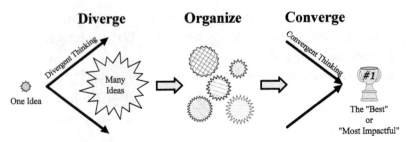

FIGURE 8.1 DOC Process overview.

process as exploring the "problem space" and the Solution Formulation process as working in the "solution space." No matter what the phrasing, one of the keys to becoming a successful serial innovator is to separate the problem from the solution. The DOC Process applies equally to discovering root-cause problems as it does to crafting creative new solutions. Given that the common experience with these creativity tools are from a solution-space perspective, the specific details of how the Diverge and Converge steps are applied to the problem space are given in Chapters 9 and 11.

The starting points of the "problem" and the "solution" are in some ways mirror images of each other. But the distinction between something and its reflection is important. Often the difference is a matter of point-of-view. The proposed solution is often from the point-of-view of the creator of the would-be innovation, while the problem *should* be stated from the point-of-view of the would-be adopter. The DOC Process first expands from the initial starting point of both the problem and the solution (extreme left- and right-hand edges of Figure 8.2) and converges in the middle of that figure to a detailed solution of a specifically defined problem. For that problem/solution convergence to take place, the detailed elements of the solution must connect to the specific aspects of the narrowed problem.

As discussed in Part I of this book, we humans are "action-oriented" beings. That means we are solution-oriented beings. It is fine if we begin thinking about a problem by starting with a solution idea. We simply cannot stop there. When a group of friends mull over where to go

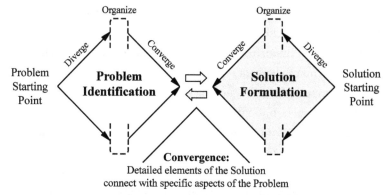

FIGURE 8.2 DOC Process application to Problem Identification and Solution Formulation.

have dinner together, the couple with the newborn might immediately suggest a restaurant; a proposed solution void of a problem definition or any solution selection criteria. They may want to go to a restaurant that satisfies their unstated criterion that they want a relative short dining experience, so as to minimize their time away from their baby. They started with a solution, restaurant B. The rest of the group of friends may have different needs, wants, or desires (i.e. "the problem" they desire to solve may be different for each of them). Some may want to go to a place where they can get a decent meal, authentically engage with the others, and not have it take all night. If that is the problem to be solved, there are likely a great many restaurants that would address those issues. Arguments about the restaurant choice will be minimized if they can first all align on the same objective. While understanding the problem is key to diversifying potential solutions, it does not mean that we always start with the problem. We often do not, as this example highlighted. Just do not be satisfied with the mirror image of the solution as the problem definition; dig deeper into the actual problem and give it more dimension.

DIVERGE

The DOC Process is a critical tool in the design of an innovation. The DOC Process involves three steps. The first is Diverge or divergent thinking. Divergent thinking is expanding our ideas from one (or a few) to many, many ideas. Most are very familiar with one version of this method – brainstorming. Groups often use various brainstorming techniques when they want to create innovative solutions. It, however, is equally important in diagnosing the issue we need to address, or in other words, Problem Identification.

Much of the work in creativity is about developing techniques to increase the breadth of ideas; to help get "out of the box" of our current thinking. What these techniques all have in common is that they help us move from a single idea to multiple ideas. Divergent-thinking techniques force us to diversify our vantage point as well as our points-of-view. Divergent-thinking techniques are most commonly used to look at potential new solutions. How can we build a better mousetrap? The technique, however, is also necessary to expand our thinking on the problem itself, to come up with a better diagnosis. Why do we need a mouse trap in the first place? What is the root cause of the mouse infestation in our house? If we can address the root cause, we can prevent future infestations. That's what we want. Not just a temporary solution – a better way to catch today's mouse. But a long-term fix, so we will not even have mice in the house going forward.

Applying divergent-thinking techniques to Problem Identification is slightly different from how it is used in Solution Formulation. The tool is the same, but the technique required is subtly different. It is, however, still a divergent thinking; step 1 of the DOC Process. When applied to the problem space, this divergent-thinking step still has the same purpose, to get us beyond our preconceived notions and consider what at first blush may appear as "crazy" thoughts. It is important to get out of our own way here, as after all, if we truly already knew the real problem and the optimal solution to it, then why is it still a problem?

ORGANIZE

Step 2 of the DOC Process is Organize. This is a crucial step in the overall process, yet it is one that is often skipped. Think about what happens during a typical brainstorming session. At the end of the session, we might have white boards full of ideas, or sticky notes pasted all over walls. Brainstorming is an invigorating step in the process. The group's energy level is high during this step. But then what typically happens next? Everyone looks at all the unjudged ideas and idea fragments on the walls and are a bit flummoxed as to how to move forward from there. Maybe the group "votes" for their favorites with colored dots or some other technique. Maybe they simply select one of the ideas to move forward, but we likely feel uncomfortable (unless the idea chosen was one of our own), with a sense that "something" else should have happened before moving forward to implement this single, half-baked, unjudged idea. That sense is accurate. There is definitely more work to do to complete the innovation design. Most of the necessary next steps require significant work and some research. Skipping these additional steps is why most brainstorming fails. Once we have completed the divergent-thinking step, that pile of ideas and idea fragments need to be organized.

The Organize step represents the transition between the Diverge and Converge steps. It is the synthesis step in the process. All the information gathered during the Diverge step, whether that information was produced via a brainstorming session or through secondary or primary research, needs to be organized. The information must first be sorted. Related concepts should be grouped together into categorizes. Once grouped together, it is easier to see how similar ideas within a group could be combined. The challenge here is that no one is providing us with the names of the category "buckets" into which we will be placing the diverse range of concepts we generated during the divergent-thinking step. We need to come up with those categories as we go; that is pattern recognition. Always create a "miscellaneous" category for concepts that just do not seem to have anything in common with any of the others. Sometimes those "odd" items end up as the most useful concepts of all!

The second thing we need to do in the Organize step of the DOC Process is to see if there are any connections between the categories or among the concepts within a category. Does one item influence the other? Is there a specific order in which things need to be done? Does an item in the list cause another to occur? Thinking of relationships between categories or items within a category forces us to think of the information as part of a system, not just isolated concepts. Impactful change is derived from understanding. The Organize step is a crucial step in developing that understanding. It takes time, but it is time well spent.

Being the transition between the Diverge and Converge steps, the Organize step has features of both. This step has convergent-thinking features in that we will be grouping our divergent ideas into categories. There will be fewer categories than there were initial concepts. This is the convergent-thinking portion of this step. The Organize step also has divergent-thinking characteristics in that we may also recognize that concepts are "missing" once we put them into categories. We thought of a variety of "face-to-face" course delivery techniques, but did not consider any "virtual" ones. We may also discover that entire categories may prove missing. Once we see items placed in a "road repair" category, we may realize that "road construction" is completely missing, although that category might have a huge impact on the quality of our driving experience. When looking for connections and causality, we may further realize that there are elements missing from our original Divergent exercise. Any of these will cause us to cycle back to the Diverge step and further diversify our ideas or information before moving forward.

Learning to see what is not there, but should be, is a very powerful innovation skill. The Organize step can be a significant aid in that skill development. Do not lose that opportunity by skipping this very important step in the process. The entire approach to the Organize step is detailed in Chapter 10.

CONVERGE

Convergent thinking is narrowing from many to the "best" or "most impactful." Of course, we will need criteria for making that selection.

Again, making the criteria conscious makes it more powerful. When we make selections "intuitively" we are not necessarily aware of our selection criteria. This makes it difficult, to say the least, to communicate to others why we believe this particular choice is the "best." It is difficult to get people on board with a decision that we cannot explain. The conspiracy theorists will always believe that we had a hidden agenda when that occurs.

Let's return to our group of friends deciding on where to go to dinner tonight. Several restaurants are suggested. Maybe some are selected because they have excellent food. Some excellent service. Others excellent vistas. Maybe some are inexpensive, while other suggestions offer a quick dining experience. How can this group possibly pick the "best" restaurant to go to that night without having a common criterion in mind? Well they cannot; each participant actually DOES have a criterion in mind, it is simply not articulated. The single person in the group is pushing for restaurant A because the waitstaff there are cute. The couple, who recently had a child, are pushing for restaurant B because the service there is quick and they can get back home to their newborn in short order. Another member of the group is pushing for restaurant C because they love the view of the city from there. Of course, none of the group members actually state their criteria, they simply push for their solution as the "best." Convergence requires that the criteria for "best" is first agreed upon. Without a set criterion, there will be no authentic convergence. Once the criteria for "best" or "most impactful" are out on the table, they can be debated and discussed. "Best" may have more than one criterion, but those criteria need to be clear to all involved.

Once the selection criteria are clear and agreed upon, the organized list of alternatives can be measured against it. This will likely involve some research. Once the research has been done, then the group can make rational decisions to narrow the organized list to one. One. Not five or ten. Few individuals or organizations have the resources to pursue multiple options simultaneously. In our personal lives, we do not even think about doing it. If we are trying to buy a family car, we do not narrow the list down to three potential automobiles and then buy all three! We narrow the list to one. However, when we are in organizations, we somehow feel we can pursue multiple paths simultaneously. It does not work. Instead organizations need to learn to rapidly evaluate options and then quickly pivot when those choices prove unsatisfactory.

Applying convergent-thinking techniques to Problem Identification is slightly different from how we would use it in Solution Formulation. Those detailed differences are outlined in Chapter 11. Whether the technique is applied to the solution or problem space, it is still convergent thinking and retains the same purpose to narrow our organized list of options to one.

COMMON MISTAKES

Each DOC Process chapter will contain a review of common mistakes in its use. The biggest mistake by far is not employing all the three steps of the DOC Process. Time after time, groups go from brainstorming directly to the selection of the best. No organization of the brainstormed ideas. No analysis to see what could be missing. No criteria from which to judge the best – and no, those criteria are not self-evident to everyone in the group. What typically occurs is a random selection and implementation of an idea that was generated in seconds. It is no wonder that most "innovations" fail. We are only doing a fraction of the work necessary.

SUMMARY

Part II of this book details the DOC Process. The three steps of this process, for which the DOC acronym stands, are Diverge, Organize, and Converge. The three steps allow us to broaden before narrowing our selection, a foundational tenet of the innovation design methodology. The DOC Process, like The Innovation Pyramid methodology itself, combines reductionism and holism, differentiation and integration; deeply engaging both sides or our brain. The DOC Process is applicable to Problem Identification as well as Solution Formulation, although most people's experience with some of the process steps is limited to generating creative new solution ideas. Chapters 9–11 will detail each of the steps, with particular emphasis on their less familiar application to Problem Identification.

9   Diverge

The first step in the DOC Process is Diverge. We will use a variety of divergent-thinking techniques to expand upon our initial concept. As with every step of the DOC Process, Diverge applies to both Problem Identification and Solution Formulation. There are subtle differences between how the technique is applied to the problem space versus the solution space. Creativity techniques often prompt us to diversify solution concepts to specific issues by creating high-level challenge statements like "How to...." or "How might we..." or "In what ways might...." or "What might be all the ways we can..." resolve the issue at hand. (See Appendix B for an extended list of divergent-thinking prompts.) The underlying assumption is that we have already properly diagnosed the situation. That is very often not the case. Rarely do we use the Diverge technique to actually identify the underlying problem which these solutions supposedly fix. But we need to do just that.

Diverging seems counterintuitive to some, particularly when we may feel that we already know what the problem is or we already have a great idea for a solution. It just seems crazy not to immediately focus on our great idea, right? Wrong. Think of every idea as an insight. That idea represents a different way of looking at the problem and/or the solution. That insight can be used to generate even better ideas. Sometimes, many times actually, we are so focused on looking in a specific direction that we do not even consider that the item we are seeking may be right behind us. How many times have we been looking for something that is misplaced, say our keys, which we just "know" it is somewhere on our messy desk, but we just cannot find it. That is because the keys are not on the desk, but on the file cabinet right behind us! Divergent thinking gives us a chance to look around, to see what is behind us, above us, below us, so-to-speak. The things we believe to be true are not necessarily so. We need to manage our own biases. Divergent thinking is one way to do that. Involving others in the process is another. It allows us to expand our thinking beyond what we "think we know" is true. It is surprising what can be discovered! The "real" problem or the "best" solution may not be staring us in the face, it may be staring directly at our backs!

Exception

There is, however, a special case in the innovation process where we can skip the initial Diverge step. Typically, the innovation process starts with a situation. That original situation may, in some cases, present itself as a great number of symptoms. What we initially need to do is to uncover the issue that is manifesting itself as all these symptoms. In this case, we already have a divergent set of information, what needs to be done first is to organize this information. In these special cases, we will start at the Organize step of the DOC Process (see Chapter 10 for details of this step). These are the times when we are faced with a plethora of data, information, and/or observations. In these circumstances, the initial "divergent thinking" has already been done. We already have a divergent set of information. Think of this situation as a patient and our organization as the physician. First, we have to diagnose the situation. What could be going on here? Sometimes we will have enough information, the patient presents enough symptoms, for us to go through a significant portion of the diagnostic process (Organize and Converge steps). Other times we may have to "run some tests" to broaden or deepen the information initially presented. Before running additional tests (additional Diverging), we will first want to organize the information we already have. In cases like this, we will need to perform the Organize step first. Given it is common to need to Diverge more after the Organize step, the "further testing" is simply a part of that postorganize divergent thinking that naturally takes place. This is the nature of a nonlinear system. Typically, we start at step 1, Diverge in this case, then to step 2, etc. But sometimes we will need to start at step 2, Organize in this case, then return to step 1, then step 2 again before preceding to step 3 (the Converge step of the DOC Process).

Consider Alternate Possibilities

There are lots of divergent-thinking tools available. The creativity movement focuses on these tools. They are meant to shift our perspective or reframe the problem, by seeing the issue from another's point-of-view or by changing our vantage point of the problem (Dorst, 2015). One approach to divergent thinking is the "brainstorming" technique popularized by de Bono (1967). All of these divergent-thinking techniques are meant to unlock us from our very rational, linear-thinking mindset. They give us a chance to let our minds be free and toss our "crazy" ideas without being negatively judged. What these techniques all have in common is that they get us "out of the box," to think about a problem differently. They help us get "unstuck," which is good as we often get in our own ways.

Divergent thinking, or reframing, comes from two basic principles: changing our perspective and/or our point-of-view. While the two are often used to mean the same thing, in this book, a point-of-view is associated to a person (or group of people). Shifting our point-of-view requires seeing the problem through another's eyes. That, in turn, requires empathy. How would our parents think about this? Our boss? Our children? The perpetrator? The victim? The newspaper reporter?

A shift in perspective, on the other hand, is defined herein as changing the mental or physical vantage point from which the observation is made. A mental shift represents a change in attitude. That obstacle in our path shifts from being a "problem" to an "opportunity for us to grow." A change in physical vantage point may mean a change of scale – zoom out to a broad purview, which reveals the "big picture" but masks the details. Zooming in narrows our purview, but it reveals much more details. Think of zooming in/out perspective changing as using Google Earth. Zoom way out to see the entire earth, or zoom very far in to see a specific street corner. As we zoom out, we broaden our purview, but lose detail. As we zoom in, more details are revealed, but we lose the bigger context. When zoomed way in we will be able to locate the veterinary clinic at the corner of Mack Drive and Rigsby Avenue, but lose track of the fact that we are in China Grove, let alone even care that it is part of the Lone Star State of Texas (Johnston, 1973). Another potential perspective change is to look at something from the inside, outside, right-side up, or upside down. This is a common car-buying or house-buying ritual. We inspect it from the outside, the inside, although we may decide not to crawl underneath it or hover above it! Points-of-view changes can be combined with perspective changes, geometrically expanding the number of ways of observing something.

The divergent-thinking techniques, as previously discussed, are most often applied to developing creative solution. What would I do if ... I were as smart as Bill Gates ... had unlimited resources ... had a magic wand ... were in charge of the world ... was the owner of the business ... was just beamed here from another planet and had no history of what was previously done, etc. Any technique that helps us to see the situation differently broadens our perspective. Appendix B discusses a number of divergent-thinking prompts.

The trap here is that we are already thinking in terms of "what we would do." Whenever we are thinking about "do" (or some equivalent verb), we are thinking of actions. That fact should trip a red flag in our minds that will tell us that we are thinking about a solution and not the problem. Thinking in terms of solutions feels "right" to us, as we humans are biased to think in terms of actions ("fight or flight"). Today's problems are more complex and more subtle. They require deeper analysis. That requires us to step through the mirror that only shows us the problem as a weak reflection of our proposed solution. We need to thoroughly explore the problem, to uncover the root-of-the-root of the real, underlying problem. Whenever we find ourselves thinking in solutions, we need to ask, "What problem does that solution address?" Followed by, "Why am I assuming that is the central problem?" Could it be a symptom or element of a larger or systemic issue? Given that the divergent-thinking techniques are subtly different when applying them to the problem space versus the solution space, the two will be discussed separately.

DIVERGENT PROBLEM IDENTIFICATION APPROACHES

The approach for applying divergent thinking to identify problems is less familiar to us than the approach used in diversifying solution ideas. It is also slightly different. Our typical starting point for identifying the real underlying issue is a description of the original situation, or more often, the initially identified issue with which we are struggling. We may already think that we know the underlying cause of the issue that is driving our present circumstance, so our instinct is to narrow from our initial starting point to something more specific. Our instinct is exactly backward. What we first need to do is broaden our perspective, not narrow it. We can diversify our initial concept by shifting points-of-view (POVs) and/or perspective. Why is this an issue from our POV? Our customers? Our supplier? We can also broaden our perspective by zooming out by asking, "Is this issue a component or factor of a larger problem? If so, what is that problem?" Such perspective shifts are illustrated in Figure 9.1. Zooming in on a broadly defined problem is the opposite, as Figure 9.1 also illustrates, as it breaks the larger issue down into its contributing factors.

We want to start with broadly defined problems to ensure we are not missing the disease by focusing on its symptoms. We can continue to zoom out by repeating our questioning technique to the answers of the previous questions. Q1. Why is employee absenteeism a problem? A1. It is part of a larger productivity problem. Q2. Why is productivity an issue? A2. It is one way that we contain costs. Q3. Why are costs an issue? ... The question is, when do we stop? We want a broadly defined problem, but not one that extends beyond the scope of the organization. The ideal, General Problem, is one

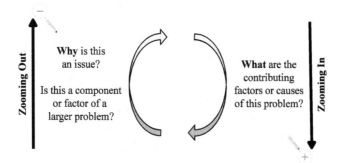

FIGURE 9.1 Zooming in/out within the problem space.

that is broad, but one that the organization is able and willing to address. Going beyond that point identifies an intractable problem from the perspective of the organization. We want to create impactful solutions. That starts with identifying broadly defined problems we can address.

Once zoomed out to the General Problem level, we are in a good position to diversify our notions of the issue. From this broader perspective, we will be zooming back in, diversifying as we do so. We are uncovering the root system of the General Problem, layer by layer, by zooming in, as illustrated on the right-hand side of Figure 9.1. The General Problem will have many contributing factors associated with it which will be revealed by asking "What are the contributing factors or causes to this problem?" We can continue to zoom in by repeating the questions to the previous question's answers. The General Problem's factors will have subfactors; those subfactors may have causes, etc., as illustrated in Figure 9.2.

We will not uncover the entire root system of the General Problem. We will be making choices along the way. We will be choosing the "best" or "most impactful" factor of those that were uncovered, and proceeding from there. We will subsequently choose the "best" or "most impactful" of the subfactors of the factor we selected, and so on, until we have uncovered a root cause problem we will be resolving. Figure 9.2 is the visual output that resulted from the application of a series of DOC Process applications (see Figure 9.3).

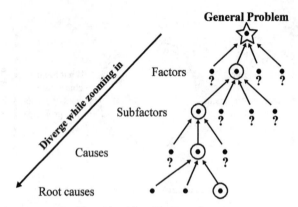

FIGURE 9.2 Problem Identification Root System.

The Diverge step is not a "brainstorming" activity, but the result of research; research that initially uncovers the primary factors of the General Problem. That research continues, layer by layer, as we dig down deeper into the root system of the General Problem. Although we may not recognize it as such, uncovering of the subfactors of the factor we selected is simply another Diverge step. And on and on it goes as we slowly uncover the root system. It is impossible to know from the start, how many "layers" we will need to dig down to before we reach the root cause level; how many applications of the DOC Process will be required. We will know we have reached that level when we have identified a problem which our organization is able and willing to address and we can articulate a clear and unique adopter group for whom the innovation resolves this problem (see Chapter 3 for details).

Certainly, the selection criteria for the Converge step of each of these DOC Process applications will need to be clearly defined. The Converge step of the DOC Process, as it relates to Problem Identification, will be discussed in detail in Chapter 11.

Yes, it is possible that the principal factor or subfactor that we select ends up being the exact initially identified issue; the issue we had described before we zoomed out to the General Problem in the first place. Although this sometimes occurs, contrary to how we

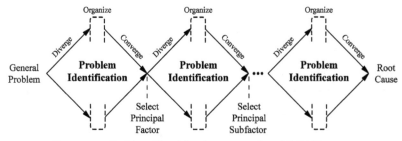

FIGURE 9.3 Problem Identification as a series of DOC Processes.

may feel, we have not wasted our time in those cases, but used that zooming-out, zooming-in mechanism to confirm that we had properly identified the correct starting issue. We now have supporting evidence and rationale for choosing that problem versus the intuitive sense we used to select it in the first place. We moved that problem selection from the "think we know" column to the "know we know" column. That's a valuable transition that was certainly worth our time.

Problem Identification, while rooted in reductionism, has several important additional characteristics. The first is that before narrowing the scope of the problem we must first zoom out. If we do not initially take this step, we are narrowing from our initial perception of the problem, which may be wrong. We will ultimately find a root cause of our initial issue. However, if we were wrong about the importance of the issue in the first place, our potential innovation will have no impact as it will not have addressed the substantive issue. Zooming out ensures that we are broadening the landscape of potential problems to ensure we are not overlooking any key components. We do not want to spend all day inventing ways to find our keys on our desk when they are, in fact, located on the file cabinet behind us.

The second additional characteristic of Problem Identification is that, once we have zoomed out, we will not be simply breaking the situation down into constituent parts and then randomly pick one as "the problem." No, we will be doing more, much more. Breaking things down into parts is a divergent-thinking step, only the divergent-thinking step of the DOC Process. The entire DOC Process needs to be applied at each level as we zoom in. The identified components need to be reorganized before applying convergent thinking. The Organize step of the DOC Process requires holistic, integrative thinking. We are certainly reducing the problem into components via divergent thinking, but we are then re-assembling those components in new ways. This re-assembly is the essence of innovation.

One point that needs to be made as we traverse from the original situation to the General Problem from which we narrow down to the root cause issue is that we are currently focused only on Problem Identification. We do not want to divert our attention, at least not yet, to Solution Formulation. However, we are clearly making choices as we go through the series of Problem Identification layers using the DOC Process. How do we make those choices if we are not considering solutions along the way? Level 1 of The Innovation Pyramid, stage 1 of the design process (Chapter 3), specifies that the problem must be one that the organization is able and willing to resolve. These conditions must therefore be part of the selection criteria for every Converge step applied to Problem Identification. There will be other criteria as well, but these two – that the innovator is willing and able to pursue a solution to the identified problem – must be part of the criteria set. For example, if we are part of a financial advising firm, and one of the potential causes to a situation we are investigating requires plant manufacturing expertise, then this cause is outside what the firm is willing or capable of addressing. As a result, when we converge on which potential cause our organization will address, this one must be eliminated. Our firm is simply not capable of addressing that issue.

While we have stayed focused on Problem Identification and diligently worked layer by layer to identify and select a root cause which we are capable and willing to address, we are not quite finished. Finding the root cause, although extremely important, is not the end of the Problem Identification process. The end objective is to uncover the unmet or under-met needs, wants, and/or desires of our Target Adopter. That Target Adopter is the one for whom we will be developing our specific innovation. That brings us to the final additional twist we are making to a standard reductionism approach to Problem Identification – the transformation of the identified root cause into needs/wants/desires of a Target Adopter.

Every problem is associated with someone (or a group of people) means that when we have identified the root cause of the initial situation, that cause will be associated with a specific group of persons. That group of persons is the Principal Adopter group. That Principal Adopter is significantly affected by the identified root cause. We, however, have one more step to take before reaching our objective of understanding the unmet or under-met needs, wants, and/ or desires of our Target Adopter. That Target Adopter will be a subset of the Principal Adopters. We therefore need one more DOC Process application to transition from the root cause of our issue to the needs, wants, and desires of our Target Adopter.

In this final DOC Process application, the perspective switches from the "cause" to the "person" impacted by that cause. That switch from the element of an inanimate "problem" to the POV of a "person" affected by that problem element is a critical one. Once that switch is made, primary research is conducted on the Principal Adopters, those dealing with or impacted by the identified cause, to uncover their needs, wants, and/or desires. Interviewing for Insight (IFI; discussed in detail in Appendix A) will be a very useful technique to apply here. We will not be solely interviewing the Principal Adopters of our potential innovation, but will expand those interviews 360-degrees around them. We seek multiple POVs: the Principal Adopter's POV, their immediate supervisor's POV, their subordinate's POV, their customer's POV, whatever is appropriate to the situation. What are the Principal Adopters doing now to accommodate that dilemma/ obstacle/challenge/difficulty? What are the shortcomings of that accommodation approach? We will not be able to satisfy all the unmet needs/wants/desires of the Principal Adopter group that we discover.

This Principal Adopter group is still too diverse. Our innovation will be targeting a subset of this group.

This open-ended interviewing process will uncover a wide array of wants, needs, and/or desires of the Principal Adopters. These interviews are the Divergent step in a DOC Process whose ultimate aim is to identify the specific adopter group for whom we will be creating our innovation, the Target Adopter. A profusion of needs, wants, and/or desires will be uncovered. That information will need to be organized. During this organization step, the categorized subsets of needs/wants/desires will be crafted into several personas (see Appendix A for details). During the Converge step, the list of personas will be narrowed down to one, our Target Adopter persona. Once the Problem Identification Root System is uncovered and utilized to identify a root cause and associated Principal Adopter group (Figure 9.2), the final stage is to complete this final transition step, as illustrated in Figure 9.4.

Problem Identification is a multistep challenge that utilizes many different divergent-thinking tools and techniques. Although these divergent tools utilized for Problem Identification are quite different from the "brainstorming" technique we are used to using when applying the DOC Process to Solution Formulation, they are simply alternate ways to employ the DOC Process. We began with an original situation or originally identified issue. We then zoomed out on this issue to identify a General Problem. Through a series of DOC Process applications (Figure 9.3), we drove those down to a root

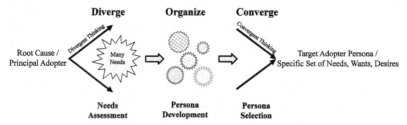

FIGURE 9.4 DOC Process application to Target Adopter persona creation and selection.

cause that we were willing and able to address. That root cause was associated with a Principal Adopter. Performing 360-degree open-ended interviews (IFIs, see Appendix A) around the Principal Adopter generated a plethora needs wants and/or desires (Figure 9.4). The diversified needs/wants/desires were transformed into adopter personas in the Organize step, from which one, our Target Adopter, is selected. That Target Adopter will have a specific set of unmet or under-met needs, wants, and desires that characterizes their condition. Details of the transformation illustrated in Figure 9.4 are provided in Appendix A.

DIVERGENT SOLUTION FORMULATION APPROACHES

The divergent-thinking tools and techniques utilized for Problem Identification ranged from primary to secondary research. They spanned the gamut from literature searches, to primary research including IFI (see Appendix A for details). The techniques utilized changed as we traversed the scope of the problem from the original situation to the needs, wants, and/or desires of a Target Adopter persona. While the application of divergent thinking is more familiar to Solution Formulation, it will still take more than a brainstorming session to design an innovative solution.

Once our Target Adopter group, complete with definitive unmet and under-met needs, wants, and/or desires, is identified, we are ready to begin formulating solutions. The next step in Solution Formulation, Level 2 of The Innovation Pyramid (Chapter 4), is to diversify the approaches to developing a solution that will benefit this Target Adopter. Those approaches must be ones which the organization is willing and able to pursue. That is a fairly straightforward process, but it is worth detailing to make sure we do not get locked into "tried and true" approaches. At this stage, we are seeking approaches, not solutions. When specific solution concepts come up in the brainstorming session (they will), group them in the organizational step by solution type. The classifications of the different groups of specific solution ideas are the "approaches" we are seeking. As with all applications of the organization step, once we start organizing the information, it becomes much easier to see what is missing. When we do find something missing, cycle back to the Diverge step.

Next, we will zoom in on our approach and drill down to a very specifically designed solution. It must be detailed enough to implement. It also must contain sufficient detail of the specific features or attributes of the proposed solution that we can articulate the solution's value proposition by mapping those solution features to the needs/wants/desires of the Target Adopter.

When diversifying new ideas, groups often get fixated on the current solution to the problem. People are dealing with the issue in some way now. The best current solution, from the adopter's POV, is their Best Alternative to a New Option (BATNO). While it is perfectly fine to start there, it becomes an issue if we get stuck at the "feature" level of Figure 9.5.

By solely exploring the feature level of a current solution, we are essentially working on a "me too" product or service. A "me too" product or service is something that is currently available, although we will try to spice it up by tweaking the features. A smartphone with a slightly better camera is still a smartphone. The new feature has some advantages, but represents an incremental improvement versus a significant change. That advantage of a "me too" solution

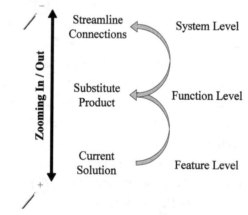

FIGURE 9.5 Divergent Solution Formulation techniques.

could be increased convenience, such as when Netflix first introduced DVD delivery to customers by mail. It was still the same product that Blockbuster offered, a rented DVD, but the customer did not ever have to leave their house to obtain it. The DVDs could be ordered online, delivered through the mail, and returned through the mail. The process offered a convenience to the customer over driving to a Blockbuster store to obtain and return the DVD. Another advantage a "me too" product might be an inherent cost advantage: lower capital requirements, lower raw material costs, and/or some economy of scale. We cannot compete solely on price unless we are differentiated on cost.

Zooming out one layer up from the current BATNO is the function level of Figure 9.5. At this level, we are not creating a "me too" offering, but a substitute. A substitute is a potential innovation that performs the same function as the current BATNO does in a different way. Streaming videos from Netflix provides the same function as receiving DVDs by mail. The streaming service, however, has many inherent advantages (quicker, more portable, etc.). Substitute products are often based on new/emerging technology. The concept simply was not previously technologically feasible. But it is not the technology that adopters want; adopters desire the function that the technology enables. Substitute products can often better at addressing an emerging or previously underserved market versus the incumbent product. Cell phones are a much more convenient way for a mobile society to stay connected than landlines and pay phones, for example.

One more zoomed-out layer up from the function level is the system level, as shown in Figure 9.5. Applying divergent thinking to this level forces us to think of the entire system from start to finish. It has us assessing all the linkages in a system and asking ourselves, can these linkages be enhanced or even eliminated? If so, how? Consider the "system" of selling used stuff via a traditional garage or yard sale. All the "treasures" are gathered up, priced, placed on a table in the garage or the end of the driveway, and then we wait for someone to come by and see if they are interested in purchasing an item. We may have even gone one step further by putting information about the sale in the newspaper or on a bulletin board at our workplace. Customer acquisition is limited to our region. Now consider eBay. Did eBay "invent" selling used goods to others? Absolutely not. But what it did was consider the entire system and realize that the weak link in the system was connecting the buyer and seller. After eBay, the geographic reach of miscellaneous goods sellers dramatically increased – eventually becoming international. Beyond expanding their reach, eBay drastically reduces the cost of customer acquisition for sellers as well as creating value for buyers by providing a breadth and convenience of their shopping experience. eBay's impactful innovation took system-level thinking. Most phone apps simplify connections and/or transactions. Whether we are seeking a ride somewhere (Uber, Lyft) or wanting to pay the babysitter without using cash (Venmo), these apps make it easier by operating on a system level. We will never create these solutions if we brainstorm solely on the BATNO's feature level.

DIVERGE EXAMPLE

This example will begin in this chapter, continue in Chapter 10 (Organize) and conclude in Chapter 11 (Converge) in order to illustrate how all three steps of the DOC Process work together. Let us say that we are charged with putting on a day-long company event highlighting the creativity of the firm's employees. The constraint given to us as the event organizing committee is that this event will take place during a normal work day. The aim is to maximize the number of employees who participate in the event, yet have an event that is not so disruptive as to prevent the employees from completing their regular work assignments on the event day.

The organizing committee brainstorms ideas as to what activities could take place throughout the day. The seemly contradictory constraints of desiring everyone's participation, but not preventing anyone from getting their work done during the day, have the committee a bit flummoxed. The result is that the brainstormed list is rather meager, containing only the eight items as follows:

- Welcome by organizers
- Ice breaker
- Create a story (each person contributes a sentence)
- Put up a "What is *your* art?" board
- Invade offices with "pink slips"
- Jam Bands
- Treasure Hunt
- Puzzle / "Mosaic" of sticky notes

Now what? Do we simply pick things to do from the list? Do we do them ALL? Do we "vote" on which ones we like the best? No, no, and no. This is the point where most divergent-thinking processes break down. The tendency is to begin creating the event based on this list, or to start ordering the list in a certain "agenda" order. That is essentially jumping to Level 3 of The Innovation Pyramid – Plan. We are not ready to start executing this event. We have not even yet begun to design it! What we *do* need to do next is organize the list. This example will continue in Chapter 10, "Organize."

COMMON MISTAKES

Divergent thinking is more than a high-energy group brainstorming session. Way more. It requires multiple perspectives and multiple POVs. The biggest mistake groups make is to not perform divergent thinking on Problem Identification. Maybe they will do an initial factor analysis and generate a vague problem description, but will almost never drive it all the way down to a Target Adopter persona with specific unmet or under-met needs, wants, and/or desires.

For Solution Formulation, the main issue is staying at the feature level of the current best solution option. Breakthrough innovations come from zooming out to the function and system levels.

SUMMARY

Diverge is the first of three essential steps in completing the nonlinear DOC Process. It is the step that is typically performed first, unless we are coming upon a situation that is already awash in symptoms and we first need to Organize that information (second step of the DOC Process) before proceeding.

Like all DOC Process steps, divergent thinking applies to both the problem and solution spaces. It simply requires different techniques when seeking to identify a root cause problem versus attempting to come up with a new impactful problem-solving approach. For Problem Identification, we will be diverging as we zoom in from the General Problem. A series of DOC Process applications are required to transition from the General Problem to identifying a root cause of it. Once the root cause is uncovered, a shift is made from the problem element to the POV of the persons most impacted by it – the Principal Adopters. The IFI technique is leveraged to identify unmet or under-met needs/wants/desires for those Principal Adopters. Those needs are organized via the development of personas. Ultimately, a Target Adopter persona, with clearly identified unmet or under-met needs, wants, and/or desires, is selected from the organized set of personas. That specific target will be the ones for whom we develop the innovation.

10 Organize

The second step in the Diverge-Organize-Converge (DOC) Process is Organize. The Organize step is the transition step between the divergent and the convergent processes. The Organize step has characteristics of both the divergent and convergent steps, as was discussed in Chapter 8. The Organize step, however, is much more than solely a transition step. This is the step where the information generated in the Diverge step is synthesized. This step requires holistic and integrative thinking. It is a crucial step in refining either the problem or a solution. This step is also key to creating personas from the abundance of needs, wants, and desires that were uncovered through the Interview for Insight technique. This step keeps us from getting overwhelmed by the details, particularly early in the design process. Organizing the detailed discoveries of the Diverge step allows us to zoom out a bit and stay focused on a bigger picture. Toward the end of this chapter, the example begun in the previous chapter will be continued.

In the divergent step we were reserving judgment. In brainstorming, in particular, the objective is not to discuss ideas as they arise, but just to get them out. Brainstorming is an ideation exercise. The less conversation the better. Organize is the opposite. We will need a great deal of discussion with our team to successfully accomplish this step (Figure 10.1). It will also take research – both primary and secondary.

THREE COMPONENTS OF THE ORGANIZE STEP

The Organize step has three components. These components are hierarchal as they have a distinct order of application. The three components in the order of application are: Categorize, Connect, and Cause. Applying each of these process components to the

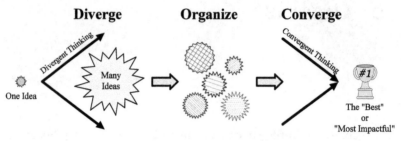

FIGURE 10.1 DOC Process overview.

diverged information further refines that information. It also puts the information in a state where the next step, Converge, is more readily achieved.

Categorize

The starting point of the Organize step is to categorize the information generated in the Diverge step. Start by grouping related concepts together. In solution brainstorming exercises, multiple ideas are often created that are similar. Separately they are idea-fragments, but together they may make one great idea. Putting these similar idea-fragments together in a category is the first step in recognizing that fact. Alternatively, if a piece of information may be placed in one or more categories, then do that. If sticky-notes were used for the Diverge exercise, make duplicate sticky-notes for the information that should be in multiple categories. There will always be "odd" items that just do not quite seem to belong with the others. These odd ideas often generate the most insight, so do not throw them out. Instead, create a "miscellaneous" category and put them there.

When we first look at a brainstormed list of concepts, it is easy to get overwhelmed. The list may be expansive – some doable, some crazy, and some that are, well, just hard to judge. The first thing we need to do now is organize this list. When initially organizing information, it is often simpler to start by first sorting the information into broad categories or buckets. Once this first separation is made, it is easier to see how these large categories can then be further subdivided into smaller categories. Trying to find a dozen independent categories from a random list of concepts in a single step is a very difficult task. Take it a step at a time.

The next thing to do is to name the created categories. Naming the categories is important for two reasons. First, it puts an overarching description on the group. Secondly, it helps us see if something is missing. Items within a category may be identified as missing or entire categories may be missing. If we are planning activities for children and created a category of activities named "outdoor activities," it is easier to see that the inverse group, "indoor activities," is completely missing. If items or groups of items are missing, return to the Diverge step to generate more concepts.

Always look for opposites or mirror images when assessing groups, outdoor/indoor, synchronous/asynchronous, individual/team, etc. Including opposites will ensure the Diverge session is sufficiently broad. There is opportunity in thinking juxtaposed to the norm. When the entire golf industry was focused on making golf balls fly farther, one innovative firm thought about making them fly less far. Crazy? Not in an area where land is at a premium. If a golf ball that flies half the distance of a normal ball can be produced, then a golf course that provides golfers with equivalent shot-making challenges on half the required landmass of a regular golf course can be developed. Dyson gave us another example of taking the opposite approach. When an entire industry was wrestling with how to prevent vacuum bags from clogging up, Dyson thought about eliminating them entirely. As crazy as thinking in "opposites" can seem when first proposed, there is often an innovation opportunity in doing so.

Categorizing is also the first phase of persona creation. In the second design stage (Level 2, Chapter 4), preforming 360-degree Interviewing for Insight (IFI; detailed in Appendix A) around the identified Principal Adopter will uncover many specific needs, wants, or desires. Once this divergent discovery process is completed, we will need to search for patterns in the gathered information; classify those diverse set of needs/wants/desires into related groups. Once this categorization phase is completed, the connect phase of the Organize step, described next, is applied to transform combinations of those categories into personas. While the categorize component requires pattern recognition, the connect phase is all about identifying relationships.

Connect

After the Organize step is complete, we will be moving on to the Converge step of the DOC Process. That convergence will require that we set selection priorities. The connect phase of the Organize step is our first movement toward that objective. During the connect phase, we are seeking to understand if there are any connections between the categories or among the information within a category. Does one item influence the other? Are there natural sequences? Is there an order that items need to be or should be performed? We are, after all, seeking to optimize our impact. Regardless of whether we are applying this technique to the problem space or the solution space, understanding how things connect and flow will help us prioritize our efforts and maximize our impact.

For example, we are having issues with our customer service. The customer service team's categories of needs turn out to be lack of training, lack of motivation, overextended personnel, etc. If we can identify, for example, that "lack of training" influences the other two categories, then focusing on resolving that one issue will allow us to impact all three categories. Understanding these relationships also makes our Converge step of the DOC Process much more straightforward. Similarly, the Pareto Principle ("Understanding Pareto," n.d.), also known as the 80/20 rule, suggests that 20 percent of the input creates 80 percent of the result. If we can identify the categories of those 20 percent, we will be able to significantly increase our impact.

Creating personas from organized categories of uncovered needs, wants, and desires is another use of the connect technique. Once the divergent information obtained from the IFIs is classified, we need to combine categories into personas. In persona development, we are not seeking to identify categories that connect to each other, but rather we seek to identify a combination that is associated with – and therefore defines – a persona. Automobile shoppers, for example, make purchasing decisions based on different automobile characteristics which satisfy different needs/wants/desires. Yes, they all need their car to transport them from point A to point B; that is the primary need of an automobile. It is the secondary needs that differentiate most products and innovations. "Soccer-mom Mary" and "Player Paul" would be two personas that are looking to satisfy very different needs from an automobile. The Mary persona's needs would be an aggregation of reliability, minimal per trip operating cost, minimal insurance cost, maximum people capacity, and protection from accidents. The Paul persona's needs would be more along the lines of status enhancement and performance.

The objective is to create a persona that represents a specific adopter segment. This is accomplished by identifying unique or contrasting combinations of needs categories that define a persona. Clearly, we do not want our persona to be "everyone," and we also do not want it to be so narrowly defined that it basically describes just one person. It is a challenging balance to maintain, but like other skills, this one too will improve with practice. Appendix A covers persona development in more detail.

Cause

If we are working on finding the true, underlying problem, then we need to dig deep. We need to find the root of the weed we are trying to exterminate. Chopping off the weed's flower will only temporarily solve the problem. The issue will return. If, however, we can dig deep and find the root of the root, then we will eliminate a number of issues that have been manifesting from this sole cause.

During the Diverge step, we changed perspective by zooming out and asking "why is this a problem?" and by zooming in and asking "what is causing this problem?" Now that we have our ideas categorized and connected, we need to dig deep to see if we can uncover causes of the categories. To dig deeper ask "what could be causing this category?" This analysis needs to be performed on each category. Finding causal elements that manifest themselves as our identified categories is the "holy grail." It is also difficult to accomplish. If we sufficiently zoomed out, then appropriately diverged as we zoomed back in, then the root categories may already have been identified during the connect phase. Still, because of the huge impact uncovering such fundamental causal categories will have, it is worth spending extra time at the cause phase to try to dig one layer deeper than what we currently have uncovered.

Uncovering causal drivers is not a twenty-minute group exercise. It takes some reflection and very likely some research. If working with a large group, consider breaking that group into small subgroups and have these subgroups spend a few days contemplating and discussing potential underlying causes. Once this has occurred, the entire group can get back together and each of the individual subgroups can report back to the whole. Energized with the findings of the subgroups, the whole group may be able to add additional insights.

Do not be discouraged if a causal element or category is not identified at this stage. The better the Problem Identification Root System (Figure 9.2) we created as we zoomed in/diverged from the General Problem, the less likely we will find a previously unidentified causal category at this stage. That said, the impact of such a discovery is so significant on the situation we are addressing that it is always worth spending the time attempting to make such a discovery. The pressure of wanting to move on to the "solution" and the "implementation plan" combined with the unlikelihood of discovering a yet-to-be-uncovered causal element or category results in many groups skipping this step entirely. Resist that temptation! The impact of an insight at this point is SO significant that it is worth spending the time searching, even if the odds of discovery are low.

LEVEL THE PLAYING FIELD

It matters not if we are working in Problem Identification or Solution Formulation, it would be a waste time and energy to detail all the identified concepts to an executable state; we are simply not at that point yet. Most of the concepts at this stage will eventually be discarded. We want to make sure, however, that we understand the concept in enough detail to be able to give it a fair evaluation in the Converge step which will follow this Organize step. To do this, we want to create a "level playing field" for all the ideas. The ones that we held near-and-dear before this process ever started will be clear in our mind. The point of the Diverge step was to broaden our thinking, to get ourselves out of the box of our current perspective. We do not simply want to toss all that diversity away just because a new concept is less complete than the one we thought was "right" from the beginning.

Creating a level playing field for ideas means that we will need to combine and/or refine the idea fragments that were produced during the rapid-fire divergent-thinking activity. Some of the idea fragments will combine into more complete ideas. Some will be similar to others in the category and be dropped altogether. Create enough detail in the description of all the concepts to make sure they can compete equally with our original thoughts at the Converge step. This may take some time and research to accomplish. It is worth that time. We will be applying selection criteria to the concepts during the Converge stage, so we want to be able to evaluate all the ideas equally against those criteria.

For example, if we know that we will be choosing the "best" runner, then in order to put all the runners on a level playing field we will want to know our criteria for "best." There are lots of ways to describe runners: how tall they are, how muscular, what sex they are, where in the world they were born, what color of track suit they prefer to wear. All these are legitimate details to describe the runners. If, however, our criteriacriterion for determining the best is based on their 100-meter dash times, then that is the descriptor that every runner must have. All other descriptors are superfluous at this point. That is the detail that puts all the runners on an evaluative level playing field.

The point is that we do not need full descriptors of every diverged concept. Generating those details would be a colossal waste of time as most will be discarded. We do, however, need to level the playing field so that each can be judged fairly against the other.

ORGANIZE EXAMPLE

Let us now return to the example of our company's "creativity day" that we started in Chapter 9. When organizing information, it is simpler to start by first creating a few categories and then later refine and subdivide the categories that contain many items. For example, we can first organize our brainstormed activity list from Chapter 9 into two large categories: individual activities and group activities. Once that information is organized, it is easier to see that when the brainstorming was being done, we were thinking about people physically participating. But the employees still have work to do on the day of the event, so how about events that people can contribute to virtually – synchronously (in real time with others) or asynchronously. We need to go back and expand our thinking on these.

During the brainstorming, the "raid offices with pink slips'" comment did not resonate with anyone. We initially put it into a "miscellaneous" category. But upon reflection, we may recognize it as being part of a "preactivity" teaser. Once we recognized this category, we could come up with other less threatening ways to get people interested in this upcoming event. Of course, once we recognize the category of "preevent" activities, we will notice the opposite is missing – "postevent" follow-up and/or activities.

Having now categorized our initial list of eight concepts, our organized list now appears as follows.

Individual, asynchronous activities
Physical participation

- Create a story (each person contributes a sentence)
- Put up a "What is your art?" board
- Puzzle / "Mosaic" of sticky notes

Virtual participation

- ???

Group (synchronous) activities

Physical participation

- Welcome by organizers
- Ice breaker
- Jam bands
- Treasure hunt

Virtual participation

- ???

Preactivity "teasers"

- Invade offices with "pink slips"
- ???

Postevent follow-up and/or activities??

Categorization has organized and simplified our original divergent-thinking list. It has also highlighted the need for additional divergent thinking. The goal of brainstorming is to put forth unjudged ideas so as to uncover better ones. The Organize step is our first opportunity to thoughtfully shape those unfettered ideas. It starts by categorizing them and proceeds by looking for connections and causes.

Our initial organization of the "creativity day" data makes it clear that we need to return to the divergent-thinking mode to expand on our original list. This time, however, it is more of a directed search as we are looking to flesh out the categories that we recognized as missing and expand the options to the existing categories. This additional divergent-thinking activity is likely not another brainstorming session. Instead it will likely leverage both primary and secondary research. We could do some Internet searching (secondary research) to see what other creativity activities others have tried. We could also interview others in the company (primary research activities) to see what they may be interested in doing on a company-wide "creativity day." Of course, if we are trying to keep the event a surprise, we may not be able to do the primary research or will need to do it in a less direct way – like asking employees questions about how they like to express their creativity.

Once the additional information is gathered, we will return to the Organize step and rework the list again. Did something come up that we did not recognize before? We may go back-and-forth between the Organize and Diverge steps several times before proceeding forward to the Converge step.

COMMON MISTAKES

The most common mistake is skipping the Organize step entirely! Over and over, groups will "brainstorm" and then befuddledly stare at the wall full of sticky-notes. Eventually one or two of the brainstormed ideas will be chosen. That choosing could be random, or by some sort of "voting" mechanism, but the mistake is choosing a raw, unrefined idea by any means. Those ideas need to be shaped and refined. Recall that brainstorming required us to "not think." Now we are going to implement an idea that was created without thought? It makes no sense if we think of it in this way. Unfortunately, most groups simply do not take on that perspective.

The second most common mistake is not categorizing the raw ideas that came out of the Diverge step. Before we detail the brainstormed idea, they should be categorized. Once categorized, it is easier to see similarities between ideas; recognize idea fragments that should be combined. It is also easier to spot a category that we may have overlooked entirely during the original divergent-thinking process. Once the categories are set, we need to see if there is any relationship between categories: Do they follow any particular sequence? Is one an underlying cause of another?

The last common mistake in this step is that ideas are not put on a "level playing field." Given we are more likely to pick the devil we know versus the devil we don't, we need to put all the ideas on an equal footing with respect to the criteria we will be using to evaluate them. Of course, this likely means we will have to jump ahead to the "Converge" step to select the criteria and then return back to the "Organize" step to make sure they are fully described with respect to this measure. That is the nature of a nonlinear process.

SUMMARY

Remember that innovation is a nonlinear process. The DOC Process is also nonlinear. We will need to cycle through the three steps, at times in different order, as we work through the process. Just make sure that each step is eventually completed.

Unlike the divergent-thinking step, which is often completed quickly and requires delaying judgment on the ideated concepts, the Organize step requires thoughtful judgment. It is not possible to thoroughly complete this step in a twenty-minute group session. It often takes additional research, both secondary and primary. The Organize step is more than a transition step between the divergent-thinking and convergent-thinking steps on either side of it. This step has elements of both divergent thinking and convergent thinking, but most importantly, this is the step that synthesizes the information gathered in the Diverge step.

The Organize step has three components – categorize, connect, and cause. The first task of this step is to categorize the information generated via the divergent-thinking activities. Creating and naming categories make it easier to see what is not there but should be. The connect component is the second phase of the Organize step. In this phase, we are looking to connect idea fragments that were previously categorized together. We can also assess whether or not there is any connection between the categories. We are seeking insight on relationships between categories. Is there a logical sequence that needs to occur? These insights will provide us prioritization insights for the Converge stage. The connect phase is an important one in persona development. Here unique combinations of organized categories of needs, wants, and desires are connected to, or more accurately, associate with an archetype adopter (also known as a persona). The final phase of the Organize step is cause. In this phase, we are assessing whether there is a causal relationship between the data categories. Causal relationships are powerful, if determined, as they set a clear selection priority in the Converge step.

Finally, before moving to the Converge step, we want to create a level playing field for the concepts. That means that we want all the concepts described in enough detail to ensure they can compete equally at the Converge step. We do not, however, want to waste a lot of time detailing items that we are about to discard. This will require that we temporarily move forward to the Converge step to articulate the selection criteria. Once that is done, we will move back to the Organize step and ensure all the items are described in equal detail with respect to that criterion. We want to avoid picking the devil we know out of fear of picking the one we do not. Ensure we know them equally, at least with respect to the decision criteria that will be applied in the Converge step.

Lastly, the criterion that we must always apply to every concept is "can WE do something about it?" Does it fall within our circle of influence? If not, can we move it there? Are we able and willing to pursue this option? Discovering things for others to do is not impactful. As former US President Theodore Roosevelt was credited with saying (Roosevelt, n.d.), "Do what you can with what you have, where you are." If we want to see impactful change, we – our group, our organization – must create it.

11 Converge

The third step of the Diverge–Organize–Converge (DOC) Process is Converge. The DOC Process, as we have already seen, is a nonlinear process inside the nonlinear methodology, that is, The Innovation Pyramid. The consequence of this nonlinearity is that it is not a sequential march through the D-O-C steps. Once in the "Organize" step, it is often necessary to return to the Diverge step for additional divergent thinking. Similarly, we will need to jump ahead from the Organize step to the Converge step to define the criteria by which we will be selecting the "best" so as to create a level evaluation field for all concepts that will be judged. Then return back to complete the Organize step to complete our work there. Now that we are in the Converge step, we may find the need to again return to either the Diverge or the Converge step, or both.

Do not be disturbed by this back-and-forth between steps. It is all part of the natural "flow" of the process. Rather than focus on where we are in the process, focus on the desired outcomes for the ultimate completion of each step. They are:

Diverge
    Generate many concepts (problem or solution, depending on the
        space we are working)
Organize
    Categorize. Group similar concepts; identify categories.
    Connect concepts within categories and/or ascertain if there are
        any relationships between categories. Determine if there is any
        desired sequence among the categories.
    Cause. Seek to identify causes of the identified categories. For
        Problem Identification are there underlying causes or factors

of the identified problem categories? Or put another way, can we dig down one more layer of the Problem Identification Root System? (Figure 9.2)

Generate a "complete" description (with respect to the selection criteria) for each concept so that it may be judged on an equal evaluation basis with the others.

Converge

Define criterion or criteria for which "best" will be judged.

Choose the "best" concept with which to move forward.

As was the case with the Organize step before it, the Converge step will take some time and research. We need to move things across the columns of Figure 11.1. There may be things we "believe" we know, but we will have to do the research necessary to move them to the data-supported column of "things we *know* we know." That must be done before convergence is initiated.

The research necessary to successfully perform this step will likely begin as secondary research: searching the Internet or other references for the appropriate information. As we continue to zoom in on the problem and/or a specific solution, conducting primary research will be increasingly necessary. The Interview for Insight technique (discussed in detail in Appendix A) will also be applicable here. Among other research initiatives, this technique will be helpful in judging how the potential innovation adopters view their current Best Alternative to a New Option (BATNO). The key objective of this step is to make informed decisions, not visceral ones; fact-based and data-supported decisions, not gut-based ones. That outcome requires us to be honest

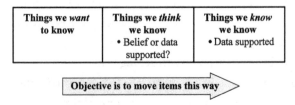

Things we *want* to know	Things we *think* we know	Things we *know* we know
	• Belief or data supported?	• Data supported

Objective is to move items this way

FIGURE 11.1 Hypothesis-directed discovery.

with ourselves regarding our beliefs. We need to remind ourselves that what we want to know or what we believe that we know is simply not definitively true unless and until we have the data to support it.

Be conscious that understanding comes before problem-solving, insight before resolution. We may be tempted to give short shrift our understanding or skip it altogether in our pursuit of a quick resolution of the issue. Resist that temptation. In and of itself, understanding often feels like the "booby prize" as it may make us feel better about the problem, but does not provide any resolution of it. Remember, however, that we humans are action oriented. We have to fight that "natural" feeling. Knowing why hurricanes are formed is simply not much comfort when our island has been decimated by one (or two). But understanding "why" is an important step along the path toward knowing "what" to do to minimize their destructive impact. It is the "what" that we desire ... what will we do about this. But it is the "why" that will lead us toward our desired outcome. "Why" comes before "what" in the development of impactful solutions, although it is not in that order in the dictionary. It is only if we stop at understanding "why" and do not leverage that understanding to determine "what" we need to do, that we end up with the booby prize.

DEFINING THE "BEST"

The ultimate outcome for the Converge step of the DOC Process is to make a choice. Choose the "best." This is true whether we are working in the problem or solution space. In the Problem Identification mode, we want to pick the "best" (or "most impactful") problem. In Solution Formulation, we want to solve that problem in the "best" way. The first thing we need to do, therefore, is to define how we will measure the "best." And very likely we will be applying more than one criterion simultaneously to our definition of "best." If, for example, we were evaluating our options to satisfy our late-night hunger cravings, our criteria for "best" may include "relatively fast" and "relatively inexpensive." It simply would not do us much good to add "favorite" to that criteria list if our "favorite" burger joint was 1,000 kilometers away. It may be our favorite burger place in the world, but that is not where we will be going tonight for our midnight burger fix!

Setting criteria for evaluating the organized concepts of the Organize step is critical. We simply cannot select the "best" if we cannot define what that means. What measure or attribute makes one better than another. We need to be objective, rational, transparent, and clear. We need more than our gut instinct; we need to start with some very definitive criteria for the "best."

Our overarching goal is to create an impact. Innovative problem-solving is about creating impactful solutions. At a zoomed-out perspective, we want the "best" problem or the "best" solution to be one that will lead to the greatest impact. The "best" problem, or probably a better way is to say it, the "most impactful" problem is one that is the most connected. A problem that is the root of the root of many other issues will create a significant ripple effect if we can resolve it. Similarly, the "best" solution is ideally one that is also the most connected. It either addresses the most number of potential adopters and/or has the most profound impact on those that are touched by this solution.

The "best," however, gets more complicated when attached to other constraints like timing and resources. Do we want to see an impact quickly or over centuries? The "best" choice for our late-night burger run will not be the same as the one we make for our last meal on earth. Timing maters. It forces us to weigh and balance criteria. The same is true for monetary and other resource commitments. The best we can do with $1,000 is different from the best we can do with $1 million. Given that specific criterion is subtly different when applied to the problem space versus the solution space, we will address each space separately.

Problem Identification Criteria

The world is full of challenges. We cannot solve them all. We also cannot move entire mountains all at once. Yes, "world peace" and "eliminating global hunger" are worthy aims, but we have no magic wand that will allow us to solve them in one fell swoop. We need to break them down and find smaller issues that contribute to the overarching causes that we desire to impact.

First and foremost the problem has to be within the innovation creator's circle of influence. As Covey (1989) defined it, something within our circle of concern is like the weather. It may be something we care about, but it is not something we can do anything about. Items within our circle of influence, however, are items we can impact if we choose to do so. Those items in our circle of influence are a subset of those in our circle of concern.

Identifying a problem which we (or our organization) can do nothing about is not impactful. Identifying a problem that we think someone else should solve is not impactful. The identified problem must therefore fall within our circle of influence. If it is outside this circle, and we really want to take on this problem, then we need to expand our circle of influence so that we *can* do something about the problem. That expansion becomes the first problem we need to work on. That expansion may require obtaining new skills, relationships, financial resources, etc. We will need to go all the way back to the beginning of the DOC Process to begin working on this newly identified problem.

Another way of evaluating "circle of influence," from a structured organizational perspective, is to assess whether or not the problem is aligned with the organization's vision, long-range goals, or short-term objectives. As a result, assuming the organization is the innovation creator, one criterion for the "best" is the degree to which the problem is in alignment with its vision, goals, and/or objectives. The problem must be one the organization is both willing and able to commit to resolving. That alignment speaks to the "willing" portion of that statement. For the organization to be able to resolve the issues infers that the organization has the Capabilities (assets, know-how, relationships, and aspirations) to potentially resolve this problem. Both "willing and able" criteria must be met.

A second clear criterion for screening problems is determining what impact solving this problem will have on the potential adopters of the innovation. One measure of this impact is the perceived value of solving the problem from the adopter's point-of-view. Is this a high-value problem for them? In other words, is it a big deal or a minor annoyance? Is this life-threatening "cancer" or a minor "headache"? A better, yet still nonideal solution to a "big deal" problem is going to have a much greater impact than an ideal solution to a problem that is only a minor annoyance to folks. The consequence of the problem is one measure of its importance. The more dire the consequences of having the problem, the "better" the problem (from an impact-generating perspective).

Another element of what makes a problem a high-value one is its frequency. Is a problem faced once in a blue moon or every day? If the problem is infrequent, like changing a flat tire, the potential adopter is more willing to grind through the problem with a less-than-adequate solution. If the problem is frequent, we want a better, easier solution. We may never have a flat tire on our car, but we will need to start it often. If starting our car was as difficult as changing a tire, people would be screaming for better solutions. It is simply a question of frequency. Manufacturers often try to reposition the problem's frequency as part of their marketing campaign. If the problem is a higher value one, we will be willing to pay more for the solution. Braun, the maker of men's shavers, had an ad a few years ago that basically said, "shaving is not something you do for three minutes, it is something you do every day." Their point? Shaving is not a low-value problem that men only spend three minutes resolving, but it is a high-value problem that men encounter every single day. The advertisement's real intent was to reframe the problem as a higher value one and therefore raise the value of resolving it. How much would men pay for a problem that they currently only have to spend three minutes to resolve. Not much. It is just not that big of a deal. But a recurring problem that they have to deal with every single day of their adult lives? Oh, that is a much higher value problem that they may be willing to spend much more to resolve. That's reframing.

A third element of a measure of impact is the sheer number of potential adopters of the innovation. Will there be millions of potential adopters around the world or only a few? If two problems are both high value from the adopter's point-of-view and the first problem impacts a large number of adopters while the second problem impacts only a few, resolving the first problem would clearly have more impact. Where the waters get murkier is trying to judge the impact of resolving a low-value problem that impacts a large number of potential adopters versus a high-value problem that impacts a significantly smaller number.

Yet another common criterion for screening problems is what impact solving this problem may have on our organization. Yes, on the creator of the innovation. When we think of problem selection, we rarely consider this criterion. However, if from an organization's perspective solving this problem does not benefit the organization in some way, it is unlikely the project team will receive support from within the organization necessary to pursue it. Altruism is great, but it has limits. Even nonprofits have to be pragmatic. If they cease to exist, it is impossible to fulfill their mission.

If we select either impact on the adopter or impact on the creating organization as components of our selection criteria set, then we must define how these will be measured. How does it make a difference? Short-term number of clients served? Long-term? Impacts on the organization: Reputation? Revenue? Market share? Units or service-hours sold? For the adopter: Money saved? Time saved? Access gained? There are many, many potential measures. We simply need to define them for the issue we are addressing as we want to be transparent on the decision criteria we are using to make our selection of the "best."

The greatest impact, however, may be due to the fact that this unsolved problem, as we discovered in the Organize step, directly or indirectly causes other problems. Solving this particular problem would eliminate or reduce those other issues. It would have a systematic ripple effect. This is the importance of identifying connections during the Organize step. The greater the connections, the greater the multiplier effect resolving the issue will have. The following list sums up the generic selection criteria when working in the problem space.

Generic Problem Identification criteria

- Is our organization able and willing to address this issue?
- Is it connected to the most other issues (root-of the root)?
- What impact will resolving this problem have on the adopter?
  - What is the perceived value of the problem's resolution to the adopter?
  - How is that adopter value measured?
  - How many potential adopters would be impacted?
- What impact will solving the problem have on our organization?
  - How will we measure that?

Solution Formulation Criteria

Setting criteria for solutions will come much more naturally than setting them for problems. There are two reasons for this; first, we are more comfortable with choosing between "actions" ("fight" or "flight," remember). Second is that we do it more frequently. Whenever we shop, we are choosing and in choosing we are, consciously or unconsciously, setting criteria for the choices we are making. What we need to ensure when selecting solution options is to set clear and conscious criteria for the selection. We want to make explainable, reasonable, and rational choices; not visceral ones. Generic Solution Formulation criteria are listed as follows. These are not, of course, the only criteria for selection. In addition, they must be made specific to the problem we are considering.

Generic Solution Formulation criteria

- Least expensive to implement.
- Quickest to implement.
- Aligns best with the organization's Capabilities.
- Longest lasting solution (long-term view).
- Most impactful solution (must define).
  - Whose point-of-view? Innovator's or Adopter's?

- Biggest improvement versus the adopter's current BATNO
  - As measured how?
- Garners the most recognition or Facebook "likes."

Selection Tools and Techniques

Even with the generic selection criteria, it can still be quite intimidating to choose the "most important" problem or the "absolute best" solution from a large group of alternatives. Fortunately, there are many tools and techniques available to assist us with this challenge.

T-Chart

The T-chart is most commonly used when trying to decide whether to commit or not to a single course of action. Two columns are typically drawn, one "pro" and one "con." The different aspects of the decision are listed in rows. If the "pros" outweigh the "cons"," then the decision is made in the affirmative. A graduate student once created a T-chart to decide whether to ask his girlfriend to marry him. It had pages of specific line items. That is probably taking use of the tool too far.

Paired Comparative Analysis

It is often easier to compare two items to each other than to an entire group. The paired comparative analysis ("Paired Comparison", n.d.) lets us do that by comparing alternative A to alternative B, then A to C, etc. We then assess B versus C, etc., until every option has been compared to every other option. In this approach, we are only comparing two items against each other, a stressless task. The overall result, however, is a matrix that will provide the optimal choice.

Decision Tree

In Chapter 9, we developed the Problem Identification Root System (Figure 9.2) as a means of driving down from the General Problem to a root cause issue. This is an augmented version of a classic decision tree ("Decision Trees", n.d.). In a decision tree, the options branch (divergent thinking) at each analysis juncture. The choices made at each juncture (convergent thinking) create a path that leads to a unique location at the bottom of the root system. The specific examples described over Chapters 3 and 4 illustrate the power of this tool in identifying root causes.

Pareto Analysis

Pareto analysis is a technique used to help prioritize choices. The analysis looks for connections and causes (two of the three phases of the Organize step). The item that is most connected is determined to have the greatest overall impact, as resolving that issue will also influence the resolution of those issues connected to it.

There are many more decision-making tools. A couple solution-specific tools that are commonly used in decision-making are listed.

Cost–Benefit Analysis

This is a financial analysis that compares the cost of creating the solution to the financial impact that would result from its implementation. The challenge with this method is in creating realistic financial measures for the impact, or the benefit side of this equation. The cost-side estimates are typically easier to obtain and, as a result, are much more accurate than the estimates of the benefit values.

Decision Matrix

Decision matrix ("Decision Matrix", n.d.) is a familiar product feature comparison chart. It compares features of different alternative solutions. Manufacturers position their offerings so that their product has the longest list of features compared to those being compared. But does that make it better? That's a question the consumer is left to ponder.

CONVERGE EXAMPLE

Let us return, once again, to our example of our company's "creativity day" that we began in Chapter 9 and continued in Chapter 10. When organizing the brainstormed information (Chapter 10), we discovered that we had originally brainstormed activities that required people to be physically present. We had both individual, asynchronous activities and group synchronous activities, but both required a physical presence. Performing the Organize step made this situation clear. The committee then returned to the Diverge step to flesh out more options for the event day.

We will recall that the original concept was to create a day that highlighted the creativity of the organization's employees. The organizing committee was initially charged with the seemly conflicting goals of maximizing employee participation while minimizing the impact on the employees' regular work schedule. These goals will be part of the selection criteria during the Converge step. The committee, however, decided to seek clarification from the organization's senior administration for more specific guidance on the selection criteria. That is when the administration informed the committee that there would be no "live" portion of this event. All the employees would participate "virtually," so as not to disrupt their work day. This also meant that there could be no "synchronous" elements of the day, where everyone could attend at one time. The criterion of "minimal interruption of the employee's day" was implemented in two ways. One, there would be a limited number of engagement activities beyond the welcoming messages. Second, each engagement activity would require less than five minutes of the employees' time.

This new, more specific, criterion caused the committee to go all the way back to the Diverge step. Once there, they reframed the "physical participation" activities into "virtual" ones. They also eliminated one item from the list as it did not fit the criterion of "highlighting the creativity of the employees" but was instead an exercise in creativity. New items were added to the list developed in Chapters 9 and 10, but subsequently eliminated as they either did not fit the criterion or were judged not to be "as good" as the items that made this list originally. The list was intentionally limited so as to minimize distraction of the employees' regular work responsibilities.

Event activities
- Prerecorded video welcome message by the organization's president.
- Prerecorded video "how to engage" throughout the day from the committee.

- Create an aggregate story where each person adds a sentence.
- Create a virtual "What is your art?" poster. Everyone contributes a line item describing how they express their creativity.
- ~~Create a virtual "Mosaic" with individuals contributing a colorful piece~~
- Prerecorded individuals or groups demonstrating their art (three to five minutes each).
  - o Music: Groups or solo
  - o Poetry reading
  - o Stand-up comic acts
  - o Acting skits

Pre-event activities
- Viewable, prerecorded messages by the committee posted on the organization's website.
- Online written announcements.
  - o E-mail messages
  - o Posts on organization's website

Postevent activities
- Follow-up, online survey

The committee now has a set of activities that fit within the criteria and scope of the event. That set is purposefully limited. This, however, is not an event. It is a proposed solution. Level 3 of The Innovation Pyramid is where the execution plan is created, or in this case the event is developed. Now that the solution has been identified, that is the next task at hand.

COMMON MISTAKES

The biggest mistake made, as noted in Chapter 10, is skipping the Organize step before moving on to the Converge step. By far the most common mistake made in the Converge step is not setting conscious and public criteria. The commonly used "voting" technique commits both of these errors. Not only is the Organize step completely skipped, but when brainstorming participants are asked to vote on their favorite idea, no criteria are set. No boundary conditions or limitations are imposed. The disastrous results are predictable.

Another offense common to this stage is to first viscerally select a "best" and then rationalize the choice afterward. This technique is often used to convince others that their intuitive choice is the optimal one. Sometimes the original chooser does, to their credit, have a criterion in mind, it is simply not a public one. Criteria need to be set before the choice is made. We do not all have identical points-of-view. We need to agree on criteria before the selection process is begun. Senior administrators will typically assume that every employee will consider both "cost" and "organizational alignment" as unspoken elements of the project's criteria set. They may not. The full set of criteria must be clear to everyone involved and void of any unspoken elements.

The final common error related to setting criteria in the Converge step is shifting or outdated criteria. These two mistakes are different, but related. There are times when a group is charged with a task and also initially given a clear set of criteria. Those criteria then change before the completion of the group's assignment. This is fine, as in the example, if the criteria change is clearly communicated. What is not acceptable is the case where the group's results are ignored after their work is complete, because the criteria shifted. Related to this error is using outdated criteria. The "we successfully did this 10 years ago" argument blatantly ignores the fact that the environment – both for the innovator and for the adopter – may have changed. The process results are again ignored because "everyone knows" they are wrong. Changing circumstances call for updating selection criteria. In both cases what ideally should occur is that the Converge step is repeated with the new, updated criteria.

SUMMARY

Converge is the third and final step of the DOC Process that is illustrated in Figure 11.2. The nonlinear DOC Process is repeatedly

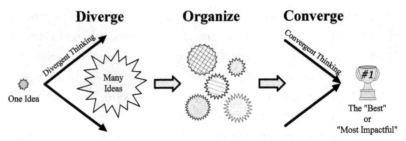

FIGURE 11.2 Diverge–Organize–Converge Process overview.

applied throughout The Innovation Pyramid methodology. The nonlinearity of the DOC Process means that we may travel between steps several times before the overall process is completed. The DOC Process is applied to both Problem Identification and Solution Formulation. The aim of the Converge step is to narrow the organized group of information down to a single choice, the "best" choice.

In order to choose the "best" factor of the General Problem to address, or select the "best" solution to that problem, we need to first define the "best." Those criteria must be clear and conscious. If we are working in an organization, the criteria should also be public. We may start with the generic criteria for the problem or solution space later, but we will have to make them specific to our organization, the adopter we are targeting, and the current environment for both the innovator and adopter.

Generic Problem Identification criteria
- Is our organization able and willing to address this issue?
- Is it connected to the most other issues (root of the root)?
- What impact will resolving this problem have on the adopter?
  o What is the perceived value of the problem's resolution to the adopter?
  o How is that adopter-value measured?
  o How many potential adopters would be impacted?
- What impact will solving the problem have on our organization?
  o How will we measure that?

Generic Solution Formulation criteria

- Least expensive to implement
- Quickest to implement
- Aligns best with the organization's Capabilities
- Longest lasting solution (long-term view)
- Most impactful solution (must define)
  - o Whose point-of-view? Innovator's or Adopter's?
- Biggest improvement versus the adopter's current BATNO
  - o As measured how?
- Garners the most recognition or Facebook "likes"

We do not want to make intuitive, visceral decisions, but rather conscious, rational, and reasonable ones. In order to accomplish that desired outcome, we need to choose a complete set of selection criteria. These criteria must be current and complete, but most importantly conscious.

12 Book Summary

The Innovation Pyramid is a methodology to assist individuals and organizations in learning to become better serial innovators. Creating an innovation requires three elements: people, environment, and methodology. The Innovation Pyramid is a learnable, repeatable, nonlinear, iterative, knowledge-based methodology for generating innovations. A method is not a guarantee for reaching an impactful solution. A methodology is a system of procedures and/or techniques that allow the accomplishment of a set of tasks without guarantee of a specific outcome. A repeatable method controls for a number of innovation project variables, but not all of them. Those variables not controlled for will require our judgment. Judgment remains an important element in innovation development. Repeatable use of a consistent method provides a means to improve our judgment and therefore improve on our ability to become serial innovators.

The design thinking-based Innovation Pyramid, which is detailed in Part I of this book describes this needed overarching guide. This section presents the macro-level view of innovation development. Part II of the book details the creativity-based Diverge–Organize–Converge (DOC) Process essential for implementing The Pyramid methodology. While the most common use of this process is in ideating new solutions, it is equally applicable to identifying problems. The book's appendices further detail techniques useful in implementing the DOC Process and consequently The Innovation Pyramid. Altogether the elements create a learnable, implementable, repeatable means for developing true innovations – impactful, original solutions to real problems.

PART I REVIEW

The learnable, repeatable, nonlinear, iterative, knowledge-based methodology for generating innovations is presented in this section. The design thinking-based Innovation Pyramid represents an overarching guide for producing innovations. The methodology divides innovation into two main activities: design and execution. Each of those general activities is, in turn, further subdivided, creating four macro-level categories of innovation activities. The design method separates the problem from the solution, producing the two design stages: Problem Identification and Solution Formulation. The execution method separates the creation of a plan of execution from its implementation, forming the two execution stages: Plan and Perform. These four stages are represented by the four layers of the inverted, triangular pyramid. From top-to-bottom, beginning at the widest portion of the inverted pyramid and descending down to the narrowest, are Problem Identification, Solution Formulation, Plan, and Perform.

The inverted triangular Innovation Pyramid has three faces. The Pyramid faces represent the "Who," the "What," and the "How" of the activities performed at each Pyramid layer. Slicing The Pyramid between the "Who" and the "How" faces and laying it flat results in the view of Figure 12.1. The "Who" face describes those who are leading and/or are impacted by the activities of this stage. The "What" Pyramid face describes the desired outcome of each stage, and the "How" face describes how those desired outcomes of each level will be achieved. Level-specific assessments are performed at each of the four stages. These assessments represent the solid core of The Pyramid that binds the surfaces together.

While the physical structure of The Innovation Pyramid lays out the four macro-level categories in a clear order, the methodology is both nonlinear and iterative. The methodology is nonlinear because, while there is a general top-to-bottom "flow" through The Pyramid, there is no sequential step-by-step checklist to follow. It is quite common, for example, to start at either of the two design stages. The

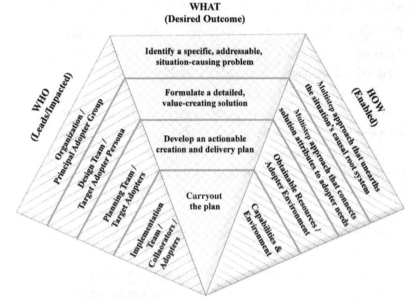

FIGURE 12.1 The Innovation Pyramid laid flat.

detailed activity order is not as important as ultimately completing every segment of The Pyramid.

The methodology is an iterative process of discovery in that completing a level further down The Pyramid, say at the Plan level, may reveal insights that cause us to return and re-do the previously completed design stages. While it is not uncommon to traverse through The Pyramid levels multiple times in the development of an innovation, it is guaranteed in the development of a prototype or pilot program. In these cases, all levels of The Innovation Pyramid will be completed during the development of a prototype or pilot program. After the program's review, all levels of The Innovation Pyramid will again be completed for the development of the final innovation.

Since this is a methodology, and not a predictable outcome recipe, even though assessment is performed at each level of the methodology, the overall outcome – the anticipated overall impact the innovation had hoped to create – may not end up being what was initially desired. The final project assessment is a systematic review of the entire Pyramid methodology, revealing how choices made at each layer may have led to the nondesired outcome. Once the root cause issue is uncovered, the innovator iterates back to the appropriate level, alters their original choice, and proceeds again from that point.

Pyramid Levels

The four macro-level activity categories of The Innovation Pyramid consist of two design stages and two execution stages. The two design stages are Problem Identification and Solution Formulation. The two execution stages are Plan and Perform.

Problem Identification

The first level of The Pyramid, which is the first stage of the innovation's design, describes a procedure for identifying and defining root causes of larger situations. Similar to The Innovation Pyramid, this five-step procedure for Problem Identification is a nonlinear, iterative process of discovery. These steps also incorporate a core tenet of The Pyramid which is diverge before converge. The Pyramid methodology consistently prompts us to broaden our purview before narrowing it.

Step 1: Clearly state the starting situation or issue.
Step 2: Zoom out to define the General Problem.
Step 3: Draft a neutral problem statement.
Step 4: Zoom in, layer by layer, to a root cause.
Step 5: Identify the Principal Adopter.

Solution Formulation

The second design stage focuses on creating an impactful solution. The first step is to narrow The Principal Adopter group, the general group for whom the innovation is being created, identified at the end of Level 1 to a Target Adopter persona with specific needs, wants, and/or desires. The Target Adopter is the specific group for whom the innovation is designed and creates value. The five-step guideline for completing this stage is as follows:

Step 1: Describe a specific Target Adopter persona.
- Identify Principal Adopter's current Best Alternative to a New Option.
- Perform open-ended interviews to obtain insight.
- Craft personas from the unmet or under-met needs, wants, and/or desires uncovered during the interviews.
- Select a Target Adopter persona.

Step 2: Determine a solution approach.

Step 3: Craft a detailed solution.

Step 4: Establish a clear value proposition.

Step 5: Quantify the Target Adopter group size.

The fifth and final step is not recommended to be completed until it is absolutely necessary, which is typically in the Plan level (Level 3) of The Innovation Pyramid. Our aim is to keep the innovation's description qualitative as long as possible. This is because our human nature is that we will resist pivoting from a design after we have spent significant time and effort determining the adopter volumes and innovation costs. During those hours, we will have convinced ourselves that our Target Adopter choice and our design are perfect. To avoid being prematurely locked into a specific design, it is recommended that we proceed to Level 3, the planning stage of execution stage, before completing this step. This is yet another example of the nonlinearity of the methodology.

Plan

The aim of this level is to develop an innovation creation and delivery plan. The plan must not only include how the innovation will actually be created, but also articulate how that created innovation will be delivered to the adopter. That plan may vary in detail, depending on the complexity of the innovation, but it must always contain the following four components.

- Operations. How will the innovation be created?
- Delivery. How will the innovation be delivered to and acquired by the adopter?

- Resources. What resources, inside and outside our organization, will be needed to complete the creation and delivery of this innovation?
- Risk. Description of the risks associated with the creation and delivery of this innovation.

The plan we create in this level must be detailed enough to be executable. If a detailed plan cannot be crafted or the resources cannot be committed to the project, then the design must be altered by returning to the design stages of The Innovation Pyramid.

The plan is also a way to communicate and sell the project to potential supporters, collaborators, and detractors. The value of the innovation project is not self-evident to all that we need to involve. We must communicate its value to them. This section also outlines various levels of pitching the innovation project we can use to transfer our enthusiasm for the project to those who can aid us in creating its ultimate impact.

Perform

Carrying out the innovation creation and delivery plan that was created in the first execution stage is a project management challenge. Launching new innovations has challenges beyond those of a typical internal company project in that they generally involve collaborators and adopters outside the innovation creating organization. This means that multiple environments and multiple points-of-view, in addition to the innovation creator's internal environment and point-of-view, must be appraised.

Systematic Pyramid Review

In the end, the usefulness of The Innovation Pyramid, like any tool, comes down to how well we learn to use it. The more we learn about its application to our organization and our innovations, the more useful it becomes. The Pyramid structure, fortunately, is equally useful as a diagnostic tool. It is useful in guiding the identification of a well-rationalized choice made during the design and execution of the innovation that may have inadvertently caused us to veer away from our overall, macro-level, desired impact on the original situation. The distinguishing characteristics of The Innovation Pyramid – separation of the problem from its solution and the innovation's design from its execution while simultaneously considering both the innovation creator's and adopter's points-of-view – aid in its usefulness as an overall project assessment guide. Rather than searching for someone to blame for the project's failure, the organization should embrace this opportunity to search for deeper understanding. This deeper discernment requires a critical analysis of the entire innovation system – every decision taken between the initial situation and overall outcome must be reviewed. Fortunately, The Innovation Pyramid provides a streamlined approach for accomplishing that analysis. It is this systematic Pyramid review that leads to the learning that improves our innovating judgment. That improved judgment, in turn, allows us to develop into successful serial innovators.

PART II REVIEW

This section describes the creativity-based DOC Process that is used repeatedly throughout The Pyramid methodology. The DOC Process, like The Innovation Pyramid, is also nonlinear and iterative. The DOC Process has three steps as illustrated in Figure 12.2: Diverge, Organize, and Converge. Chapters 8–11 describe the DOC Process and its elements in detail. Appendix A illustrates how the DOC Process, particularly when combined with the Interview for Insight technique, can be utilized to create personas of archtype adopters.

Diverge

Divergent thinking, as illustrated in Figure 12.2, is aimed at expanding ideas. As with every step of the DOC Process, Diverge applies to both Problem Identification and Solution Formulation. Most often this technique is used to "brainstorm" new solutions to problems. Rarely it is used to actually identify the problems which these solutions hypothetically fix. Both, however, are necessary. The

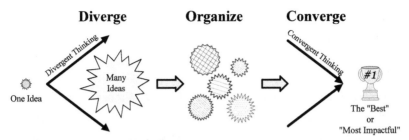

FIGURE 12.2 DOC Process overview.

subtle differences between how we can apply the technique to the problem space versus the solution space are detailed.

Problem Identification divergence occurs via the development of the General Problem Root System. A series of DOC Process applications are required to transition from the zoomed-out General Problem to identifying a zoomed-in root cause of it. Solution Formulation divergence, on the other hand, requires both point-of-view and perspective shifts. To truly diversify solution ideas, we must also brainstorm on the feature level, function level, and system level around any solution concept. Specific divergent techniques are expanded upon in Appendix B.

Organize

The Organize step, the second step of the DOC Process, is the important transition step between divergent thinking and convergent thinking. The Organize step has three components: categorize, connect, and cause. The first task of this step is to categorize the information generated via the divergent-thinking activities. Creating and naming categories makes it easier to see what is not there but should be. The connect component is the second phase of the Organize step. In this phase, we are looking to connect idea fragments that were previously categorized together. We can also assess whether or not there is any connection between the categories or if the categories fall in a particular sequence. The final phase of the Organize step is cause. In this phase, we are assessing whether there is a causal relationship between the data categories. Causal relationships are powerful, if determined, as they identify potential impact-creating domino effects.

Converge

Converge is the third and final step of the DOC Process. The ultimate desired outcome for the Converge step is to make a choice, to choose the "best." This is true whether one is working in the problem or solution space. An important element of this step, therefore, is to consciously define the criteria by which we will be selecting the "best" so as to create a "level evaluation field" for all concepts that are being judged. We do not want to make intuitive, visceral choices, but rather conscious, rational, and reasonable ones. In order to accomplish that desired outcome, we need to choose a complete set of selection criteria. These criteria must be current and complete, but most importantly conscious. It is not uncommon that the criteria selection causes us to iterate back to either the Diverge or the Organize step. Despite the number of iterations through the steps, the DOC Process ultimately ends with a single choice.

SUMMARY

Anyone, or any organization, can improve upon their abilities to become serial innovators. Innovators are both problem identifiers and problem solvers. Innovators create new, impactful solutions to clearly identified root cause problems. Creative problem-solving is not enough. To generate impact, those solutions must also be adopted: no adoption, no impact; no impact, no innovation.

Innovating is a learnable, not an innate, skill. Innovating takes the right people, in the right environment utilizing the right methodology. The focus of this book is the description of a learnable, repeatable, nonlinear, iterative, knowledge-based methodology for generating innovations, The Innovation Pyramid. It is the oft-missing guide necessary to becoming a serial innovator. A guide that integrates creation and adoption. A guide that includes root cause problem identification and solution formulation. A guide that can be adopted by individuals, groups, or large organizations.

The design thinking -based Innovation Pyramid methodology is laid out in Part I of this book. Its implementation utilizes the creativity-based DOC Process described in the second half of this book. The appendices, in turn, describe specific techniques that apply to the DOC Process. The structure of this book reflects the multiperspective approach to innovating captured by The Innovation Pyramid methodology.

Individually, corporately, and society-wide, we face increasingly critical and complex problems. We long for new solutions that will generate meaningful and lasting positive change. Not just solutions that are different or creative, but those that are impactful. We need innovators to create them. This book is aimed at aiding in their development.

Appendix A: Interviewing for Insight and Persona Development

It would be great if people would just tell us their fundamental needs, wants, and/or desires and their true, root-of-the-root basis upon which they make choices. It would be especially great if we could simply survey them to find out these secrets. But we cannot, for two reasons. The first is that they are humans like us. That means they also think in terms of solutions and not in terms of underlying problems and definitely not in terms of fundamental needs, wants, and desires. Hence, the famous Henry Ford quote that states if he asked the customer what they wanted they would respond by saying a "faster horse" holds true. That response is a solution. Furthermore, it is an incremental improvement based on the solution with which they are already familiar. Do not expect your potential adopters to be innovators. Just as we needed to learn how to separate the problem space from the solution space, we will need to learn how to gain insight into the adopter's needs, wants, and/or desires through the solutions they offer. For it is this insight we seek, not the potential adopter's proposed solution.

The second reason our potential adopters cannot tell us their underlying needs is that such information is tacit knowledge. We all know things that we cannot put into words. How do you balance on a bicycle? How do you generate that unique guitar sound? How do you operate that complex piece of machinery? The next time you find yourself at a comedy club laughing at the comic, ask yourself why one joke was funnier than another. Odds are you will have a difficult time articulating the difference, yet you *know* the difference. Knowledge which is intrinsic or difficult to transfer to another person in words is called "tacit knowledge." Tacit knowledge is often know-how and know-what. Explicit knowledge, on the other hand, is knowledge that is codified, written down. Explicit knowledge is essentially anything we can Google. If we cannot Google it, odds are it is tacit knowledge. Sometimes explicit knowledge can become tacit in an individual. When the factory worker first learned how to operate that complex piece of machinery, he likely started with an operator's manual. At the beginning, he could likely recite the process, but over time he developed his own techniques and it became "muscle memory" or "instinct" to him. It became tacit knowledge.

Uncovering adopter needs is an exercise in tacit knowledge discovery. Once the problem space has been narrowed down to a root cause that impacts a Principal Adopter, we need to transform that cause into unmet or under-met needs, wants, and/or desires. Those would-be adopters, unfortunately, will not be able to tell us, at least not directly. It is tacit knowledge. The information we want is inside them, but they cannot articulate it in such a straightforward way. What we seek is nearly impossible for them to put it into words. As a result, we need to get inside their heads and tease the information out. What we will eventually acquire from them is not "facts" but "insight" as to how these potential adopters think and choose. Acquiring such information is simply not possible using a written tool, like a survey. We need to have a conversation with them. We need to coax out the information we seek. We will then have to make some inferences from the information we gather, for we will not be able to get at the root-of-the-root directly. We need to use Interviewing for Insight (IFI).

Once we have developed this insight into our potential adopter, we will then start generating ideas for an innovation that will satisfy their needs/wants/desires. At that point, it will be helpful to envision how our Target Adopter will directly engage with our innovation. To do that, it is convenient to personify the Target Adopter group, to create an image of an archtype adopter – a persona – that makes decisions based on the needs/wants/desires we uncovered. That persona we are creating is a composite, a representative of our Target Adopter group, and typically not any individual that we interviewed during the data-gathering phase. This appendix will detail how to develop this persona as well as obtain the foundational information we need to do so by the IFI.

DOC PROCESS APPLICATION

Both IFI and Persona Development are elements of a specialized application of the Diverge–Organize–Converge (DOC) Process discussed in Part II of this book. While the IFI is definitely not "brainstorming," this primary research technique, like all research, is a divergent act. We will be uncovering a plethora of adopter needs, wants, and/or desires during the interviews. The next step is to organize these needs/wants/desires. Persona development is a specialized way to organize this diverse information, as will be detailed in this appendix. Several personas will be created in the Organize step of the DOC Process. The Converge step is then applied to select a single adopter persona from the several that were created. That selected adopter is the Target Adopter. That Target Adopter has defined unmet or under-met needs, wants, and/or desires as defined by its association with a specific subset of categories of the needs/wants/desires that were uncovered. Once the persona for the Target Adopter is clear, the focus of design methodology shifts to Solution Formulation. The most innovation solutions come from the clearest understanding of the Target Adopter. It is therefore worth investing our time in the IFIs and persona development.

HYPOTHESIS DEVELOPMENT

Part of our preparation for our interviews with potential adopters involves secondary research: gathering explicit knowledge. That may include industry and association reports, market reports, academic papers, or other articles we have discovered on the World Wide Web. While we are reading this material, we will start to formulate beliefs. We will have beliefs about the real problem, the best solution to that problem, and our Target Adopter. Be aware that these beliefs make up our hypotheses. These hypotheses may be purely speculative,

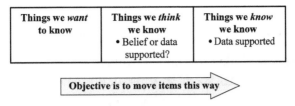

Things we *want* to know	Things we *think* we know	Things we *know* we know
	• Belief or data supported?	• Data supported

Objective is to move items this way

FIGURE A.1 Hypothesis-directed discovery.

conjectured from some preliminary understanding, or they may be fact-based understanding that is rigorously supported by evidence. In other words, we will have things that we know, things that we *think* we know, and things we would like to know, as illustrated by the three columns of Figure A.1. Those conjectures that we think we know may turn out to be more fantasy than fact. As Figure A.1 illustrates, we want to move from items we want to know column to data-supported understanding by creating and testing hypotheses. This hypothesis-testing will be done via the IFIs.

Organizing information in this way allows us to better understand what items require more research and which are supported by data. Creativity trainers often put things into two columns using the "know/wonder" tool: one column for things we "know" and one for items we "wonder" about. As we continue to do research and obtain more information the conjectures shift from the "wonder" column to the "know" column. The three-column format is more specific on the "know" part by ensuring we have supportive information to ensure we really "know" what we may simply think we know. The tool, however, is less important than the practice of keeping information organized during the research process.

In addition to the things we know and wonder about, there are items that may turn out to be important that, as of this moment, we are completely unaware. As former US Secretary of Defense Donald Rumsfeld stated (Rumsfeld, 2002) at a press conference in 2002:

> [T]here are known knowns; there are things we know we know.
> We also know there are known unknowns; that is to say we know

there are some things we do not know. But there are also unknown unknowns – there are things we do not know we don't know.

These unknown unknowns are the "things we don't know we don't know" (Khosla, 2002). We need to obtain information on the known unknowns. In doing so we must keep our eyes open to try to see the unknown unknowns. That is to say we seek information that provides insight to the questions we know we do not currently have answers to in addition to uncovering the questions we do not yet know to ask.

INTERVIEWING FOR INSIGHT

Discovering what people think and know, revealing their tacit knowledge, is critical to testing our hypotheses and an important part of the innovation process. It is how our known unknowns become known knowns and how the unknown unknowns become known unknowns. Uncovering what is in people's heads is a key component to gathering the information we need to support or disprove our working hypotheses. We are not asking our interviewees to confirm the brilliance of our hypothesized solution. We are seeking evidence that will do so. This is detective work. We are not asking the suspect directly if they committed the crime. We simply cannot trust their response to that blunt question. Instead, we are seeking evidence that incriminates or exonerates them.

The interviews are also key to truly understanding the problem from the potential adopter's point-of-view; a critical step in the process of creating impactful solutions. We have likely developed a point-of-view from our secondary research. We need to set that aside, and through empathy, truly listen to and try to understand the interviewee's point-of-view. A questionnaire will not uncover this deep understanding. Our questions would be nothing more than a reflection of our own biases. What would we possibly ask to uncover unknown unknowns? We need to engage directly with people in a discovery-driven dialog to uncover what they may not even realize they know. Such dialogs achieve three objectives.

First, they offer the chance to meet and talk with people who can deepen our perception and understanding of the issues. Second, these dialogs create the opportunity to learn and mutually explore specific needs and frustrations. Finally these are hypothesis-driven learning opportunities. These interviews are definitely not sales calls where we are promoting or seeking reaction to our preconceived innovation.

Interview Preparation

Before engaging in these IFIs, we need to prepare. While this conversation is not a pitch of our ideas, we still need to bring something to the table. It should be a conversation, albeit a directed one, and not a rambling soliloquy on the part of the interviewee. To prepare for this dialog, we need to do our homework. We need to research and read and uncover as much explicit knowledge as we can so as to be knowledgeable enough on the topic to hold up our end of the conversation. We also do not want to have our initial dialog with one of the world's experts. We need to work up to these key individuals by building knowledge and understanding as we go. We do not want our first dialog about smartphones to be with Tim Cooke of Apple!

This is a conversation not an oral questionnaire. While it is fine to prepare an opening statement or question, do not prepare a ten-question list as it will tempt you to simply run through the list regardless of the interviewee's responses. Imagine a conversation with a friend that just went to a new restaurant that you are curious about, but one to which you have not yet been. You will be interested in your friend's take on the food, the service, the ambiance, etc. You will likely start the conversation generally as in "how was your experience at the restaurant last night?" When your friend answers, "it was great, but on the way home we became part of a ten-car pile-up," you would not immediately follow up with, "yes, interesting, so was the food good?" You do not go down a checklist of questions, you go with the flow of the conversation. As IFIs are directed conversations, you may need to steer the interviewee back to the topic of interest, but it has to flow.

Stay focused on the goal of seeking insights versus obtaining "facts." Ask open-ended questions. Be wary of asking direct, specific questions. Answers to these questions can be misleading, as they may not be the "right" question to ask. If, for example, we are trying to figure out why a company's product sales are not increasing as was expected, we may be tempted to ask someone if manufacturing is a problem. They may say, "yes," as manufacturing is always challenging. That information would "confirm" our hypothesis that the firm could sell more if it could only manufacture more. That hypothesis is very likely wrong and the "fact" used to confirm it is misleading at best. The big issue may lie in the distribution of the product, which would never be revealed with such a specific question. The IFI is a process of discovery that will lead to the underlying issues. It is not a true–false test. The objective is to evaluate and readjust our hypotheses from the information gathered in this dialog. This is the essence of the scientific method. We hypothesize, we experiment, we evaluate the data, adjust the hypotheses, and repeat the process. The "experiment" in this case is the interviews, the IFIs. We want to gain insight as to how potential adopters think and choose so that we can gauge their reaction to our new innovation even before the prototype is created.

These dialogs are best done with one person at a time. Groups, like a conversation, can be dominated by a single individual. If that occurs, tacit knowledge of the others will remain obscured by the loudest voice in the room. Although interviewing a single person, we may want to have a partner with us. That way we can keep in the flow of the conversation, while our partner records the information. Alternately, we may also, with the interviewee's explicit permission, record the interview on our phone. Interviewing for Insight with a partner, however, will allow us to obtain two points-of-view on the nonverbal cues. Nonverbal cues are powerful, yet easy to miss if our head is down writing notes. If we do take a partner to an interview, it is important that we guide the conversation and they just listen. We should also introduce our respective roles to the interviewee before we start so that there will be no confusion as to who is leading the conversation on our side. Clearly, since we are seeking nonverbal as well as verbal cues, the interviews are best performed face to face. A video-linked interview is the next best alternative, but phone interviews limit nonverbal cues which are a large portion of our communication.

Who to Interview

The primary focus of our interviews will be potential adopters of our potential innovation. The original situation from which we started was reduced, through a series of DOC Process applications, to a root cause. The Principal Adopters are the group most directly affected by the identified root-cause. The IFIs will be primarily performed on the Principal Adopters. We also want to include, however, people who represent 360-degrees around these Principal Adopters. That 360-degree list will vary, but the Principal Adopter's current solution provider will likely have useful insights if it is practical to interview them. Industry experts and other thought leaders in the field should also be considered as we want to cast a broad net in our understanding of the problem. There may also be environmental restrictions (real or perceived), such as laws or company policies, that the Principal Adopter identifies as barriers to a better solution. Individuals who can speak to those issues should also be interviewed as we seek a fully informed description of the problem.

We will need to perform many IFIs to get a thorough understanding of the landscape. While there is no magic number of interviews that should be performed, ten IFIs is a good place to start. These interviews are the Diverge step of the DOC Process. As with all applications of this process, when we begin organizing the findings, we often discover that we are missing information and have to return to the Diverge step. That will be the case here as well. When we start to organize the unmet and under-met needs, wants, and/or desires that we uncovered into personas, we may find that we could use more information or that there is an important perspective that we failed to obtain. In those cases, we will have to perform a few additional IFIs.

Contacting the Interviewee

Engaging in deep, one-on-one conversations with people we do not know may sound intimidating. Like any other skill, we will get better the more we do it. People are generally very open and responsive to such engagements. People love to be listened to; they love that we are interested in their perspective. They equally get annoyed and shut down if they sense we are secretly trying to sell them something, which is why cold sales calls are so difficult.

Start the discussion about their participation in the IFI by stating what we are trying to accomplish. For example, you may say, "I would like to have a confidential twenty-minute conversation with you about current offerings in marketing communications." It sets expectations in terms of time and content. It tells our interviewee that we are really interested in their opinion, their insights, and are not going to be selling them a new idea.

We always need to introduce ourselves and provide our motivation for the conversation. If you are a student, play the "student card." People love to help students, especially students from their alma mater. You can say "I'm a student studying business at the University of Michigan and I'm doing a research project related to consumer demand for iPhone applications and would like to spend twenty minutes talking to you to gain your insight on this topic." Your responses will be surprisingly fabulous.

Setting the Scope of the Interview

Every issue has an existing solution. At the very least we want to identify our potential adopter's current best solution, their Best Alternative to a New Option (BATNO), and understand what is satisfactory and dissatisfactory, from their point-of-view, about this solution option. While these responses will provide us with some insight as to their unmet and under-met needs, wants, and/or desires, such a discussion will only lead to incrementally improved solution ideas. To broaden the potential innovations, we need to take a step back from their BATNO and broaden our purview.

The type of innovation (incremental to radical) that we will eventually design, is an outcome determined, in part, by how we identify and define the problem we are seeking to resolve. The narrower the scope of our interview, the more likely the innovation will be incremental. If we ask people what they like and do not like about their cell phone, their answers will help us innovate at the feature level. But it will not lead us to anything other than a "better" cell phone. The result will be, at best, an incremental innovation. If, on the other hand, asking what is working and not working for them regarding staying connected to their globally distributed business team will provide us insights that will enable us develop a more radical innovation. Either way, the potential innovation is partially dependent on how narrow or broadly we are identifying the problem we are attempting to resolve.

Unless we are only interested in improving on today's solution features, we need to broaden our questions from specific questions about our potential adopter's likes and dislikes of their current BATNO. To broaden our purview, we need to ask what issue does the BATNO resolve for them, generally speaking? What does their BATNO allow them to accomplish? If their current BATNO is a mobile phone, the more general issue is communication. If they frequent a certain restaurant, what are they getting out of it? Is it a convenient means to get a quick bite to eat or is it a place to meet up with friends and family? A narrowly scoped IFI will lead to an incrementally improved solution. Broadening the scope of the IFI will provide us broader insights which will, in turn, lead us to more diverse solutions.

Interview for Insights not Solutions

Remember that the adopters will likely speak in terms of solutions and innovation features, so we will need to push them to explain why their proposed solution is better than the BATNO. In what way is it better? What does it provide that the current solution does not? The point of the conversation is not to have the adopter design the innovation for us. We are the innovators and we will do that. To do so, however, we will need insight as to the potential adopter's unmet or under-met needs/wants/desires and their relative importance in making choices of these needs/wants/desires. That will take some stealth investigating. Try not to jump to conclusions about why we think their current BATNO is not working for them, but we need to push the interviewee to articulate that for us.

Do not fall into the temptation of pitching your solution idea. The objective is to learn about the needs/wants/desires of the potential adopter, not sell them on a specific solution. The interviewee will often describe the problem as a solution. "It would be better if they did ... or we had...." When that occurs, we will be tempted to interject our own solution concept. "Don't you think ... would also work?" Do not go there. Instead, dig deeper. What does their solution solve that the current solution does not?

In addition, try also to better understand the assumptions the interviewees are making. What have they gotten used to that they no longer even see as part of the problem or artificial constraints to alternate solutions? Most of us are apologists or survivors (Cooper, 1999). We quickly adapt to our environment and accept it, limitations and all, as fixed. We are unable to fix problems we cannot even "see." How does the person we are dialoging with consider alternatives? We need to be curious about what we hear. Follow up with questions to find out more detail about their answers, particularly those that surprise us. As Tom Kelley says, "think like a traveler" (Kelley, 2008). When we travel to a new place we are often in this hyper-aware state where we see things anew, like a child. That is the mindset we need to have for a productive IFI experience.

Also be aware that context creates bias and experts are highly contextualized. If we are having a dialog with the world's expert in diesel combustion, they will not likely lead us to believe that the future power source of personal transportation lies in solar, natural gas, or any other potential automobile power plants besides diesel. That does not mean that we should not engage with experts; quite to the contrary. These experts are great sources of knowledge, including the limitations of the current solutions.

Nonverbal Cues

During a dialog, we have to be keenly aware and read between the lines. Pay particular attention to emotionally expressed annoyances (Schmitt, 2006). These annoyances may be revealed through nonverbal cues as much as verbal communications. Fifty-five percent of communication is nonverbal (Covey, 1989). Watch for signs of excitement or discomfort on the part of the interviewee. Thirty-eight percent of communication is how we say the words. Listen for an increase in the cadence of the speech, increased volume, as hints that we have hit upon something important to the interviewee. The greater the emotionally charged response, the more important the issue is to the interviewee. When we hit upon an issue or annoyance that evokes an increased emotional response, it is time to drill deeper with a series of "why" questions to get further understanding. The best way to think of the why questions is to think like a six-year old. Some questions that can help in this pursuit include:

- Why?
- Please tell me more.
- Then what happens? What is next?
- Why is that a problem for you?
- What do you spend time on?
- Why don't you seem to have time to do that?
- What is preventing you from doing ...?
- If you had a magic wand....
  (Note that it is not the answer to this "magic wand" questions that is important, but the underlying "why" they think their "magic wand" answer would be better.)

Be Patient

The last caution in seeking understanding through dialogs is to be patient. Noise comes before illumination. Tacit knowledge is difficult to communicate. Interviewing for Insight is a developed skill. We will need to perform many IFIs. Do not expect all the information we gather to lead us on a direct path to a world-changing innovation.

We need to make some inferences from the insights we are gathering. The more insights, the better the inferences. In addition, IFI, like The Innovation Pyramid itself, is an iterative path forward. Hypothesize, gather data, assess the data, rehypothesize, and repeat. Be diligent and persistent, we will get there.

PERSONA DEVELOPMENT

People have problems and people will adopt solutions to those problems. If we want to innovate, we need to know for whom we are innovating. Interviewing for Insights is an important technique for uncovering the specific needs/wants/desires of our potential innovation adopters. We cannot create innovation, however, that satisfies all needs for all people. When innovating, Everyone = No One. If we are designing an innovation for everyone, we are, in reality, designing for no one. The corollary to this axiom is that 10 percent of everyone is equal to 10 percent of no one. We cannot say that we are targeting 10 percent of some vaguely described group, like 10 percent of the tourists who visit St. Thomas, USVI. That is, 10 percent of "everyone," which means we are, in truth, targeting 10 percent of no one. Successful innovation design is like archery, we need a target at which to aim.

The IFIs will allow us to better understand the needs, wants, and desires of the people we interview. It is not, however, the final step in the innovation process. Far from it. The IFIs are a divergent thinking tool. The first step of the DOC Process. The more interviews we perform, the more data we will acquire. Increasing the number of interviews will also likely increase the diversity of the data we obtain. If we properly organize these findings, the more data we have, the clearer the description we will obtain of the needs/wants/desires of the specific adopter for whom we are designing. The next step is therefore organizing the data we uncovered during the IFIs.

Given we are designing for people, we need more than a curated list of needs/wants/desires, we need to be able to describe the specific group of people for whom we are designing our innovation. To accomplish that, we will be creating adopter personas. The personas we will create will embody a subset of needs/wants/desires that we uncovered during the IFIs. A persona is an archtype adopter. It is specific. Our personas will aggregate those with similar decision-driving needs, wants, and/or desires. These personas will *not* be based on a demographic description of a person (sex, race, age, etc.), although those characteristics can become part of the persona description.

Our innovation design goal is to identify a design target; those people that think and choose alike. We want to build a picture of that representative person. What desired outcomes do they value? We want to make sure to include both rational and emotional impacts – it saves them time, it saves them money, it makes them feel good, etc. How do they make decisions? What are their annoyances? What are they attracted to? Repulsed by? The personifications we create from the needs/wants/desires data we gathered during the IFIs will more than likely be a mash-up of some of the people we interviewed.

We will be creating several personas from the disparate IFI data. These persona creations will be how we ultimately organize this diverse information. Each persona will be connected to a unique combination of need/want/desire categories. Creating those categories of needs/wants/desires from the needs/wants/desires uncovered from the IFIs is the first organizing step.

Persona Development Process

Performing many IFIs will reveal a plethora of different needs, wants, and/or desires. The next step is to categorize these needs/wants/desires. This is the part one of the Organize step of the DOC Process. It may be easier to first put the interview data into broad categories. We can then subdivide these large, broad categories into smaller subgroups. There will always be a few needs/wants/desires discoveries that simply do not fit in any particular category. Do not discard these findings, rather put them in a "miscellaneous" category.

Once the categories of needs/wants/desires have been created and populated, part two of the Organize step is to create adopter personas from combinations of these categories. Typically, when organizing the data, this second phase involves finding connections between the created categories. How do the categories relate to each other? Is there a specific sequence that needs to take place? But in persona identification, we are not seeking connections between the categories, but connecting the categories to a persona. What unique combination of need/want/desire categories maps into a single persona? Clearly, we do not want to connect every need/want/desire category to a single persona. That would leave us with too broad of a persona and would not segment our adopter group very well. We also do not necessarily want every single need/want/desire category to connect with a different persona, as that might create too narrow of a persona group. Finding the right balance will take some practice. Let's look at two car buyer personas which we'll call "Soccer-Mom Mary" and "Player Paul." Our two car buyers would make car-purchasing decisions based on a very different set of needs/wants/desires. Mary's need/want/desire categories would relate to safety, passenger capacity, and costs – both operating costs and initial car price. Player Paul's need/want/desire categories would be quite different. The combination of categories that map to his persona would relate to performance and image. He is likely not concerned about safety or operating costs. It is perfectly acceptable to have certain categories connect with more than one persona, although that was not the case in this example. Naming the created personas is powerful, but not required. Naming the personas gives them life and makes it easier to imagine how they would interact with our innovation.

Before we begin innovating, however, we will need to narrow down the list of personas to a specific target by choosing one of the developed personas. This is the "Converge" step of the DOC Process. We will, of course, need explicit criteria for choosing the Target Adopter persona for which we will be innovating. That Target Adopter will have, as all the created personas will, a unique set of unmet or under-met needs, wants, and/or desires as defined during the Organize step of the DOC Process.

Once our target persona is clearly articulated, the Solution Formulation of our innovation design can begin. With a clear target in mind, a clear persona description of our Target Adopter, it is possible to create an impactful solution. A clear Target Adopter with a well-articulated set of needs/wants/desires makes it straightforward to understand how the attributes of our innovation will connect to their unmet or under-met needs, wants, and/or desires. Personifying our Target Adopter by giving them names will allow us to empathize with them and improve our ability to "see" them interacting with our proposed innovation. It will also make it easier to construct a story of their engagement with our innovation. What is their situation, their annoyance? What is the experience they will have with our innovation? How will the outcome be better/different for them with our innovation versus their current BATNO? Without a clear target, the archer will likely not hit anything important. Because we are designing for people, that design target should be a persona – an archtype adopter that represents a specific group of people.

Persona Development Example

Let us say that in the investigation of our slipping product sales, we discover that our repeat customers are on the decline. The root cause of that turns out to be that our repeat customers feel like they are receiving poor service from the customer service team. That team is the Principal Adopters of whatever "fix" we will ultimately employ. Too often, at this point, organizations will make moves to resolve the problem. We, unfortunately, do not actually know the problem. We know the outcome of the problem – poor customer service. We simply do not yet know what is causing that outcome. As a result, we simply are not yet ready to move to the solution space, but need to stay in the problem space just a little bit longer. Our next step is to perform interviews of the Principal Adopters and 360-degrees around them. In this case, we will perform the IFIs on the customer service team members, their supervisors, their colleagues, and, of course, the customers.

Part of that discussion with the Customer Service Team will include their current BATNO in addressing their perceived challenges. Most of every problem that exists is currently being addressed somehow. It may not be addressed in a very elegant or effective manner, but it is being addressed. Leverage a discussion regarding the primary adopter's current BATNO to assist in teasing out their underlying needs. Why is the current BATNO not satisfactory in addressing their needs/wants/desires? Let's say that one of the needs that the customer service team articulates is the need for better training. In our research, however, we discovered that the firm has online training modules available. Why are those not working for them? Those answers will provide us with further insight as to the real unmet needs of the customer service members. Remember that this is tacit knowledge that we are seeking. Tacit knowledge is not easily communicated, so be patient. Also remember that we are seeking insight and not "answers." We are looking for unmet or under-met needs, wants, and/or desires not "solutions."

For our customer service team, let us say that we were able to categorize need/want/desire data we uncovered during the IFIs into five categories. We will say those identified categories are better training, improved work environment, affinity for the assigned job, work task prioritization, and a miscellaneous category. Some items in the miscellaneous category included distractions the employees were feeling coming from outside the office. These distractions varied widely from childcare to parent care.

The next step is to create several personas that represent the customer service team. It is helpful to name those different personas as that makes them feel more "real." For simplicity, we will say that we can create three different personas from the needs/wants/desires categories: "Poorly trained Peter," "Unmotivated Uma," and "Overcommitted Olivia," as illustrated in Figure A.2. Peter is simply undertrained. He is bright, energetic, and personable, but no one has shown him how he can effectively do his job. The "training" category of needs/wants/desires connects with Peter. A couple of different need/

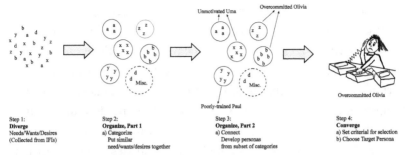

FIGURE A.2 DOC Process from the IFI to Target Adopter selection.

want/desire categories map to "Unmotivated Uma." Each category, in some way, impacts her motivation to perform well at her job. One category is the work environment and another is her affinity for the job. Uma has little interest in the firm or its products and is working for the pay. She also feels that the work environment is depressing, as she is alone all day in a gray cubicle that company policy does not allow her to personalize. "Overcommitted Olivia," in this example, also has two categories of needs/wants/desires connected to her. One category is that she is charged with multiple tasks to perform within the company. She does customer service, but she also does data entry. The two jobs get in the way of each other as she can only do one thing at a time. She also has two supervisors, one for each job responsibility. Each of her two supervisors believes that Olivia should give top priority to the work they need her to do. The other category impacting Olivia is that she is besieged by outside work distractions. Olivia is a single mother with a newborn in childcare. Her childcare firm is contacting her multiple times in a day with issues related to her child. Each outside call interrupts her work flow, making her less efficient, and more likely to forget the details of the customer call she just cut short to take the call from her childcare facility.

Let us say that in our example, the majority of our customer service team can be described as the "Overcommitted Olivia" persona. Our criterion for selection was to choose a persona that will have the most significant impact on our customer service. Since this persona represents the majority of our team, we will select "Overcommitted Olivia" as our Target Adopter. We could have made our selection based on different criteria. We could have selected the issue we could resolve most quickly, or most inexpensively. Whatever the selection criterion, make it a conscious one. In this case, we chose the biggest impact and, as a result, chose to address Olivia's needs/wants/desires. We should now do some more interviewing before resolving her issues. Is her biggest issue her dual responsibilities inside the firm or the distractions coming from the outside? We may want to split the "Olivia" persona in two, but we will need to perform more IFIs before we can take this action. Olivia has a couple of very different issues to resolve. One innovation will not likely be able to address both. This is the nonlinear nature of the process. We often have to step backward before moving forward. We are, however, much closer to defining the real issue and being able to create an impactful solution to the issue than when this was framed as a "customer service" issue.

CONCLUSION

Interviewing for Insight and Persona Development are nothing more than unique techniques applied to the DOC Process which is described in Part II of this book. But they are powerful techniques that allow us to take the final step in reducing the original situation to a specific group of people for which we will be creating an impactful solution. For it is people who have problems and it is people who will adopt solutions to their problems. Creating impactful solutions, innovations, means addressing people's unmet or under-met needs, wants, and/or desires.

The original situation is first reduced to a root cause which is impacting a group. That group is the Principal Adopters of our would-be innovation. That group, unfortunately, is still too large and too ill-defined for us to create a specific design. Like the archer, we need to aim at something small and specific if we are going to generate the outcome we desire. We need to reduce this Principal Adopter group to a specific target.

We accomplish this transformation from this broad Principal Adopter group to our Target Adopter, with a very specific set of needs/wants/desires, by performing a specialized version of the DOC Process. Like all applications of the DOC Process, we diverge before we converge. In this special application, we first diverge by uncovering the needs, wants, and/or desires of the Principal Adopter group by performing a number of IFIs. We are seeking insight from these interviews; insight as to their underlying needs/wants/desires which our interviewees may not be able to directly articulate for us. Through these one-on-one, face-to-face interviews we will try to tease out this group's underlying needs/wants/desires. It will not be easy as this is tacit knowledge that we seek. Compounding this problem, our interviewees will likely speak in terms of solutions, not underlying needs/wants/desires. It is up to us to coax them to articulate the reasons behind their suggested solutions. We will, of course, talk to them about their current BATNO as every problem has some sort of solution today. But we also want to take a step back from that BATNO and talk to our interviewees more broadly so that we are not limiting ourselves to simply improving on the current solution.

Once a plethora of needs/wants/desires has been uncovered via the IFIs, we will finish the DOC Process by first Organizing this information into Personas and then and then Converging to a single persona – the persona that represents the Target Adopter for which we will be innovating. The persona creation process is a technique used to organize the needs/wants/desires information we obtained through the IFIs. Those need/want/desire insights are first organized into categories. Unique combinations of those need/want/desire categories are then mapped or connected to individual personas. These personas are archtype adopters who think and choose alike. Naming these personas helps make them more real and improves our ability to relate to them. Finally, one of those developed personas is selected based on a specific criterion. The criterion can vary, but it must be conscious. That selected persona is our Target Adopter and embodies a specific set of needs/wants/desires, which is a subset of those uncovered during the IFIs. Once that Target Adopter is identified, we are ready to design an impactful solution for them that will satisfy their unmet or under-met needs, wants, and/or desires.

Appendix B: Divergent Thinking Prompts

The design thinking-based Innovation Pyramid, detailed in Part I of this book, is an overarching guide or roadmap for producing innovations. The methodology leverages the creativity-based Diverge–Organize–Converge (DOC) Process detailed in Part II of this book. The two elements work synergistically together. The Innovation Pyramid is the overarching pathway for developing an innovation, and the DOC Process is an important tool utilized in transforming that construct into reality. The divergent step of the DOC Process, which can be applied to both Problem Identification and Solution Formulation, is critical in ensuring that we can get "out of the box" in how we are looking at either the problem or the solution. This appendix highlights approaches to prompt that divergent thinking.

Too often when people refer to being "innovative" what they really mean is thinking divergently. Divergent thinking is certainly an important step in the DOC Process. The DOC Process is, in turn, a useful tool in the application of The Innovation Pyramid. While being able to think divergently is important, it is by itself, not innovating.

Divergent thinking approaches are aimed at altering our approaches to understanding the problem or to crafting its potential solution. Most approaches come down to two key points: encouraging us to shift our perspective or our point-of-view. While it is common to use these words interchangeably, recall that in this book we defined them differently. Perspective is a vantage point for looking at something. It is a mental or physical place from which we view the situation. Are we looking at the "big picture" (zoomed-out perspective) or assessing its details (zoomed-in perspective)? Are we looking at the issue as a problem or an opportunity? Are we seeing the alternative solution as "rational" or "crazy?" Point-of-view, on the other hand, as used in this book, is whose "eyes" through which we are looking at the issue or solution. Are we looking at the problem through the eyes of the innovation creator or the potential innovation adopter? Empathy is key to authentically observing from any point-of-view other than our own.

APPLICATION TO PROBLEM IDENTIFICATION AND SOLUTION FORMULATION

Our familiarity with divergent thinking is in its application to generating diverse problem solution ideas. Part II of this book demonstrates how it is equally applied to Problem Identification and Solution Formulation. The techniques utilized to apply divergent thinking are subtly different for both spaces. As discussed in Chapter 9, the search for a root cause of the General Problem required that its root system be uncovered. As we zoomed in on the problem, layer by layer, we were diverging as illustrated in the right-hand side of Figure B.1. The discovery of multiple factors to our initial problem is divergent thinking. It is certainly not "brainstorming," but the research that leads to the uncovering of these factors results in this diversification. We then looked for factor of the factors, then causes of the subfactors, etc., diversifying the potential problem as we zoomed in.

Chapter 9, Diverge, also discussed divergent thinking's application to Solution Formulation. That chapter leveraged a perspective change to think about the potential solution by comparing

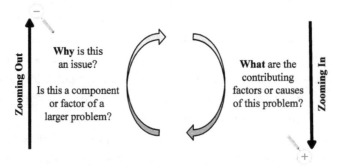

FIGURE B.1 Zooming in/out in the problem space.

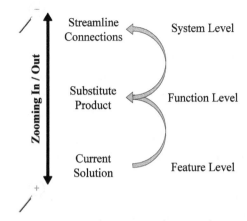

FIGURE B.2 Divergent Solution Formulation techniques.

it with the potential adopter's current Best Alternative to a New Option. We can think of improving the features of the current option (feature level), think about creating something that could serve the same purpose of the current solution (function level), or zoom way out and think about how to improve the connections in the entire system (system-level thinking), as illustrated in Figure B.2.

This appendix will illustrate some techniques for accomplishing this divergent thinking. Most of the techniques will only have application to formulating new solution ideas. That fact does not in any way reduce the importance of divergent thinking to Problem Identification.

CHALLENGE QUESTIONS

We were careful, in the Problem Identification, to state the problem in neutral language. This was done so as not to bias us toward any particular solution. However, such statements, such as "our energy consumption exceeds our generation capacity," do not necessarily get our creative juices flowing. When trying to diversify solution ideas, it is often easier to start with challenge questions (Grivas and Puccio, 2011):

- How to...
- How might we...

- In what way might...
- What might be all the ways we could...

... resolve the issue we have identified. We do not want to lose the problem neutrality we worked hard to create. As a result, we may need to create multiple statements ... "How might we reduce our energy consumption?" in addition to "What are all the ways that we could generate more power?" Before crafting any challenge question, as discussed in Chapter 9, we had better clearly identify the correct problem first!

The remainder of this appendix will highlight various ways to shift points-of-view and perspective.

POINT-OF-VIEW SHIFTS

Innovating requires the ability to shift points-of-view. DeGraff and Quinn (2007) and their colleagues at the University of Michigan developed the opposing values theory for creative teams. That framework illustrates the value in forming innovative teams with conflicting points-of-view. The framework's four quadrants ("collaborate," "create," "compete," and "control") represent the chief ambition for four different groups of people. Teaming people with tendencies to view the world from these divergent desired outcomes will certainly create tension. However, if that tension is properly managed, their different points-of-view will diversify the group's thinking. The consulting firm, Foursight, similarly, crafted four personas (clarifiers, ideators, developers, and implementers) who focus on different innovation development aspects.

While it may give one comfort to put themselves into a quadrant of the Michigan model or identify with a persona of the Foursight approach, locking into one point-of-view is counterproductive. Being an innovator means being self-aware; knowing our natural tendencies is an important aspect of that. That understanding of our natural tendencies is not enough, but we must be careful not to get trapped by our own biases, that is, the opposite of what we need to do to innovate. To innovate, we need to learn to shift our point-of-view beyond our own tendencies, which requires that we empathize with our innovation adopters as well as our innovation creation-and-delivery collaborators.

There are a number of techniques for shifting our point-of-view. The Kelley brothers (2013) suggest "thinking like a traveler." When we travel, especially to a foreign country for the first time, our senses are on "high alert" as nothing is "normal." In our everyday lives, we do not always "see" what is all around us. Forcing ourselves to be truly aware of our environments is enlightening. To put it another way, "Paying attention to the world around you will help you develop extraordinary capacity to look at mundane things and see the miraculous" (Michalko, 1991). In addition to asking surgeons and nurses about their surgical environment, a surgery equipment firm often employs people unfamiliar with medical procedures to observe surgeries. Why? These "travelers" see things that the others simply overlook or take for granted as part of the normal surgical environment. The insights these "travelers" provide positively impact the ultimate redesign of the surgical unit's equipment.

Another way to shift our perspective is to separate yourself from your own point-of-view. Asking, "what would "x" do?" where "x" could be Steve Jobs, or our parents, or even a fictional character allows us to shed our own view. Linkner (2019b) took this one step further by suggesting we ideate as that person (real or fictional), in what he called "rolestorming" – brainstorming as someone else. Whatever technique helps get us beyond our own point-of-view is beneficial.

PERSPECTIVE SHIFTS

Beyond point-of-view shifts, we also need to consider perspective shifts. Edward de Bono (1967), widely acknowledged as the "father" of brainstorming, was a proponent of taking on different perspectives. His "Six Thinking Hats" force users to consider different perspectives:

- "White" – just the facts.
- "Red" – only feelings.

- "Yellow" – values and benefits.
- "Black" – potential challenges with the proposed solution.
- "Green" – creativity, new ideas.
- "Blue" – next steps, action plans.

When we are in the divergent thinking mode and someone jumps to a planning activity, we can say "thank-you for that input, but we are currently wearing our 'green' thinking caps" and will not shift to "blue" until we get to Pyramid Level 3.

Other ways to shift our perspective is to change the "rules." We often get in our own way by putting constraints on our thinking. Some constraints may be real, others may exist only in our minds. We may, for example, stifle ideas that we think may be "too expensive." Those ideas, however, could turn out to be the seeds of ideas that could also be inexpensively implemented. von Oech (1983) suggests we "be foolish" and disregard "reality" during the Divergent steps. We can always bring "reality" back in during the Converge step of the DOC Process. Trying to simultaneously ideate and edit our ideas is ineffective.

Another "rule-breaking" perspective shift is the "judo flip" (Linkner, 2019b). In this technique, we first list all the traditional ways we would approach the challenge before us. List the standard industry approach, our organization's approach, etc. Then draw a line down the page, and for every "practical" solution idea or approach, list the opposite. The industry is all pursuing golf balls that fly further, what could be the benefits to ones that flew less far? That could be quite valuable to creating a similar golf experience to those in a land-constrained region. There is power in "opposite" thinking, as discussed elsewhere in this book, do not be afraid to list them.

One of the powers of the multistep DOC Process is it separates the process's contradictory objectives into a series of independent steps. In the Converge step, we will be picking "the best" option. We do not have to worry about that in the Diverge step. In divergent thinking, our aim is to produce as many ideas as possible. This is where we need to get out of our own way and let our imaginations run wild. Tap that inner child within us all, the one that is full of questions and believes anything is possible. We can put "adult" constraints on those ideations later, but for divergent thinking – be free.

Bibliography

Ackoff, Russell L. (1999). *Re-creating the Corporation: A Design of Organizations for the 21st Century*. Oxford: Oxford University Press.

Adner, Ron (2012). *The Wide Lens: What Successful Innovators See that Others Miss*. New York: The Penguin Group.

Anderson, Monica (2017). Two Dirty Words: Reductionism and Holism. June 26. Retrieved on February 6, 2020 from https://artificial-understanding.com/two-dirty-words-6703aee8e323

Anthony, Scott (2012). *The Little Black Book of Innovation: How It Works, How to Do It*. Boston: Harvard Business School Press.

Assembly Line History. (n.d.). Retrieved on February 5, 2020 from https://science.jrank.org/pages/558/Assembly-Line-History.html

Berkun, Scott (2010). *The Myths of Innovation*. Sebastopol, Canada: O'Reilly Media Group.

Bohm, David (1957). *Causality and Chance in Modern Physics*. Philadelphia: University of Philadelphia Press.

Bohm, David (1980). *Wholeness and the Implicate Order*. London: Routledge & Kegan Paul, Ltd.

Briscoe, T., Baccineli, C. and Chambless, J. (2000). Best Practices – Project Review Process. Paper presented at Project Management Institute Annual Seminars & Symposium, Houston. Newtown Square: Project Management Institute.

Brown, Tim (2009). *Change by Design: How Design Thinking Transforms Organizations and Inspires Innovation*. New York: HarperCollins Publishing.

Camp, Justin J. (2002). *Venture Capital Due Diligence*. New York: John Wiley & Sons.

Center for Disease Control. World Cancer Day. Retrieved on Febuary 5, 2020 from www.cdc.gov/cancer/dcpc/resources/features/WorldCancerDay/

Chesbrough, Henry (2003). *Open Innovation: The New Imperative for Creating and Profiting from Technology*. Boston: Harvard Business Review Press.

Christensen, Clayton M. (1997). *The Innovator's Dilemma*. Boston: Harvard Business School Publishing.

Christensen, Clayton M. (2003). *The Innovator's Solution.* Boston: Harvard Business School Publishing.

Clifton, Jim and Badal, Sangeeta B. (2014). *Entrepreneurial Strengths Finder.* New York: Gallup Press.

Collins, Jim (2001). *Good to Great.* New York: HarperCollins Publishing.

Collins, James and Porras, Jerry (1996). Building Your Company's Vision. *Harvard Business Review*, September–October.

Cooper, Alan (1999). Cognitive Friction. In *The Inmates Are Running the Asylum: Why High Tech Products Drive Us Crazy and How to Restore the Sanity,* 19–38, Chapter 2,. New York: Sams.

Cornell University, INSEAD, WIPO (2019). Global Innovation Index 2019: Creating Healthy Lives – The Future of Medical Innovation. Retrieved on February 7, 2020 from www.wipo.int/publications/en/details.jsp?id=4434

Couros, George (2015). *The Innovator's Mindset: Empower Learning, Unleash Talent and Lead a Culture of Creativity.* San Diego: Dave Burgess Consulting, Inc.

Covey, Stephen R. (1989). *The 7 Habits of Highly Effective People.* New York: Simon & Schuster.

Covey, Stephen R. (2008). Quote. Retrieved on February 6, 2020 from http://studio2d.com/quote-all-things-are-created-twice-says-stephen-r-covey/

Csikszentmihalyi, Mihaly (2007). *Creativity: Flow and the Psychology of Discovery and Invention.* New York: HarperCollins Publishing.

Davila, A. and Foster, G. (2012). How to Structure Companies for High Growth. *IESE Insight*, September 15.

de Bono, Edward (1967). Dr. Edward de Bono, Brain Training and Lateral Thinking Pioneer. Retrieved on February 6, 2020 from www.edwddebono.com/

de Jouvenel, Bertrand (1967). *The Art of Conjecture.* New York: Basic Books, Inc.

Engel, Jerome S. (Ed.) (2014). *Global Clusters of Innovation: Entrepreneurial Engines of Economic Growth around the World.* Boston: Edward Elgar Publishing.

Decision Matrix. Retrieved on February 1, 2020 from https://en.wikipedia.org/wiki/Decision_matrix

Decision Trees. Retrieved on February 1, 2020 from www.mindtools.com/dectree.html

DeGraff, Jeff and DeGraff, Staney (2017). *The Innovation Code: The Creative Power of Constructive Conflict.* Oakland: Berrett-Koehler Publishers.

DeGraff, Jeff and Laurence, Katherine A. (2002). *Creativity at Work.* New York: John Wiley & Sons.

DeGraff, Jeff and Quinn, Shawn E. (2007). *Leading Innovation: How to Jump Start Your Organization's Growth Engine*. New York: McGraw-Hill.

Dorst, Kees (2015). *Frame Innovation: Create New Thinking by Design*. Boston: The MIT Press.

Drill, Baby, Drill. (2008). Retrieved on February 11, 2020 from https://en.wikipedia.org/wiki/Drill,_baby,_drill

Drucker, Peter F. (1954). *The Practice of Management*. New York: HarperCollins Publishing.

Drucker, Peter F. (1985). *Innovation and Entrepreneurship*. New York: Harper and Row Publishers.

Drucker, Peter F. (1990). *Managing the Non-profit Organization*. New York: HarperCollins Publishing.

Dyer, Jeff, Gregersen, Hal and Christensen, Clayton (2011). *The Innovator's DNA: Mastering the Five Skills of Disruptive Innovators*. Boston: Harvard Business Review Press.

Einstein, Albert. Quote. Retrieved on February 2, 2020 from www.brainyquote.com/quotes/quotes/a/alberteins103652.html

Ellenberg, Jordan (2014). *How Not to Be Wrong: The Power of Mathematical Thinking*. New York: Penguin Group.

Eller, Karl (2005). *Integrity Is All You've Got: And Seven Other Lessons of the Entrepreneurial Life*. New York: McGraw-Hill.

Evans, Phillip B. and Wurster, Thomas S. (1997). Strategy and the New Economics of Information. *Harvard Business Review*, September–October.

Faley, Timothy L. (2015a). *The Entrepreneurial Arch: A Strategic Framework for Discovering, Developing and Renewing Firms*. Cambridge: Cambridge University Press.

Faley, Timothy L. (2015b). Best Practices Are Killing Innovation… and How to Fix It. LinkedIn Pulse, August 2. Retrieved on February 2, 2020 from www.linkedin.com/pulse/best-practices-killing-innovation-how-fix-timothy-tim-faley

Faley, Timothy L. (2016a). *Entrepreneurial Finance: An Entrepreneur's Guide*. Seattle: Kindle Press.

Faley, Timothy L. (2016b). Leading Institutional Change: A Case Study of the Creation of Innovation Centers at the University of the Virgin Islands. International Conference on Leadership, Management and Strategic Development Conference Proceedings, Vol. 1, May. St. Thomas, US Virgin Islands.

Faley, Timothy L. (2016c). Future Industry Cluster Design Methodology. *Journal of Economic Development in Higher Education*, 1 (1)3–14.

Faley, Timothy L. (2017). Leading Innovation Development. International Conference on Leadership, Management and Strategic Development Conference Proceedings, Vol. 1, May.

Fitzgerald, Eugene, Wankert, Andreas and Schramm, Carl (2011). *Inside Real Innovation: How the Right Approach Can Move Ideas from R&D to Market – And Get the Economy Moving.* New York: World Scientific Publishing, Co.

Fitzgerald, F. Scott. Quote. Retrieved on February 6, 2020 from www.brainyquote. com/quotes/f_scott_fitzgerald_100572

Ford, Henry (2013). Quote. Retrieved on February 5, 2020 from http://blog. thehenryford.org/2013/03/henry-fords-quotations/

Foster, Richard and Kaplan, Sarah (2001). *Creative Destruction: Why Companies that Are Built to Last Underperform the Market – And How to Successfully Transform Them.* New York: Random House.

Foursight (n.d.). What Kind of Creative Thinker Are You? Retrieved on February 6, 2020 from https://foursightonline.com/

Fried, Jason and Hansson, David Heinemeier (2010). *Rework.* New York: Random House.

Fuller, R. Buckminster (1981). *Critical Path.* New York: St. Martin's Press.

Gardner, Howard (2006). *The Five Mind of the Future.* Boston: Harvard Business School Press.

Gladwell, Malcolm (2008). *Outliers: The Story of Success.* New York: Hachette Book Group.

Global Smartphone Sales Reached $522 Billion in 2018. Retrieved on February 11, 2020 from www.gfk.com/insights/press-release/global-smartphone-sales-reached-522-billion-in-2018/

Grenny, Joseph, Patterson, Kerry, Maxfield, David, McMillan, Ron and Switzler, Al (2013). *Influencer: The New Science of Leading Change.* New York: McGraw-Hill.

Grivas, Chris and Puccio, Gerald (2011). *The Innovation Team: Unleashing Creative Potential for Breakthrough Results.* San Francisco: Jossey-Bass Publishers.

Hamel, Gary (2007). *The Future of Management.* Boston: Harvard Business School Press.

Hamermesh, Richard G. (2002). Note on Business Model Analysis for the Entrepreneur. Harvard Business School Case 9-802-048.

Hasso Platter School of Design Thinking (n.d.). What Exactly Is Design Thinking? University of Cape Town Website. Retrieved on February 5, 2020 from www. dschool.uct.ac.za/what-design-thinking

Hatfield, David (2012). Coined the Terms "Zoom-in" and "Zoom-out" in the Context of Evaluating Businesses from Various Perspectives. Personal Communications.

(2011). *HBR's 10 Must Reads on Change Management*. Boston: Harvard Business School Publishing.

Heathfield, Susan M. (2019). 10 Key Tips for Effective Employee Performance Reviews. June 25. Retrieved on February 1, 2020 from www.thebalancecareers. com/effective-performance-review-tips-1918842

Hiatt, Jeffrey M. and Creasey, Timothy J. (2012). *Change Management: The People Side of Change*. Loveland: Prosci, Inc.

3M. History of 3M Corporation. Retrieved on February 5, 2020 from http:// solutions.3m.com/wps/portal/3M/en_US/3M-Company/Information/ Resources/History/

Johnston, Tom (1973). China Grove [Song] on the Doobie Brother's the Captain and Me [Album]. Warner Records. Lyrics. Retrieved on February 6, 2020 from www.azlyrics.com/lyrics/doobiebrothers/chinagrove.html

Kahneman, Daniel (2011). *Thinking, Fast and Slow*. New York: MacMillan Publishing.

Kawasaki, Guy (2004). *The Art of the Start: Time-tested, Battle-hardened, Guide for Anyone Starting Anything*. New York: Penguin Group.

Kawasaki, Guy (2013). How to Create an Enchanting Pitch. January 9. Retrieved on February 6, 2020 from https://guykawasaki.com/how-to-create-an-enchan ting-pitch-officeandguyk/

Keeley, Larry, Pikkel, Ryan, Quinn, Brian and Walters, Helen (2013). *Ten Types of Innovation: The Discipline of Building Breakthroughs*. New York: John Wiley & Sons.

Kelley, David (2001). Presentation at Stanford University. October 10.

Kelley, Tom (2008). Presentation at Stanford University. November 12.

Kelley, Tom and Kelley, David (2013). *Creative Confidence: Unleashing the Creative Potential within Us All*. New York: Random House.

Khosla, Vinod (2002). Presentation at Stanford University. April 24.

Kindlon, Audrey E. and Jankowski, John E. (2017). Rates of Innovation among U.S. Businesses Stay Steady: Data from the 2014 R&D and Innovation Survey. NSF 17-321. August 28. Retrieved on February 6, 2020 from www.nsf.gov/ statistics/2017/nsf17321/

Larson, Elizabeth and Larson Richard (n.d.). 10 Steps to Creating a Project Plan. Retrieved on February 6, 2020 from www.projecttimes.com/articles/10- steps-to-creating-a-project-plan.html

Lathem, Edward C. (Ed.) (1969). *The Poetry of Robert Frost*. New York: Holt, Rinehart and Winston.

Leung, Ing. C. H. (2007). Evolution of the Business Model. Retrieved on February 3, 2013 from http://alexandria.tue.nl/extra1/afstversl/tm/leung2007.pdf

Linkner, Josh (2019a). Nine Simple Pre-game Questions to Maximize Your Business Results. April 14. Retrieved on February 2, 2020 from https://joshlinkner.com/2019/nine-simple-pre-game-questions-to-maximize-business-results/?utm_source=CONSTANTCONTACT&utm_medium=BLOG&utm_campaign=APRIL15

Linkner, Josh (2019b). The 12 Secret Brainstorming Techniques of Billionaires. October 29. https://joshlinkner.com/2019/the-12-secret-brainstorming-techniques-of-billionaires/

Martin, Roger (2009a). *The Opposable Mind: How Successful Leaders Win through Integrative Thinking*. Boston: Harvard Business School Press.

Martin, Roger (2009b). *The Design of Business: Why Design Thinking Is the Next Competitive Advantage*. Boston: Harvard Business School Press.

McGrath, Rita Gunter and MacMillan, Ian C. (2009). *Discovery Driven Growth: A Breakthrough Process to Reduce Risk and Seize Opportunity*. Boston: Harvard Business School Press.

McKinsey, Dave (2014). *Strategic Storytelling: How to Create Persuasive Business Presentations*. Charleston: CreateSpace Independent Publishing Platform.

Michaelides, Doug (2012). Mission and Vision: A Means to an End. May 27. Retrieved on February 6, 2020 from http://stratfordmanagers.com/mission-vision-strategy/

Michalko, Michael (1991). *Tinkertoys: A Handbook of Creative-thinking Techniques*. Berkeley: Ten Speed Press.

Moore, Geoffrey A. (2005). Presentation at Stanford University. April 6.

Moore, Geoffrey A. (1991). *Crossing the Chasm*. New York: HarperCollins Publishers.

Munro, Eileen (2018). Presentation at Stellenbosch University. February 19. Retrieved on February 6, 2020 from www.sun.ac.za/english/Lists/news/DispForm.aspx?ID=5446

Nagel, Thomas T. and Holden, Reed K. (1987). *The Strategy and Tactics of Pricing: A Guide to Profitable Decision Making*. New York: Prentice-Hall, Inc.

Naisbitt, John (2006). *Mindset!* New York: HarperCollins Publishers.

Nunes, Paul and Breene, Tim (2011). *Jumping the S-curve: How to Beat the Growth Cycle, Get on Top and Stay There*. Boston: Harvard Business School Publishing.

Paired Comparison Method. (n.d.). Retrieved on February 5, 2020 from www.toolshero.com/decision-making/paired-comparison-method/

Pareto Analysis. https://en.wikipedia.org/wiki/Pareto_analysis

Porter, Michael E. (1980). *Competitive Strategy: Techniques for Analyzing Industries and Competitors*. New York: The Free Press.

Porter, Michael E. (1985). *Competitive Advantage: Creating and Sustaining Superior Performance*. New York: The Free Press.

Porter, Michael E. (1990). *The Competitive Advantage of Nations*. New York: The Free Press.

Porter, Michael E. (2003). The Economic Performance of Regions. *Regional Studies*, 37 (6&7), 549–578.

Porter, Michael E. (2014). Reshaping Regional Economic Development: Clusters and Regional Strategy. Keynote Presentation at the Mapping the Midwest's Future Conference, Minneapolis, September 29. Retrieved on February 6, 2020 from www.youtube.com/watch?v=mF2CsUcwFrw

Prahalad, C. K. and Hamel, Gary (1989). Strategic Intent. *Harvard Business Review*, May–June. Retrieved on December 21, 2013 from https://www.academia.edu/29536366/Strategic_Intent

PWC (n.d.). The 2018 Global Innovation 1000 Study. Retrieved on February 6, 2020 from www.strategyand.pwc.com/gx/en/insights/innovation1000.html

Reinholz, Matthias (2016). 7 Questions to Shape an Effective Innovation Team. December 9. Retrieved on January 31, 2019 from https://bookmachine.org/2016/12/09/7-questions-to-shape-an-effective-innovation-team/

Rogers, Everett (1995). Attributes of Innovation and Their Rate of Adoption. In *Diffusion of Innovation*, 204–251, Chapter 6. New York: The Free Press.

Roosevelt, Theodore. (n.d.). Quote. Retrieved on February 2, 2020 from www.brainyquote.com/quotes/theodore_roosevelt_100965

Rumsfeld, Donald (2002). Quote Made at a Press Briefing. February 12. Retrieved on February 5, 2020 from http://en.wikipedia.org/wiki/There_are_known_knowns

Schaver, Eric (2014). The Many Definitions of Innovation. June 6. Retrieved on February 5, 2020 from www.ericshaver.com/the-many-definitions-of-innovation/

Schmitt, Larry (2006). *Driving the Innovation Process*. Presentation at the University of Michigan. January 16.

Schumpeter, Joseph A. (1934). *The Theory of Economic Development*. Boston: Harvard University Press.

Schuster, Steven (2018). *The Art of Thinking in Systems*. Seattle: CreateSpace Publishing.

Senge, Peter M. (1990). *The Fifth Discipline: The Art & Practice of the Learning Organization*. New York: Doubleday.

Shane, Scott (2008). Top Ten Myths of Entrepreneurship. Retrieved on December 21, 2013 from http://blog.guykawasaki.com/2008/01/top-ten-myths-o.html#ixzz0ea35EGW5

Simms, Peter (2011). *Little Bets: How Breakthrough Ideas Emerge from Small Discoveries*. New York: Free Press.

Sinek, Simon (2019). *The Infinite Game*. New York: Penguin Random House.

Sutton, Robert I. (2007). *The No Ass-Hole Rule: Building a Civilized Workplace and Surviving One that Isn't*. New York: Business Plus Publishers.

Tacit Knowledge Definition. Retrieved on February 12, 2020 from https://en.wikipedia.org/wiki/Tacit_knowledge

T-charts. Retrieved on January 12, 2019 from www.enchantedlearning.com/graphicorganizers/tchart/

TEC (The Executive Connection) (2018). The Five Issues Concerning CEOs the Most. TEC.com.au, December 11. Retrieved on February 2, 2020 from https://tec.com.au/resource/the-5-issues-concerning-ceos-the-most/

Teece, David (1986). Profiting from Technological Innovation: Implication for Integration, Collaboration, Licensing and Public Policy. *Research Policy* 15(6) 285–305.

The Five Basic Methods of Market Research. Retrieved on February 2, 2020 from www.allbusiness.com/marketing/market-research/1287-1.html#axzz2JfvaT3Cf

The Wizard of Oz (1939). Movie Quote. Retrieved on February 6, 2020 from www.moviequotedb.com/movies/wizard-of-oz-the/quote_26269.html

Turner, Natalie (2018). *Yes, You Can Innovate: Discover Your Innovation Strengths and Develop Your Creative Potential*. London: Pearson Education, Ltd.

Understanding PEST Analysis with Definitions and Examples. (2013). Retrieved on February 6, 2020 from https://pestleanalysis.com/pest-analysis/

Understanding the Pareto Principle (the 80/20 Rule). (n.d.) Retrieved on February 3, 2020 from https://betterexplained.com/articles/understanding-the-pareto-principle-the-8020-rule/

von Hippel, Eric (2005). *Democratizing Innovation*. Cambridge: MIT Press.

von Oech, Roger (1983). *A Whack on the Side of the Head*. New York: U.S. Games Systems, Inc.

Young, James Webb (1940). *A Technique for Producing Ideas*. Seattle: Amazon Press.

Index

CPSIA information can be obtained
at www.ICGtesting.com
Printed in the USA
LVHW022125170121
676736LV00004B/41